Perspectives on Transforming India-Central Asia Engagement
Prospects and Issues

Perspectives on Transforming India-Central Asia Engagement:
Prospects and Issues

Editor

Brig Vinod Anand (Retd)

Published for

Vivekananda International Foundation

New Delhi, India

Vij Books India Pvt Ltd
New Delhi, India

Published by

Vij Books India Pvt Ltd

2/19, Ansari Road, Darya Ganj
New Delhi - 110002
Phones: 91-11-65449971, 91-11- 43596460
Fax: 91-11-47340674
e-mail : vijbooks@rediffmail.com
web : www.vijbooks.com

© **2011, Vivekananda International Foundation, New Delhi**

First Published : 2011

ISBN 13 : 978-93-80177-79-3

TABLE OF CONTENTS

FOREWORD

In the global re-configuration of power in the offing, Central Asia will both substantially influence and get influenced by geo-strategic power shifts. Located in the Eurasian heartland, historically, it has profoundly influenced power politics and the rise and fall of civilisations in the Asian land mass, though rarely being a seat of power or of an empire itself. Its unique setting acquires added import as China, Russia and India, three of the six BRICS countries, seen as emerging powers that will influence global power shift, lie in its close vicinity. Close proximity to a volatile Af-Pak region, its hydro-carbon reserves, Russia's Eurasian ambition in the wake of declining Europe are likely to contribute to its political and strategic relevance.

For a brief period following the end of Cold War and dismemberment of the Soviet Union the region remained internally in a state of disarray and externally out of global focus. Talibanisation of Afghanistan and growth of Islamic Radicalism in Pakistan, culminating in 9/11 attacks in US brought it to centre stage. As Muslim majority states in a state of flux in a setting where the West was engaged in a fight against the Taliban and Al Qaeda in Afghanistan, Russia against Chechens, China against *Uighurs* and India against Pakistan sponsored terrorism in J&K, Central Asia became an area of concern for all, albeit for different reasons.

In the war against terror Uzbekistan particularly emerged as a front ranking state to support US efforts in its counter-terrorist operations in Afghanistan. The new relationship involved facilitation of military supplies to Afghanistan, stationing of US troops, use of bases for US air planes, launching of offensive strikes on terrorist groups in Afghanistan etc. Other states also played supportive roles in varying degrees in this fight against terror. With the reliability and capacity of Pakistan to take on the fight against Islamic terrorists under serious doubt and the West's supply routes for International Security Assistance Force (ISAF) seriously threatened the Central Asian Republics have become all the more important. This role is likely to become still more crucial in the post US withdrawal phase from Afghanistan.

Hydro-carbon reserves and other mineral wealth is another factor that has aroused greater global interest in the region. While Kazakhstan, Uzbekistan and Turkmenistan are rich in hydrocarbons, Tajikistan and Kyrgyzstan have abundant hydro power potential. China with its long border with Central Asian Republics and its global hunt for energy resources, views Central Asia with considerable interest. Other countries in search of energy security view the potential with interest. Russia, in its long term geo-strategic calculations, considers Central Asia as its strategic backyard. Enjoying many advantages like a long common border, an influential Russian speaking population, historical links, economic and technological complementarities it would not like outside influence in the region growing beyond a point to its detriment. Besides its import in the fight against Islamic extremism, the West also considers the region strategically significant in the context of its long term China policy and Russia's Eurasian vision in the context of the declining power of Europe.

India, however, views the region from a different perspective. As a status-quoist power, with centuries old cultural, economic and historical links with the people of Central Asia, it looks at the region much beyond the prism of geo-political and economic interests. It considers the emergence of Central Asian Republics as strong and viable states enjoying decisional autonomy, economic prosperity and political stability to be essential for the development and stability of Asia. It also believes that insulation of these predominantly Muslim states from the pernicious influence of jehadi extremism inundating its Southern neighbours is important for India. For all this to happen, it will be important for these states, helped by international community to be stable and secure. They need to be supported to (i) develop their economic infrastructure which has considerably corroded in last two decades; (ii) strengthen the institutions of democracy and governance making them more transparent, accountable and people friendly; (iii) undertake human resource development programmes focusing on education, health care, nutrition, food security etc. and (iv) increasing regional cooperation, including security cooperation to contain religious extremism. According to a study undertaken by International Crisis Group, one of the factors that have contributed to the current predicament is that "As part of the Soviet Union, the five countries were tightly woven into a single system. These interdependencies have proven difficult to unravel, and have produced serious imbalances. Education and healthcare suffered with the end of the social safety net. Most importantly, governments across the region seemed to feel their Soviet inheritance would last forever, and the funds earmarked for reforms, education, training and maintenance were often misused and insufficient". India feels that this is the deficient area where international players, including India, could have a role.

India has been a late starter on the Central Asian firmament even though it established diplomatic relations with the CARs soon after their independence. However, India considering Central Asia as part of its extended/ strategic neighbourhood has many commonly shared interests with them. Their relations are based on a shared commitment to open and progressive societies, human rights and freedom, democracy and inclusive growth to improve the lot of common people. They also share a common approach to fight against terrorism, drug trafficking and other areas of security concern. India's soft power approach to address the concerns of CAR nations strikes a positive chord among these nations.

Afghanistan, part of the larger Central Asian construct, is inextricably linked with India's and Central Asian Republics' security concerns as it shares boundaries with Tajikistan, Uzbekistan and Turkmenistan. Dangers arising from intricately intertwined threats of Islamic radicalism, jehadi terrorism, drug trafficking, gun-running, use of non-state armed groups by some countries in the region to achieve their politico-strategic objective etc. pose a serious danger. India has formalized its security relations by establishing Joint Working Groups on counter terrorism and has signed defence cooperation agreements with some of the Central Asian States. Institutional arrangements in security cooperation often degenerate into ceremonial rituals unless the governments and the people consider the cooperation vital for their security. For creating this security awareness and promoting mutual interests, interaction among opinion builders, security experts, think tanks and academic bodies etc. is essential.

While security and stability in the region is of prime importance to the CARs and India, the other important driver is the economic engagement. India has the ability to help build Central Asia's capacities in areas like information technology, science and technology, knowledge industries, tourism etc. Conversely, India's increasing need for energy can be addressed by the energy-rich Central Asian countries. In the energy sector, there have been missed opportunities in the past, but India is striving to revitalize its interaction with concerned countries of Central Asia. Areas such as energy, non-conventional sources of energy and agro-based industries are promising spheres of cooperation. Joint ventures in cotton and agriculture can be established which could benefit the entire region.

Problem of direct connectivity between CARs and India is one of the factors inhibiting relationships to grow to their full potential. There is a need to enhance this connectivity through multi-modal corridors and multi-state arrangements. In a sense, it will recreate past history of the region when robust trading activity was a dominant feature. Afghanistan was the fulcrum on which such activities were carried out in various directions. However, an unstable situation in Afghanistan and obtuse policies of Pakistan prevent the achievement of good connectivity between South and Central Asia.

This volume, largely based on the proceedings of an international seminar held at Vivekananda International Foundation on **"Perspectives on Transforming India- Central Asia Engagement: Prospects and Issues"** on February 14-15, 2011, dwells upon the themes of security and stability, upgrading economic engagement including the energy sector and increasing connectivity to promote trade and commerce. These broad themes, however, need to be further expanded, debated, deliberated and refined by the scholars and experts, both from CARs and India, for evolving new policy options. It is hoped that this publication will help in creating an interest among the people and scholars and trigger a discourse in the right direction.

-Ajit Doval, KC
(Former Director Intelligence Bureau)
Director, Vivekananda International Foundation

PREFACE

The geo-strategic salience of Central Asia has been recognized since the days of British strategist Hartford Mackinder when he propounded the 'Heartland Theory'. According to him whoever ruled the heartland rules the world island. The same concept was later expanded upon by Zibignew Brezenski in his book to underline the importance of Central Asia to America's strategy. Notwithstanding the above Central Asian region consisting of the nascent nations of Kazakhstan, Uzbekistan, Turkmenistan, Kyrgyzstan and Tajikistan have been of abiding interest not only to India but also to all its neighbours. After gaining independence from the erstwhile Soviet Union they have been following multi-faceted policies to engage their neighbours and the international community. They are in the process of nation building which by no means is an easy task. Diverse ethnicities and cultures, complex historical legacies and problems of command economy are impacting the nation building processes. Major powers are forging political, economic and security ties with these nations which at times is viewed as a great game to absorb these nations into their spheres of influence. These countries have become members of a number of security and economic groupings in order to address their security, political and economic concerns.

Admittedly, India preoccupied by its economic problems in early 1990s was somewhat of a late starter in engaging the Central Asian nations even though it has had a long history of cultural, economic and people to people contacts with these nations. During Soviet Union era also such exchanges between India and Central Asia had received a fillip. Further discovery of hydrocarbons and region's potential for natural resources made it an attractive destination for investment by growing economies like India and others. Another important factor which compelled India to enhance its engagement with Central Asia was the rising specter of fundamentalism, extremism and terrorism in the region driven by Pakistan and Afghanistan based groups like Taliban which came to power in Kabul in 1996. When the American and coalition forces moved into Afghanistan in the aftermath of 9/11 attacks India supported Northern Alliance. The US and NATO/ISAF troops were provided basing facilities and transit rights for their operations in Afghanistan. Fight against Taliban remains inconclusive even after a decade of war because of many contextual factors the major one being Pakistan's support to Taliban. Central Asian nations and India remain concerned with spill over effects of the instability in Afghanistan especially if Taliban was to come back in power in Kabul.

While the security issues remain of utmost importance to both India and Central Asian nations they are also seized with the need to enhance their economic engagement. One of the major factors militating against increased trade and commerce is the lack of connectivity. Even though Pakistan has entered into a trade and transit treaty with Afghanistan allowing Afghan goods to be sent overland to India it has not allowed India the same facility in the reverse direction. India has been finding ways and means to connect to Central Asia through Iran and Afghanistan but the unstable situation there is not of much help in this regard. The International North South Transport Corridor is yet to be realized fully. Further, there are some hopes of Turkmenistan-Afghanistan-Pakistan-India gas pipeline fructifying in not too distant a future. But then the security situation in Afghanistan would have to improve substantially before Central Asia and South Asia embarks on the path of becoming an integrated region and benefits from the synergies thus obtained.

In keeping with the world wide trend the environmental issues and other non-traditional threats to security are receiving much attention in Central Asia. Whether it is water security, drug trafficking, social conflicts or terrorism there is a great scope for India and Central Asian nations to cooperate and share experience and information on these matters. India has been involved with Central Asian nations both at bilateral and multilateral levels to address these issues. Apparently India has been more successful at the bilateral level in purposefully engaging the Central Asian nations rather than say on the multilateral platform of Shanghai Cooperation Organisation (SCO) where India is an observer. However, India has applied for full membership of the SCO and it may be granted this status along with Pakistan in the coming years. The SCO membership would definitively confer some advantages which would help India in enhancing its engagement with Central Asian region.

This volume commences with an introduction to India-Central Asia engagement by Lt. Gen Ravi Sawhney (retd.) who provides a perceptive overview of the entire gamut of India-Central Asia relationship. This is followed by perceptions and views of Ambassadors of Kyrgyzstan, Turkmenistan, Uzbekistan and Afghanistan to India. Further, the current geo-political and strategic scenario is in a state of flux. The current geo-political and geostrategic scenario in Central Asia can not be but part of the larger dynamics occurring at both global and regional levels. A former Ambassador to Russia, Kanwal Sibal presents an overview of the strategic environment in Central Asia. The same theme is further amplified in the following chapter. A perspective from Russia is offered by Dr. Alexander Lukin who examines Russian and Central Asian relationship incisively. He looks at the Russian interests in Central Asia. Chinese interests in Central Asia have been examined by Amb. TCA Rangachari in the next chapter. He takes note of only the positive aspects of the Chinese approach and stated policies of China's political leadership towards Central Asian nations. Perspective from Kazakhstan is provided by Dr. Lerov Tarakov who analyses the problems of regional and global security and Kazakhstan's successful multi-vector policies. Some of the geo-political and geo-economic issues in the context of India-Central relations are analysed by Dr. Nivedita Das Kundu in the next paper.

Afghanistan occupies a key strategic location between Central Asia and South Asia; it can easily be viewed as part of both South and Central Asia. Continuing instability in Afghanistan and the possibilities of its spill over effects to the neighbourhood is a cause for concern. The next section of the book looks at the situation in Afghanistan and role and stakes of Central Asian republics in Afghanistan and the way forward. Dr. Davood Moradian, strategic analyst from Afghanistan evaluates the security situation there while Uzbek expert examines the role and stakes of various stakeholders in the Afghan imbroglio. Kanwal & Ghosh discuss possibilities and ways of conflict resolution while Arun Sahgal paints alternative future scenarios of Afghanistan and what actions could be taken to resolve the issue.

The third section of the book covers the non-traditional security threats to Central Asian nations. The entire range of of non-traditional threats has been avidly looked at by Prof. Nirmala Joshi who is a well-known expert on Central Asia. The same subject has been further elaborated upon by Dr. Arun Mohanty. Dr Sanjay Kumar Pandey has examined in detail the water security issues in the Central Asian region.

The last section of the book examines the problems of connectivity between India and Central Asia and the endeavours so far made in this direction. Eminent experts like Prof. Gulshan Sachdeva look at the economic engagement between CAR and India and hoe it can bring peace and prosperity in the region. Prospects of energy security cooperation are analysed by Dr. Jyotsna Bakshi; advantages, disadvantages and prospects of India joining Shanghai Cooperation Organisation have been explained by Dr. Meena Roy whereas the last chapter is a summation of the entire volume wherein Amb. Satish Chandra suggests the way forward for India if it wants to intensify its engagement with the Central Asian nations.

The Central Asian region remains very important to India for a variety of reasons which have been dealt at length by eminent contributors to this volume. Effort has been made to cover very comprehensively the entire spectrum of issues that impacts the India-Central Asia relationship and I am quite sanguine that this volume will strike a positive chord in the strategic community, the academia and among the practitioners of statecraft besides students of geo-politics and geo-strategy.

-Vinod Anand
Senior Fellow,
Vivekananda International Foundation

INDIA CENTRAL ASIA ENGAGEMENT: AN INTRODUCTION

Lt. Gen. Ravi Sawhney

Central Asia has immense geo-political significance for us. In the past, friendly ties with Soviet Union took care of India's strategic concerns and interests in this region that lies in our extended neighbourhood. After the Central Asian States gained independence in 1991, India's concerns were focused at the developments on the global and regional level. These were; the strategic shift from Europe to Asia as well as significance of natural resources, especially energy which had assumed critical importance. On both these counts, Central Asia had assumed consequential priority.

Importance of Central Asia in understanding world history too has been recognised by all strategic thinkers. As a landmass connecting Asia with Europe, it played a vital role in the evolution of many civilisations in ancient times. Many of the contemporary languages trace their origins one way or the other to this region. During the mediaeval period, invasions that originated from Central Asia changed the course of history in many regions of Eurasia including India. The "centrality" of Central Asia as a connecting point for many trade routes that linked Asia with Europe, especially the Silk Route, continued up to the 16th century till technological developments and the industrial revolution shifted the gravity of power to the West. The changing configuration of the states in Central Asia and the division of the region between Russian and British colonial powers pushed it into the background since the 19th century. Though the 70-odd years of the Soviet period radically changed the face of Central Asia, the region remained somewhat isolated from the rest of the world.

The collapse of the Soviet Union towards the end of the 20th century brought Central Asia into the foreground once again. Though it was impossible for the region to regain the "centrality" of the earlier period, nevertheless, many developments since then have brought the region into the focus of international relations. Three aspects assume importance in analysing the post-Soviet Central Asia: the internal transformation in the states of Central Asia vis-à-vis society, polity and economy; the security situation in and around Central Asia, particularly in the context of the prevailing situation in Afghanistan; the activities of major powers, especially the United States (US), Russia and China; and, the competition among these powers to gain strategic control over the vast hydrocarbon resources of the Caspian region. Instead of competing for actual control over a geographical area, pipelines, tanker units, petroleum consortiums and Internal Dimension contracts are the prizes now.

Afghanistan has a unique strategic location which makes it both a part of South as well as Central Asia. It connects Europe and Asia and any instability in this country has a profound influence on the Central Asian Republic's, hence no study of this region is complete without including Afghanistan in it. It can also be said that Afghanistan is part of the greater Central Asia region.

Internal Dimensions

The political systems that evolved in these states exhibit the features of authoritarianism with minor differences. All the states adopted new Constitutions, which institutionalised the presidential form of government. Discipline and order have taken precedence over democratic norms and systems. All other centers of "authority," including the legislature and the judiciary, are subordinate to the executive branch of the state. The leaders of the Central Asian Republics have supported their authoritarianism by arguing that in the transition times, the concentration of power in a single centre is an absolute necessity. Thus, everything is described by the popular Russian proverb about not changing horse's midstream. Since opposition has been suppressed or co-opted, the elections in some of the republics have assumed a less than fair nature. The presidents of these states have often preferred to get reelected through referendums.

While acknowledging the achievements of the Central Asian leaders, especially in the preservation and consolidation of national independence and sovereignty, the failure to bring material welfare to the people and corruption along with nepotism have diminished the "oriental trait of respect for state leadership" among the common people. However, there is a requirement to go beyond the contemporary political situation by tracing the issues and trends related to future succession in the Central Asian Republics. The coming few years are going to be crucial for an orderly succession as the extended terms of the presidents of the Central Asian states would be expiring. Would these countries be affected by the type of current upheavals in Egypt and rest of Arab world?

Lesson from the current situation in the Arab World may be equally applicable to Central Asia and hence care a matter of concern. These are thwarting the development of democratic institutions which eliminates the possibility of political change being effected without a convulsion. Secondly, the unpredictability of succession breeds instability.

Economic Dimensions

Understanding the economic dimensions would offer more advantage to an observer of Central Asia as these would tend to strongly influence the social, political and security environment of the region. Unlike political change, the transformation from the erstwhile Soviet command economy to a market economy has not been smooth as it ruptured the existing industry, trade, agriculture and communication systems. The nature of previous Soviet economic development has been partly responsible for the problems faced by the post-Soviet Central Asian economies, at least on four accounts. Firstly, during the Soviet times, limited industrialisation was accompanied by employment of a workforce from the European parts of the Soviet Union and not so much by the creation of an indigenous one. Secondly, the Soviet policies, oriented towards the state's goal of vertical integration of regions with the central economy, without much concern about local needs and traditions, resulted in serious distortions in the social and economic spheres; 60 to 65 per cent of the indigenous population was still employed in agriculture.

Thirdly, the agriculture sector was distorted with the monoculture of cotton. Fourthly, in the Soviet economic complex, not a single regional sub-system, especially the smaller republics, possessed the traits of autonomous reproduction. Hence, after the break-up of these linkages of a unified chain, isolated functioning of many enterprises became practically impossible. The strategies adopted by different regimes to reform the economy are to a large extent influenced by their ability to cope with the transformational challenges.

International community and Central Asia

The disintegration of the Soviet Union left the vast Eurasian space open for geo-political competition and contestation. Initially, the international community's interest in Central Asia largely focussed on four key areas: (1) addressing the security threats emanating from the transnational *Jihadi* forces, particularly the Taliban and Al-Qaeda; (2) gaining control over the region to enhance global influence; (3) controlling the hydrocarbon reserves of the region; (4) increasing their market presence for trading goods and services.

Apart from the US and Russia, Central Asia's neighbours, China, India, Iran, Turkey and Pakistan, have vital stakes in developments within the region as one way or the other they influence the interests of these states. The initial differences aside, the post-9/11 context witnessed a sort of convergence in the understanding of security threats emanating from the Taliban and Al-Qaeda, and extending mutual support in tackling these forces. As the militarily weak regimes of Central Asia could not handle some of the security threats on their own, the US, Russia and Iran extended their support to these states.

However, it is the competition between regional and extra-regional powers, mainly the US, Russia, Iran and China, to gain control over the "power vacuum" left by the Soviet Union's disintegration that has been the characteristic feature of the post-Soviet Eurasia's strategic environment. Termed as the "New Great Game," this competition is largely in tune with the global and regional aspirations of these powers where each actor has a vital stake in the outcome. Since gaining control over the development, production and transit of hydrocarbon resources of the Caspian Basin, considered as the "Persian Gulf of the 21st Century," to a large extent will decide the outcome, each actor is playing "The Game" to eliminate the other from this key area. As the land-locked Central Asian countries have to depend on one or the other for energy exports, the competition of major powers to bring them into their fold is adding to the post-Soviet foreign policy dilemmas of the region's leaders. The US policies in gaining control over the Caspian basin's energy sector have also not come up to its expectations. Its objective of decreasing Russia and Iran's influence from transiting oil and gas has not met with success due to Russian assertiveness and lack of a conducive atmosphere in Afghanistan which would otherwise have provided an opportunity to largely sideline Iran.

While the US is trying to establish itself in the Central Asian region, Russia is boldly asserting to strengthen its position in what it calls its "traditional sphere of influence." Russia's foreign policy under Vladimir Putin is taking a proactive role. In tune with the policy objective of maintaining its status as a leading power in the Eurasian region to meet its global ambitions, Russia has put in place a coherent "multi-vector" strategy in which it has effectively combined incentives with "soft coercion" towards its neighbours. By effectively using multilateral structures and improving bilateral economic and military cooperation, Russia is trying to enhance its position in the "Near Abroad." While accepting the presence of US forces in the Af-Pak area, Russia is clearly expressing its reservations about "security partnerships" in the region with "non-regional states."

The other major player in Central Asian geo-politics is China. By sharing territorial boundaries with three of the five Central Asian states, Kazakhstan, Kyrgyzstan and Tajikistan, China has emerged as a major player in the Central Asian strategic context, especially from the middle of the 1990s. The major objectives of China's policies towards Central Asia are: enhancing its position as an emerging global power, expanding the market opportunities, procuring natural resources at low costs and containing security threats emanating from Uighur unrest in Xinjiang province.

The structure of the SCO provides an opportunity for China to expand its economic presence in the Central Asian region, and to ensure that it gets influence, power, hegemony and profits in this area.

Afghanistan and Central Asia

All five Central Asian Republics perceive their own national security as directly tied to developments in Afghanistan because of the transnational threats that originate in that country, or just beyond in Pakistan. They are equally worried due to possibility of a force vacuum after the intended US/ NATO withdrawal from Afghanistan in future. The three states that border Afghanistan (Tajikistan, Turkmenistan, and Uzbekistan) have the greatest level of concern. While each of these countries wants the US and international coalition to succeed, broader national interests shape the degree and kind of national participation that has been offered by individual countries. Leaders in all five states believe there are risks as well as potential benefits associated with participation in US activities against terrorism. Nonetheless, each has been willing to participate, albeit always mindful of the possible impact on the relationship with Russia and on its own population. In particular, Uzbekistan, Tajikistan, and Kyrgyzstan have rented airfields to NATO. Only Kyrgyzstan's are still in use, although the French International Security Assistance Force (ISAF) contingent makes more limited use of the Dushanbe commercial airfield in Tajikistan. Uzbekistan, Kazakhstan, and Tajikistan also all play major roles in facilitating transport of non-lethal cargo along the new Northern Distribution Network. Turkmenistan, which pursues a foreign policy based on "positive neutrality," will not provide direct support for ISAF military activities, but it has permitted the transport of humanitarian cargo and grants limited over-flight and emergency landing or other facilities.

In the long run, however, if Afghanistan is to be helped and made a viable state in the interest of regional security, expansion of the transportation corridors in and around the country are essential. These would permit not only Afghanistan but all the regional states to benefit from the rapidly expanding Chinese, Indian and other Asian economies by becoming either new sources of raw material exports to these states or new markets for their own goods or even by simply enjoying transit fees for commodities passing in any direction through their territories. This idea and efforts for exploiting economic opportunities to enhance regional security, however, invariably peter out – and for good reason. The evidence, thus for suggests that at least one critical state, Pakistan, has consistently valued its security driven relative gains more than any absolute gains emerging from enhanced regional trade. Consequently, here too, desired goals of regional integration have been blocked, because of Islamabad's fears about its own narrow political interests not being served as a result of increased prosperity accruing to others; even if Pakistan itself flourished in the process, have prevented it from cooperating in the manner that votaries of economic integration imagined it should. This particular attitude requires to be tackled at both regional and global levels.

India and Central Asian Republics

The emergence of independent states in the Eurasian region has thrown up new foreign policy challenges for India. To an internally liberalised and externally pragmatist India, the Central Asian region has offered opportunities as well as challenges to deal with. The Central Asian region has become an important factor in the foreign policy priorities of India, partly because of its geo-political location and partly because of the nature and character of its neighbouring states. Four objectives have become critical in its policy priorities for the Central Asian region: (1) while neutralising security threats emanating from the transnational *Jihadi* forces and drug traders, achieving peace and stability in the region by extending bilateral and multilateral cooperation, technical and humanitarian assistance and participating constructively in the region's development process; (2) finding a fine balance between the priorities of the major powers (the US, Russia and China) that are actively engaged in this strategically competitive region to establish their supremacy; (3) developing transportation and communication links within and beyond the region for enhanced access and connectivity; (4) maximising the share of economic benefits the region offers to the global market, particularly in the energy sector.

India has been striving to develop a transport corridor to the Central Asian region without which long-term stable trading relations are impossible. The agreement concluded among India, Russia and Iran on September 12,

2000, to build an International Transport Corridor (ITC), better known as the North-South Transport Corridor, is a significant development in this context. The corridor stretches from ports in India across the Arabian Sea to the southern Iranian port of Bander Abbas, where goods then transit to ports in Russia's sector of the Caspian. From there, the route stretches along the Volga River via Moscow to northern Europe. Once it becomes fully operational, it will reduce both time and cost of delivery. The project has the potential to incorporate other interested states, including the Caucasian countries, Central Asia, and Eastern Europe. The problem in this project is less than enthusiastic participation by Iran. The other possible corridors could be (a) Access through Xingiang (b) Through Pakistan: Access through Gwadar Port, Karakoram highway. These however, have quite a few impediments which require to be surmounted. The other policy objective of importing the hydrocarbon resources of Central Asia has met with little success due to the costs involved and the prevailing instability in the Afghanistan-Pakistan border areas. Out of the three options available to India to build transit pipelines to bring energy resources from Central Asia via Iran and Pakistan, via Afghanistan and Pakistan, via China's Xinjiang province - so far, only TAPI has shown progress.

For India, the independence of the Central Asian states has opened a new opportunity to renew its rich legacy of historical ties and cultural contacts. For India, these states are part of its extended/strategic neighbourhood. Common commitments to peace and stability, open societies, secularism and similar perception on security threats and their origin bind India and these states together. Increasing linkages between India and CARs, Afghanistan's membership to the SAARC, and its emergence as a potentially important player in facilitating regional economic cooperation is shaping India's *"Look North Policy"*. There is a need to connect India with Central Asia through multi-modal corridors, particularly, in the transport and trade sectors. In a sense, it recreates the past history of the region when robust trading activity was a dominating feature. Afghanistan was the fulcrum on which such activities were carried out in various directions. However, an unstable situation in Afghanistan and obtuse policies of Pakistan prevent achievement of good connectivity between South and Central Asia.

The following chapters in the book authored by eminent experts in the field give their perceptions on external environment and internal dynamics of Central Asian states and the role India can play in areas of key concern to the Central Asian states, especially in their economic development; diversification of their economies, cooperation in energy sector and transport corridors as they are landlocked. There is a need to explore the prospects intensifying Indian engagement with the region. In this context, it is important to identify the tools available to India in furtherance of its objective. Can India's soft power be harnessed to benefit the ties? These are some of the issues that need in-depth understanding and analysis. These are the issues which have been deliberated upon in this book.

PERCEPTIONS AND VIEWS OF AMBASSADORS OF AFGHANISTAN AND CENTRAL ASIAN REPUBLICS TO INDIA

HE Dr Nanguyalai Tarzai
Ambassador of Afghanistan

Afghanistan has a unique geographical location in the heart of Asia where four of the most populous and resource rich region in the world converge; South Asia, Central and North Asia Middle East and Far East. In the 19th century when the British Empire was ruling this subcontinent the notion of South Asia as it is today did not exist. And Afghanistan was located between the British Empire and the Central Asian Emirates of Bahara, Hewa, Samarthan and Ferghana under the domination of the Russian Empire. With the establishment of the Soviet Union and the collapse of the above mentioned Emirates in the Central Asia, the term of Central Asia was extended to the newly established country that later achieved its independence. Due to its geographical location Afghanistan has historical relations with Central Asia as well as Indian subcontinent in South Asia. The relation reached a new phase with the independence of Afghanistan and India as well as the newly established republics of Central Asia.

The thousand of years old relation with the subcontinent has given Afghanistan a special place in the history of South Asia. Based on the historical and traditional relations, India did not spare any efforts to contribute to the infrastructure and institutional building of Afghanistan. With the contribution for $1.4 billion for the reconstruction of Afghanistan, India ranks the 6th largest donor to Afghanistan in the world. Throughout the history, Afghanistan stood central to the silk route and even today because of its vital location has emerged as a key transit route for Central Asian energy resources to South Asia and beyond. A good example is the TAPI gas pipeline project. The project envisages exporting natural gas from Turkmenistan to Pakistan and India through Afghanistan. The recently signed Afghanistan-Pakistan trade and transit agreement is another example which makes faster and cheaper Afghan goods to reach India via Pakistan. We hope with the same agreement goods from India will also be carried to Afghanistan and to Central Asia. Afghanistan is also a mineral rich country with considerable assets and potential for its economic development which can contribute to the economic development of the region and the world at large. The government of Afghanistan is committed to share the benefit of its centrality through regional cooperation with its neighbouring countries, and behind it its immediate neighbourhood.

Recently iron, coal and other minerals etc. are being extracted and a number of Indian companies are involved at different levels of these developmental activities. We look forward for investments to exploit our natural resources, which is around $3 trillion. As the most investment friendly country, Afghanistan is proud to be a partner in the collective effort in the sub regional prosperity and integration of its economy and the stability of the region and the world. To substantiate this partnership, Afghanistan has become a member of two regional organisations; the SAARC and ECO. We also have good exemplary relations with our neighbours in Central Asia and we are grateful for the assistance and help which we receive. But unfortunately Afghanistan, our region and the world as a whole are facing the challenge of insecurity caused by the menace of terrorism and together with a strong determination we can stop it. Even history has proved that peace and stability in Afghanistan is a major factor for stability and economic growth of the whole region. And I conclude with what the great thinker and famous poet of the subcontinent Al-lama Lahuri has said about Afghanistan. I just read the translation:

Asia is the body of water in soil
Afghan nation is the heart in this body
Its sorrow brings sorrow to Asia
Its happiness brings happiness to Asia.

HE Mrs Orolbaeva Irina Abdyevna
Ambassador of Kyrgyzstan

This year Kyrgyz Republic, as well as other Central Asian former Soviet republics will celebrate 20th anniversary of its independence. During this short period Kyrgyzstan has twice endured events of the revolutionary character connected with changes in polity.

Kyrgyzstan since its independence on 31st August 1991 is strictly following the course for carrying out democratic reforms. The social society is actively involved in management: in the country the NGOs are widely presented, the multi-party system is developed, independent mass media are working that does not give possibility to the Head of the State to completely usurp the power.

The events that took place in April 2010 are an acknowledgement of the fact that the people and progressive forces of the society will not suffer lawlessness and corruption which used to blossom during years gone bye.

On 6-7 April 2010 the people of Kyrgyzstan overthrew the family and clan regime of the President Kurmanbek Bakiev. The state power was transferred to the Interim Government as a result of popular will. The national referendum took place on 27th of June last year with the active participation of the society. A new Constitution was adopted by way of nationwide voting which laid the foundation of parliamentary form of governance in Kyrgyzstan.

Along with the Constitution, a decree "On President of Kyrgyz Republic for transition period" was put to the referendum. As a result the Chairwoman of the Interim Government Roza Otunbaeva was elected as President for the period till the end of 2011.

According to the new Constitution, the country has adopted the parliamentary form of government, and Kyrgyzstan has become the first parliamentary republic among the Commonwealth of Independent States (CIS) countries to bring fundamental changes in its political system.

The new constitution has taken away some powers from the post of President and devolved them on to the Prime Minister. President retains enough authority to exert significant influence on the political process.

The presidency is to be restricted to one term of six years only. An upper age limit of 70 has been set for the post. The winning parties are restricted to 50 per cent of seats in the parliament and plus five with the number of seats in legislature of 120, this limited absolute majority will be 65. The system should help to strengthen a political pluralism as it will give more influence to opposition parties.

The system is entirely based on party lists, with no individual constituencies. One important point is that new constitution reinstates the statement that Kyrgyzstan is a secular state, adding a line prohibiting religious organizations and the clergy from interfering in the work of state institutions. The Constitution is being considered as only the start of a long process which should take Kyrgyzstan away from the kind of autocratic presidential rule that sparked popular protest in March 2005 and in April 2010, in both cases leading to the Heads of State of the time, Askar Akaev and his successor Kurmanbek Bakiev, being ousted.

Parliamentary elections were held on 10th October 2010. Twenty Nine political parties participated in the election from which five parties won the race. Parliament and then the government were formed. Nowadays Kyrgyzstan has a unique chance to build a true democratic parliamentary state based on the rule of law.

A tragic event that happened after April political changes was the interethnic clash and killings in the southern region of Kyrgyzstan, bordering Tajikistan and Uzbekistan.

On January 19th 2011, seven months after violence, a National Commission was established to investigate the causes and consequences of the conflict. It has presented its findings and recommendations.

Bloody street fighting broke out on June 10th in Osh, Kyrgyzstan's second city, and raged for five days, leaving several Uzbek neighbourhoods burnt to the ground. About 100,000 Uzbeks were forced to flee the city, many crossing the border into neighbouring Uzbekistan.

In the months following the violence, Human Rights Watch, the international campaign group, has warned of "mob justice and fundamentally flawed investigations" which have overwhelmingly targeted ethnic Uzbeks.

"The tragic events were provoked not by the Uzbek or Kyrgyz people, but by people with extremist views," stressed Mr. Erkebayev, the Head of National Commission. He also suggested that there had been some prior organisation ahead of the violence.

In that difficult time, friendly India offered a helping hand as it always believes in the interests of strengthening peace and democracy. The notable humanitarian help was directed to the south of Kyrgyzstan by Indian Air Force at the time of utmost need. My government has expressed its gratitude to the Government of India.

Kyrgyz side also appreciates the Indian recognition of the parliamentary elections in Kyrgyzstan and great support extended to the new Government of Kyrgyzstan Republic. We are grateful especially for the efforts being extended to the democratic process aimed at stability and further development of Kyrgyzstan.

The strategic goal of some terrorist organisations illegally operating in Ferghana Valley is to overthrow the constitutional system in Kyrgyzstan, Uzbekistan, Tajikistan, and Kazakhstan with the view of building an Islamist state a Caliphate, with the outlook to relocate the zone of instability to China and Russia.

Kyrgyzstan along with other Central Asian states is becoming a main transit corridor for trafficking drugs to Central Asian states, Russia and then to Europe and USA. An estimated 90 per cent of heroin consumed in Russia is trafficked from Afghanistan via Central Asian countries. The main route is Gorno-Badakhshan-Osh-Andijan mountain road which is 3000m above the sea level.

Deterioration of economic situation and war in Afghanistan, Taliban insurgency in Pakistan, growing threat of radical Islamic fundamentalist groups make the security situation very vulnerable in our common region. We understand that terrorism, drug trafficking and organised crime are a serious barrier on the path to progress in the region that should focus the world community's attention.

Formally Kyrgyzstan as the participant of the anti-terrorist coalition in accordance with the agreements with a number of member countries has given its international airport 'Manas' in 2001 as the aviation base for transfer of cargo to Afghanistan. The USA is responsible for that and this military base which in 2009 was renamed as 'Facility Centre' is recognised as American base. Two years later after opening of the base the agreements have been reached on providing the Russian Air Forces with the former military airdrome in the city of Kant near the capital Bishkek, but formally the base is considered as the aviation component of the Rapid Response Forces of the countries of the Collective Security Treaty Organisation. This is considered by many abroad as collision of interests between Russia and the USA, though we consider it as balance of forces in the region on the whole. And this is the contribution of Kyrgyzstan to the common fight against terrorism.

The Central Asian countries are rich with natural resources and become more influential players in the energy development program. Kyrgyzstan does not have the reserves of oil and gas and therefore can count only on development of its rich hydropower industry.

This is a difficult time for our country due to cardinal changes in political life and system, and we would request all to appreciate our difficulties and be with us in this resolute hour during the transitional phase of change to democracy. What we need more is understanding the situation and respecting the choice of Kyrgyz people.

Our countries are united by common historic and cultural roots, which are extending into the depths of centuries, when the trade and handicrafts were flouring over the whole Great Silk Road. It means that our common history bequeath to us to continue these traditions and I want to stress once again that there is no obstacles between our countries for common prosperity.

HE Mr Salikh Inagamov
Ambassador of Uzbekistan

Recently Central Asia has been witnessing the process of transition in social and political reforms, rapid economic growth and at the same time the region has been suffering from terrorism, extremism, drug trafficking and regional conflicts. I am confident that during this seminar our distinguished participants will share their valuable opinion on recent developments in Central Asia and give their assessment on the prospects of this region. Speaking of Uzbekistan's place and its importance in the region one should not forget that for nearly 20 years of its independence Uzbekistan has been carrying out gradual reforms in all fields' social, political, economic and cultural life. At the same time Uzbekistan has been at the forefront in the struggle against terrorism, religious extremism, drug trafficking and other activities which pose a real threat to peace and stability and economic development not only of Uzbekistan but of the entire region.

It may not be necessary to go into the details of Uzbekistan's economic development or elaborate on reforms. However, I would like to briefly dwell upon the concept of future deepening of democratic reforms of establishing the civil society in the country. Put forward by President Ismail Karimov at the Joint session of parliament of Uzbekistan in November last year the concept has been widely discussed by experts and analysts in many countries and is viewed as a crucial document which defines the ways of the country's development for several years ahead. The concept covers the most important areas of reforms, visions and adoption of new laws and legislative documents at enhancing the role of parliaments and political parties in people's life, enhancing the electoral system, liberalizing judicial aid and economic life, developing mass media, in creating favourable conditions for setting up NGO's.

Among the initiatives put forward by the President, I would like to draw your attention on one that suggests the Prime Minister being nominated by a political party which secures majority in the lower house of the parliament. Following the President's approval the candidate would have to be approved by both houses of the parliament. Yet in another statement which gives the role of legislative authority, suggests that the parliament will have the right to pass the vote of no confidence against the Prime Minister. These are the initiatives of the President and are seen as the new phase of reforming and democratizing the country and go for economic reforms. Yet it proves commitment of our leadership to continue with the comprehensive reforms in the country to make Uzbekistan a truly democratic state and develop its economy.

Uzbekistan has been playing an important role in maintaining regional peace and stability. In this regard I would like to say a few words about Uzbekistan's approach on how to solve the most important security problem of the region which is Afghanistan. It is an open secret that the major threat to regional security in Central Asia comes from Afghanistan. During the years of independence Uzbekistan has been trying positively to help Afghanistan by assisting it in economic development, reconstruction and capacity building in this war torn country. Over the years Uzbekistan has implemented a number of important projects in the field of railways, IT and other important sectors of the Afghan economy. Particularly worth mentioning is that Uzbekistan has been supplying electricity through power lines which were built with the assistance of our Indian friends.

Moreover, recently Uzbekistan has concluded construction of 4th railway in Uzbekistan from Hairatan to Mazar-e-Sharif in Afghanistan. The 75kms long railway was built by Uzbekistan National Railway Company. The project cost was $180million and funded by Asian Development Bank and the Government of Afghanistan. The railway connected the border town of Termez in Uzbekistan to Mazar-i-Sharif town of Afghanistan. Commissioning of this railway shall be contributing to the enhancing of supply routes of non military cargo of NATO/ISAF troops from territory of Uzbekistan to Afghanistan. In conclusion I would like to thank the organisers for excellent arrangement and for expressing confidence in opinions which will be presented in the seminar which will be of great use in strengthening the relations between the countries of Central Asia and India.

HE Mr Parakhat H. Durdyev
Ambassador of Turkmenistan

My focus will be more on Afghanistan where we are trying to make efforts in stabilizing the country and provide assistance which may be of great importance to that country. First of all I would like to thank you for inviting to speak here in this gathering and let me express my hopes that the outcome of the seminar would be only for good or better understanding of each other. I will speak about Turkmenistan's peace efforts in Afghanistan. Turkmenistan has been contributing most actively in the global efforts to resolve the conflict in Afghanistan. As the President of Turkmenistan has stated at the Millennium Development Goals Summit in New York in September 2010 and I quote "We want to see Afghanistan as a peaceful and prosperous country, a good neighbour and partners of all countries in the region. Moreover we believe that the United Nations can and should play an active role in solving the Afghan crisis. Afghanistan related problems should be solved through peaceful means and negotiations, through developing on a long term basis new political and diplomatic mechanisms responding to modern realities."

Along with the political aspect of the problem the attention should be drawn to the need of creating mechanisms for the effective participation of the Afghan people. Particularly, these concerns of development and acceleration of long term programme for the revival of economic and social infrastructure of Afghanistan under the aegis of United Nations. This programme should first of all involve the project of developing the transport and communication network, electrification, diversification of industry, construction of schools, hospitals that will help stabilization and help in the social and economic development of the country. Taking into consideration the long border almost 900kms as well as the common roots between the two fraternal countries, Turkmenistan has far reaching plans with Afghanistan. These include projects in the energy and transport sector which is important not only to the participant countries but for the entire region as a whole. By connecting the highway and railway network Turkmenistan and Afghanistan which have the advantageous geographical location can ensure the transit of goods through their territory on the South East West corridor. The paramount task is assisting Afghanistan in developing transport infrastructure.

Our country proposes a project of constructing a road from Turkmenistan to Afghanistan and further extension to Afghan territory through the aid of international donor and aid organizations and institutions. It is difficult to over estimate our initiative of the construction of the TAPI gas pipeline. This is no longer an idea but a real project as seen in the TAPI Ashgabat summit meeting of 2010. The meeting was of the Technical Working Group, steering committee of the TAPI (Turkmenistan-Afghanistan-Pakistan- India) gas pipeline project as well as bilateral and quadrilateral meeting in Ashgabat, in Delhi and in Dubai. Couple of meetings are yet to happen but we are waiting for the next meeting to take place in Ashgabat. Asian Development Bank, which has specified the various ways and mechanisms for the construction of the new energy route is yet to formulate the basics of consortium formation, and continues to be integral part of the project.

The planned distance of the gas pipeline is 1635 kms and its capacity is 33bcm annually. The project cost is enormous some $ 7 billion but in the present international environment it could be slashed by 50 percent. Although security concerns are still relevant taking into account the ground realities of Afghanistan. The success of this undertaking is vital not only for the Central and South Asia but also for the rest of the world interested in the irreversibility of the stabilization and developmental processes in Afghanistan. The project is being pursued with the aim to bring peace and stability in Afghanistan in addition to the commercial one. Construction of the TAPI gas pipeline has the further potential of generating along the route many other infrastructure projects that would give powerful impetus to the economy and social development infrastructure in Afghanistan. In particular, it would create thousands of new jobs as a spin off from the successful conclusion of the project.

Our country also stands ready to collaborate in the exploration of natural oil and gas fields within Afghanistan. The ultimate goal is to ensure political stability in the region by economic means, expand the opportunity for attractive international partnerships for peace and security, economic and social progress and essentially have a positive impact on the international security. Other meaningful contribution by Turkmenistan is that we gave gas to our Southern neighbour at symbolic prices. Under the existing bilateral agreements Turkmenistan experts are engaged in building important economic facilities in Afghanistan. First of all this includes our transmission lines supplying Turkmen electricity to the Afghan people. We are willing to take active part in the power supply to Afghanistan; particularly power supplies to Herat will be increased in future. Also the development of the project for construction of sub stations, 500 kilowatts power transmission lines in the territory of Turkmenistan stretching for 410 kilometres along the border of Afghanistan is underway. All this is being done out of Turkmenistan's own funds and risks and involves many vulnerabilities. If anything happens we will be affected more than anyone else. But we are consciously doing it because we understand that engagement is the only way out.

Turkmenistan is ready to increase the electricity supply to Afghanistan and as well as expand our own energy infrastructure for the purpose of future installation of networks in the Afghan territory, inviting international communities represented by the UN to discuss the proposal. Contributing to the sustainable development, Turkmenistan provides assistance in training specialists and reserves a quota for the neighbouring country in the educational institutions as well as provides free medical care to the population in both the areas. We also propose to train in the UN coordinated programmes.

I reiterate Turkmenistan's commitment to actively and effectively participate in the stabilization process of Afghanistan in support of the international community especially the UN and its specialised agencies in the peaceful settlement of the problem in Afghanistan including economic development and engage in projects which would ultimately lead to political stability in this region and beyond. It is with this approach that we view initiatives in implementing large scale regional development projects such as Trans Asian pipeline that started to supply Turkmen gas to China in December, North-South railway which is to be operational in this October which will be the shortest and convenient route from Europe to South Asia in the Persian Gulf built by the joint efforts of Turkmenistan, Iran, Kazakhstan,

Russia or the possibility for supplying Turkmen gas and oil to India and Pakistan through Afghanistan as well as construction of East West gas pipeline and a variety of other projects like roads, ports, airports etc as our investments in future to regional and international integration and engagement.

I would like to go further into detail but here at the end of my short note I would like to share some brief statistics about our efforts:

- Last year we have registered 42 Turkmen-Afghan, 32 Turkmen-Kazakh, 2 Turkmen-Kyrgyz, and 13 Turkmen-Uzbek companies operating in Turkmenistan.

- Every year Turkmenistan appoints 30 Afghanis in the higher educational institutions of the country since 2003. And I believe that this number should reach 100 with effect from 2011.

- One school with 400 school children was registered in Shordepe district; Balkh province and a hospital in Garamgol district of Faryab province were built.

- The 2 km section of the Serhatabad Turgundi railway was reconstructed to the tune of $550000 and Atamurat- Imamnazar-Andhoy railway, of which 90 km will be in Turkmenistan and 36 km in Afghanistan is under consideration.

- Humanitarian aid in abnormally cold 2007-08 season became a routine affair and this practice has been followed on a regular basis since then and happened even before.

- Writing off the Afghan debts for delivered power is done on regular basis.

- Afghanistan is recipient of special discounted prices at the Turkmen Stock Exchange for every item on sale.

- Cultural exchange programs are held on a regular basis.

AN OVERVIEW OF THE STRATEGIC ENVIRONMENT OF CENTRAL ASIA

Amb. Kanwal Sibal

It is well recognized that India attaches great importance to its relations with Central Asia. But there are physical difficulties which hinder India in enhancing its relations with Central Asian Republics, essentially because these countries are land locked and there is no direct access to them. Strategic environment in Central Asia can be conceptualised in two facets: the role of major players in Central Asia and the extent and degree to which multilateral engagements have been beneficial or otherwise to the Central Asian republics.

Ever since the Soviet Union collapsed the strategic environment in Central Asia has got completely transformed. Some may recall the writings that came from the United States from people like Mr. Zbigniew Brzezinski who spoke about Central Asia being the soft underbelly of Soviet Union. The argument was that to achieve larger US strategic goals, the Soviet Union could be weakened or put on the defensive through the Central Asian countries. Whatever be the reasons for the collapse of the Soviet Union, with the emergence of Central Asia as independent countries, the strategic picture in this region has changed altogether.

As an observer, one could say that all of a sudden a power vacuum got created in Central Asia. The countries that would have interest in filling this power vacuum would have been, primarily, Russia itself. These countries were originally part of the Soviet Union, but the new Russian government under Yeltsin turned its back to the Central Asian countries, preferring its relationship with Europe. With President Putin coming to the power, Russia began to focus its attention on Central Asian states. In fact, in defining the new priorities of Russian foreign policy, Commonwealth of Independent States (CIS) and the Central Asian states were put in the most immediate concentric circle of Russian interest. Therefore, it would be normal, and remains understandable, if Russia were to look upon this area, if not as a 'strategic backyard 'because that could be misunderstood, but one where its strategic interests were deeply involved.

The other major contender who would want to establish its presence in the region is the United States of America. America is a global power, and especially after the collapse of Soviet Union, it saw itself as the only superpower left. That was the era of uni-polarity that is well known. The US focused on this region mainly because of its hydrocarbon potential, but, over and beyond that, also as a key strategic area which would, if they positioned themselves there strongly, give them a multidirectional role aimed at Russia, Iran and, of course, China in the east.

The third contender for influence is obviously China. As one can see from the map, many of these countries are direct neighbours of China. China is resource and energy hungry, whereas these countries are a source of oil and gas to power China's growth. Moreover, as a neighbour, China has clear, understandable interest in managing a better relationship with them, after having settled its outstanding border issues.

The other country that initially tried hard to become a major player, or a leader, was Turkey. Turks suddenly found that all these countries with Turkic historical and cultural links were available as a natural arena for them to build a strong bilateral political, security, and of course, cultural relationship. In the initial years they made a great deal of effort to build up these linkages with Central Asia. They were not entirely successful. Possibly, these newly independent countries were not ready to come under some kind of domination by another big brother, this time, Turkey. In terms of soft power like education and language Turkey still remains a powerful force in the region, and also in terms of trade and economic activity.

The other country that it was feared would try and fill the vacuum was Iran. Again, as a neighbour to the South, it was felt that Iran with its aggressive

Islamic credentials might wish to play an Islamic role in this area in order to counterbalance the US presence in the region, and strengthen its historical links especially with countries like Tajikistan. Being India's Ambassador in Turkey at that time, the author was privy to the discussions then on the issue of whether for India Turkey, with its secular credentials, would be a far better option as a partner for these countries than Iran as a country with an Islamist vocation. Further, Japan and Korea also have tried to establish their influence in the area.

As regards India, there has been a flurry of high level visits between Central Asian countries and India. The Presidents of most of these countries have visited India very often. From Indian side, perhaps, such visits have not been reciprocated to the same degree in terms of high level visits, but, nevertheless, there has been a great deal of activity on the ground in order to explore all possible opportunities for India to play a role.

India's goals are quite simple to understand. Firstly, India wants peace and stability in this area. When these countries were part of the Soviet Union India didn't see any strategic challenge in front of it because India had excellent relations with the Soviet Union. Even at that time when Indian delegations visited the Soviet Union, their itinerary was largely organised around the Central Asian states. India had close contacts and was very comfortable with these countries when they were part of the Soviet Union, having good understanding not only with leaders but also the society at large. Secondly, this being the period during which Islam rose as a radical force in this region at large; India would naturally feel extremely concerned if the depth of this radical extremist thinking got extended to Central Asia. Pakistan is in the process of getting radicalized; Afghanistan is unstable. If Afghanistan came under Taliban rule, extremist ideologies could over-run Central Asia. The meaning of all this for India would be that it would have very limited opportunity in the future to establish productive relations with such Central Asian regimes.

Issues related to terrorism worry India very much. The spread of terrorism, with its epicenter in the Afghanistan-Pakistan region, can destabilize Central Asia potentially. India, therefore, has common interest with Central

Asian countries to contain this menace.

Economic dimension of relationship is also very important. India is the largest economy in this area. If one looks at the map the distances are not that much. But there is the physical problem of access because of political differences between Pakistan and India. Potentially, however, India is in a position to play an important role in contributing to the economic growth of these countries. That would reinforce our larger goal of helping strengthen peace and stability in the region.

The biggest opportunity is in the oil and gas sector. To what extent can India and others exploit these hydrocarbon assets to mutual advantage? India is making a serious effort in Kazakhstan and now Turkmenistan, but the quantum of success India might achieve remains to be seen.

Russia continues to be in a very powerful position because the networks, pipelines and regional supply arrangements have been historically linked to Russia. These cannot be substantially modified in the medium term. Russia, therefore, continues to be an important factor. It would naturally want any future projects and plans not to be at the expense of minimum Russian interests. It is for Russia to define these interests taking into account the new political realities and the enhanced choice of partners that the Central Asian countries now have. It would seem Russia is taking a realistic view and is ready to adjust to competition.

For China, independent Central Asian countries have provided a wonderful new opportunity to tap into newly available resources to fuel China's growth. Pipelines have already been built for supply of gas by Turkmenistan, for example, to China, and volumes are planned to be increased. China's position in this regard has improved strategically because of its tie up with Russia itself for supply of oil and gas. After many years of hesitation and slow movement, Russia has finally decided to build a pipeline to China. It has agreed strategically that its natural resources can be used to fuel China's phenomenal economic growth.

America's ambition with regard to oil and gas resources of the region is well known. It has essentially focused on the Caspian Sea area, and especially, Kazakhstan. Further east, the Americans were interested in a gas pipeline across Afghanistan from Central Asia even when the Taliban were in power in Afghanistan. The TAPI project has been revived. The Americans have a vision of Greater Central Asia with integrative links between Central Asia and South Asia. The goal is to extract the resources of Central Asia through linkages with South Asia. This would diminish the political and economic grip of Russia and China on the resources of these countries. This US strategy caused a lot of worry to Russians when it was first unveiled because the impulse came from the Pentagon rather than the US State Department. Now such Russian concerns seem to have become attenuated.

The market size of Central Asian countries may not be big as the population size is small. Nevertheless, these are countries with large development needs. Neighbouring countries would have interest in getting a share of the available market. China, with its enormous export capacities, is dumping its products in Central Asia. What this is doing to the survival of local Central Asian economies is well-known to these countries.

The key issue is that of potential instability in this region. There are external threats as also internal political distractions, with problems, in Kyrgyzstan, Uzbekistan and, earlier, in Tajikistan. There have been problems of governance, of establishing political systems which relate directly to the needs of the people, of constructing modern democracies. All this is in the context of relatively low economic development and rising aspirations and pressures stemming from globalization that impact the internal dynamics. The region has witnessed the phenomenon of velvet revolutions with ambiguous roots and elusive results. Some positive changes are occurring as, for example, the institutionalizing of democracy in Kyrgyzstan. The threat of religious extremism is real. This remains a big problem when political and economic development is lagging, as people can easily get inspiration from extremist religious ideology and try and change the system by mobilising the disaffection and grievances of the people on an Islamic platform. India has to be concerned about these threats for obvious reasons as it is not far away.

Another country, at a distance, which is deeply worried, is Russia, and it makes no secret of its concern. It regards Central Asia as a buffer for containing religious radicalism and terrorism in Southern Russia. For Russia the disruptive forces that are destabilising Central Asia could in the next stage increase its problems in Southern Russia. The problems of terrorism and drug trafficking are causing the Russians great loss in human terms, because statistics show that 30,000 Russians die from drug abuse every year and most addicts relapse into dependency even after treatment in Russia's clinics. (These fatalities in a single year are more than twice the figure of Soviet Union soldiers who died in over a decade long war in Afghanistan). Russia has been putting the drug trafficking problem on the agenda of every international forum that deals with Central Asia and Afghanistan in a bid to get international cooperation. But they have not been fully successful in this effort.

In Central Asia Russia has played its cards rather well. In my judgment Russia is careful to respect the sovereignty of the Central Asian countries, adhering to the principle of non-interfere in their internal affairs, avoiding giving lectures to them on their political systems and exhorting them to embrace democracy. Their concern about the so called velvet revolutions affecting the former Soviet space is, of course, clear.

Russia has clear security interests in Central Asia which they have tried to secure through organisations like Collective Security Treaty Organization (CSTO). Russia has tried to secure its political and economic interests through organisations like Eurasian Economic Community (EurAsEc) and the Shanghai Cooperation Organisation. The SCO is the principal multilateral organisation in this area which seeks to focus on mutuality of interests of member countries, as well as deal with the presence of outside powers in the region. Most importantly, the SCO is a forum in which Russia and China can have an understanding on their respective roles in Central Asia.

The Russians are also apparently using their soft power to recover the ground they have lost in the region by promoting Russian language, education and culture.

There is also the relevant fact that the air space in Central Asia is controlled by the Russians as per arrangements within the CIS. This has strategic implications for operation of foreign powers in the area.

For China the main instrument for exerting its influence in the region is the economic one. China has the necessary financial resources- $2.7 trillions of foreign exchange reserves- which it can use very effectively to finance projects and to offer financial terms that no one else can match with a view to increasing its commercial footprint on the ground. It would have interest in keeping an eye on forces in Central Asia that could link with the insurgency in Xingjian.

Afghanistan has become strategically very important for the major powers involved in the difficult situation there. The access through Pakistan to Afghanistan is becoming more and more problematic for US/NATO forces for supplies. NATO is developing new routes to Central Asia through Russia and Central Asia for this purpose. They are succeeding in this effort, in cooperation with Russia which sees its larger interest served in cooperating with the US to keep the radical forces in check in Afghanistan. It was a very difficult decision for the Russian elites and the Russian armed forces to allow NATO military personnel and supplies the right of passage through their own territory.

As for India, there have been talks with the Iranian and Russian sides about the North-South corridor. The study of this project has now been joined by several countries. But, unfortunately, progress on the ground has been very slow, largely an account of Iran's limited interest in streamlining customs procedures and developing sufficiently the required infrastructure to make the corridor the reality. Not only India can have access to Russia and Central Asia through Iran but the whole of South East Asia can be connected with trade links this way. Studies have shown that given the existing dilatory and inefficient procedures the Iranians have, containers to Russia through this route take just a couple of days less than by sea. Another problem is that empty containers returning are not an economical proposition. The transit problem is important for India's trade and economic relations with Kazakhstan in particular. For our cooperation in the petrochemical sector and the implementation of agreement to buy Uranium, India needs access, and that can be most rationally through Iran.

In conclusion, the strategic environment in Central Asia remains fluid. There is political instability on the ground in the Central Asian countries, and possibly the last word has not yet been said on the kind and quality of future governmental structures there. The problem of religious extremism affects the region. The US, Europe and rest of the world, including India and China, are fighting it, but the problem will not go away easily. The problem in Afghanistan will impact this region in the years ahead. The Afghan issue will be a powerful element in the way one looks at Central Asia. Pakistan's destabilising role in this region is well-known, but suffices to say that Pakistan doesn't want to give India any significant role in Afghanistan and Central Asia. This is a huge challenge for India's future interests in this region. Finally, there is the Iranian dimension. One can talk about the North South corridor and Iran being a rational access point to Central Asia, but progress will also depend on US policies towards Iran. If relations between the US and Iran undergo change then the entire strategic landscape in the region will change.

MAJOR POWERS AND EVOLVING STRATEGIC EQUATIONS IN CENTRAL ASIA

Vinod Anand

Central Asia has been of abiding interest to major powers not only since the demise of the Soviet Union but even during the Tsarist days when British strategists like H Mackinder propounded their geopolitical theories on control of Central Asia being crucial to emerging power structures. The competition between various powers was then referred to as a Great Game which in some form or the other continues even till today. The appearance of sovereign Central Asian Republics after the disappearance of the Soviet Union and the weakness of the Russian state in the immediate aftermath of the Soviet collapse led to a strategic vacuum in the region. Many major and regional powers sought to fill the vacuum by intensifying their engagement with new nations. Meanwhile, Central Asians endeavored to associate themselves with as many multilateral organizations and foreign powers as possible in order to define their newfound independence and national identity. Engagement with the U.S. and the Western countries were considered to be a way to address their concerns about security and economic issues, in addition to emphasizing their newly acquired sovereignty. At the same time it was not easy for the Central Asian Republics to break their umbilical link with Russia. This was due to a number of contextual factors besides the dominant factor of geographical proximity. The policies of the Central Asian nations were further impacted by their internal dynamics and the difficult and turbulent process of nation-building with which they have been coping with since their birth.

The U.S. and European nations sought to absorb the Central Asian states into their orbit of influence through economic engagement and security cooperation (via NATO's Partnership for Peace Program). China, too, embarked on a similar path to enhance its strategic presence in the Central Asian states, after having first solved boundary issues with Russia and its Central Asian neighbors. By the early 1990s, such regional powers as Turkey, Iran and Pakistan were also in the fray in the Central Asian arena. With the end of Boris Yeltsin's decade and emergence of a more assertive Russia under President Putin, the Kremlin, too, began reorienting its policies towards re-claiming what it considered its 'strategic backyard.'

After the collapse of the Soviet Union, the second most significant strategic event to occur in the Central Asian arena, and at the global level as well, was the American response to the 11 September 2001 terrorist attacks, which took the form of Operation Enduring Freedom (OEF). The war against terrorism, launched in October, 2001, brought the U.S. and NATO next door to Central Asia. Central Asian countries such as Uzbekistan and Kyrgyzstan readily granted the use of bases to OEF forces. Other countries provided over-flight and miscellaneous support. This U.S. response was largely welcomed by Russia, China, the Central Asian states and India. Russia and China raised no objections to the U.S. being granted bases and logistics facilities in Central Asia since it suited their short-term strategic interests of containing the rising tide of fundamentalism and terrorism, even though they harbored concerns about the long-term strategic designs of both the U.S. and NATO.

During the heydays of the Taliban regime (1996-2001), Afghanistan had become the epicenter of terrorism, with sanctuaries and training facilities provided to the likes of Al Qaeda, the Islamic Movement of Uzbekistan (IMU), and other radical Islamic groups operating in Central Asia. Even China felt threatened by religious fundamentalist and extremist Muslim elements in Afghanistan because of its vulnerabilities in Xinjiang and its problems with Muslim Uighurs. In a broader strategic framework, U.S. intervention against the Taliban regime coincided with growing Russian and Chinese security concerns.

India was a late-starter on the Central Asian chessboard. India's preoccupation in the first half of the 1990s with its economic difficulties (leading to pledging gold reserves to the Bank of England), ongoing insurgency in J&K, and unstable political milieu prevented it from taking major political initiatives in Central Asia. Notwithstanding this, India recognized Central Asia as an area of strategic importance. The Annual Report of India's Ministry of Defense stressed Central Asia as an area of vital importance to India, not only on account of its geographical proximity and India's historical and cultural links with the region, but also because of the common challenge they all face from extremism and terrorism.

The growth of the Indian economy creates an ever-growing demand for energy and natural resources to fuel and maintain the momentum of our growth. The discovery of large reserves of hydrocarbons and other resources needed for sustaining economic growth makes the Central Asian region immensely attractive for forging a mutually beneficial cooperative relationship. Relations that are based on a shared commitment to open and progressive societies, secularism, democracy, and improving the lot of the common people, have been reinforced by a similarity of views in the fight against terrorism, drug trafficking and in many other areas of security. Also, with the intense power play taking place between Russia, China, the U.S. and the Western countries in the strategic arena of Central Asia, India's emphasis on soft power strikes a positive chord among these nations.

This paper examines the interests of leading powers in the Central Asian region to include its significance, the role of major players, the responses of Central Asian states, and India's approach in the evolving strategic scenario.

Central Asia: Geopolitical Salience

The geopolitical and geo-strategic salience of Central Asia today has been underscored by two main factors. First, Central Asia has become important because of the discovery of hydrocarbon reserves and second, it has become a major transportation hub for gas and oil pipelines and multi-modal communication corridors connecting China, Russia, Europe, the Caucasus region, the Trans-Caspian region and the Indian Ocean. Furthermore, whether it was Czarist Russia or the Soviet Union or even the present Central Asian regimes, there has always been a strategic ambition in the north to seek access to the warm waters of the Indian Ocean. Thus Afghanistan, which links Central Asia and South Asia, is a strategic bridge of great geopolitical significance.

Central Asia has never been a monolithic area and is undergoing a turbulent transitional process with a diverse range of ethnicities and fragmented societies throughout the region. These societal divisions and lack of political maturity compound the social, economic and political challenges. Security and economic issues are the two most important components of the Central Asian states' engagement with outside powers. Among the states themselves there are elements of both cooperation and competition. Historical legacies, their geo-strategic locations, and above all their perceived national interests profoundly influence the political choices of Central Asian nations. The weaknesses of the new nations in Central Asia pave the way for outside powers to interfere in their internal affairs.

Engagement of the U.S. and EU with Central Asia

After the collapse of the Soviet Union, the U.S. Congress passed a Freedom Support Act (FSA) in 1992 to provide aid to the newly independent nations. In 1999, a 'Silk Road Strategy Act' (later updated and modified in 2006)[1] and authorized economic aid, development of transportation and communication links and border controls. But this also contained riders to promote democracy and create civil societies in the South Caucasus and Central Asia. Even though these were lofty aims, the underlying desire of the U.S. was to strengthen its influence in the wake of persisting Russian weakness in Central Asia and elsewhere.

Additional objectives were to involve the Central Asian states in Euro-Atlantic institutions and to foster their pro-West orientations.[2] The U.S. encouraged the Central Asians' links with NATO, the European Union, and the Organization for Security and Cooperation in Europe (OSCE). By the mid 1990s, most of the Central Asian nations had joined NATO's Partnership for Peace (PFP) Program (four of them joined in 1994 and Tajikistan did so in 2002) and a number of PFP-style military training exercises were carried out in both the U.S. and in Central Asia.

The Central Asian nations also viewed NATO's greater engagement in the region as an opportunity to modernize their armed forces and upgrade their capacity to respond to the regional challenges of drug trafficking, religious extremism, terrorism and the proliferation of weapons of mass destruction. The development of relations with NATO also constituted a counterweight, or at least a useful alternative, to their relations with Russia.

The strategic influence of the U.S was at its peak during October 2001 and thereafter, when it was offered bases in Central Asia to fight the Taliban. It went into somewhat of a decline after the U.S. started aggressively promoting western style democracies in Central Asia and in the former Soviet republics. The high point of these policies, with negative repercussions for the U.S., was reached when it responded to the Andijon violence of May 2005 in Uzbekistan by severely criticizing the Uzbek government. In retaliation, the U.S. was asked to vacate its base in Uzbekistan. The Shanghai Cooperation Organization (SCO) in July 2005 urged all foreign forces to set a timeframe for withdrawal of their bases from the territory of SCO member states. [3] The so-called colored revolutions, such as the Tulip revolution in Kyrgyzstan, though believed to be supported by the U.S. and the West with a view to promote a pro-Western orientation, did not meet with much success. The current instability in Kyrgyzstan has also created some apprehensions regarding the sustainability of U.S airbase at Manas which supports operations in Afghanistan.

The U.S of late seems to have learnt the virtues of being pragmatic and not assertively nationalistic in its dealings with the Central Asian republics. For instance, it has been circumspect in imposing its notions of democratic norms on CARs because of the imperatives of its geopolitical interests.

As mentioned earlier, the strategic goals of the U.S. center on building energy and transport corridors that avoid Russia by going either south or west. Despite many engineering and financial challenges involved in the building of the oil pipeline from Baku, Azerbaijan, via Tbilisi Georgia to Ceyhan in Turkey, it was completed in May, 2006. The BTC pipeline was part of the U.S. policy of reducing Russia's control on the Central Asian oil and gas pipeline network by providing an alternative route to Europe. Another U.S. and EU-supported proposal for the "Nabucco" gas pipeline is under examination, with a memorandum of understanding signed on 13 July, 2009. Turkmenistan and Kazakhstan are being actively courted by the US and EU leadership for access to their hydrocarbon reserves. In October 2008, the Yolton-Osman gas field was certified by international auditors to contain gas reserves four to five times greater than the Dauletabad field. This discovery confirms that Turkmenistan can export gas to all its potential customers.[4]

Of late even Uzbekistan has granted some limited use of its airspace and air base for transport of non-lethal logistics' in support of US and NATO operations in Afghanistan. The focus of the U.S. policies is not only on hydrocarbon and resource-rich states like Kazakhstan and Turkmenistan and strategically important Uzbekistan, but Washington has paid equal attention to Kyrgyzstan and Tajikistan. The construction of the Panj River Bridge was an element of Washington's Central Asia strategy.

The countries in the central Asian region have many common concerns, such as finding sources and outlets for energy, achieving prosperity through economic cooperation, and enhancing security and stability. However, the primary goal of the U.S is built around weaning the Central Asian countries away from a unilateral dependence on Russia.

As part of its greater engagement with Central Asia, and as an adjunct to the US policy, the EU in June 2007 unveiled a new Central Asia Strategy for the period 2007-13, which revolves around promoting political dialogue, trade and economic relations and cooperation in a variety of sectors. The EU program also seeks to promote good governance and democratic norms. Earlier, in February, 2007, the EU Commission advised the EU to increase contacts with Central Asian countries in order to secure energy resources that are of "permanent strategic importance."[5] The EU intends to spend 750 million euros in the region, a sum that is unlikely to take it far. The level of interest in Central Asia varies from one EU member to another.

However, the Central Asian countries remain concerned over the EU's political agenda, even though there are practical initiatives under the

Partnership for Cooperation Agreements (PCAs) between the EU and each Central Asian nation. Observers from the OSCE have criticized the practice of democracy in all the Central Asian states but this did not deter the OSCE's Ministerial Council from granting the presidency of the organization to Kazakhstan in 2010.[6] The new EU strategy is a recognition of the fact that the EU did not exploit its initial advantage in the 1990s and has been losing influence there ever since.

The Central Asian nations cannot be said to have fulfilled their expectation of economic gains from the pro-Western policies they pursued after gaining freedom from the Soviet yolk. Meanwhile, an economically ascendant China was making important gains there, as was Russia which underwent certain resurgence due to its abundant oil and gas reserves, along with its past political and economic linkages. The Central Asian governments, in an effort to extract maximum advantage from this situation, have followed "multi-vector" policies. The emerging environment in Central Asia is further underscored by the fact that Russia has been at pains to regain its strategic space in an area that it considers as its strategic backyard or 'near abroad'. Both China and Russia have been coordinating their efforts to increase their influence.

Russia's Drive for 'Privileged Interests' in Central Asia

The decade of nineties saw the decline of Russian power in Central Asia which was largely as a result of internal dynamics and a general withdrawal from the former Soviet republics. Boris Yeltsin's reign coincided with a decline in Moscow's economic, military and political strength. There was a time in 1999 when oil reached its lowest price of US$10 per barrel, adversely affecting Russian revenues. After President Putin appeared on the scene he embarked on the process of internal balancing and of regaining a hold on Central Asia and the former Soviet republics. Besides joining the Chinese-led SCO, Putin developed Russia's own security structure, the Collective Security Treaty Organization (CSTO), for Central Asia and the former Soviet republics. It needs to be underscored that apart from the historical perspective, Russian ties with the region are driven by military and economic considerations. Central Asia is the central pillar of its Eurasian strategy and constitutes a strategic space that protects its Eastern flank. It can be thus expected to protect its security, energy, and transportation interests. The CSTO is the construct of such thinking. Collective Rapid Reaction Force exercises are carried out to showcase Russia's resolve to protect the southern belt of the CIS. Similarly, the Russian air defense command carries out regular exercises to defend strategic air space over Central Asia. A counter-intelligence center has been established at Bishkek for sharing intelligence, reviewing threat perceptions, and formulating joint strategy to combat terrorism.

The current President, Dmitri Medvedev, has also moved to reclaim Russia's former influence over its southern neighbors by reasserting its "privileged interests" in neighboring countries that were once part of Soviet Union.[7] Russia's armed intervention in Georgia in August, 2008, was a reassertion of this purported right. The response of the Central Asian states to Russia's armed intervention in South Ossetia and Abkhazia manifested their own multi-vectored policies. While individually they may have praised (for instance, Kazakhstan) the Russian intervention and accepted Russia's rationale for doing so, they refused to give diplomatic recognition to the newly-emerged entities recognized by Russia. In a fine act of balancing, they joined China at an SCO summit in August, 2008, in Dushanbe to present a common stance that reflected their shared opposition to altering present territorial borders and to interfering in the internal affairs of others. At the meeting of the CSTO in September, 2008, they maintained the same general stance. Kyrgyzstan, Kazakhstan, Tajikistan, and Uzbekistan praised the "active role of the Russian Federation in working toward peace and cooperation in the Caucasus" but refused to recognize the independence of South Ossetia and Abkhazia.[8] However, following Russia's war against Georgia, the Central Asian Republics would be less ready to defy Russia and more accommodating to Russian concerns.[9]

Moscow's push for closer military ties with the Central Asian countries has also been seen as an effort to safeguard Russian economic interests and its domination of the Central Asian energy sector. It is worth noting that oil flows in BTC temporarily stopped at the time of Russia's 2008 intervention in Georgia. Turkmen gas remains central to Moscow's energy strategy in Central Asia for it helps Russia to control gas supplies to Western Europe. The Turkmen have used China to impose much higher gas prices on Russia. Yet as was noted above, the reserves in the Yoloton-Osman field are much larger than previously thought and Russia may have largely succeeded in gaining access to this huge new source.

China: Protecting its Periphery

China has expanded its footprint in Central Asia through trade, energy deals, transport infrastructure, and the gradual enlargement of the scope of the SCO to include both security and economics. It has a long-term perspective and is willing to cooperate with Russia in order to make gains in Central Asia. However, many Chinese scholars view Russia's Eurasian Economic Community and CSTO as direct competitors of SCO. The main stimulus of Sino-Russian cooperation continues to be the shared objective of offsetting U.S. influence, which neither can accomplish alone. While China still needs Russian arms, technologies, and natural resources, Russia needs China to balance the West.[10] In practice, the U.S. and the West's approach to Russia shapes Russia's level of cooperation with China.

China has also to manage its security relationship with Russia in order to protect its vulnerable northern and western flanks. Beijing also sees the U.S. presence in Central Asia as a part of a specific policy designed to constrain China's rising power.

Securing and stabilizing its periphery is central to China's plan for developing its western area. Enhancing its influence in Central Asian Muslim nations also helps China address its security concerns regarding separatist Muslim movements in Xinjiang. Besides Uyghurs, China's source of concern is the Fargana Valley, the main fountainhead of Islamic fundamentalism in the Central Asian region, which is not far from China's borders. Preventing separatism, extremism and terrorism (which China classifies as the 'three evils') is China's key security concern. Hence, through the Chinese-led SCO it carries out border management training and joint exercises with the Central Asian armies. To promote stability China supports the current political regimes in neighboring Central Asia, [11] which reciprocate by acknowledging China as a regional and international leader seeking a 'harmonious world'.

China looks to Russia's and Central Asia's energy reserves to fuel its growth. China has built a 988-km-long pipeline from Kazakhstan (Atasu) to Xinjiang designed to carry 10 million tons of oil annually. It also struck a deal with PetroKazakhstan, which granted access to vast reserves of Kazakh oil.[12] Plans are also afoot to connect this line to Tengiz on the Caspian coast. In October 2006, China negotiated to acquire another oil field in Kazakhstan.[13] Earlier, in April 2006, China signed a deal with Turkmenistan to supply 30 billion cubic meters of gas for a thirty-year period from 2009 onwards via a new 7,000 kilometer pipeline.[14] This deal broke Gazprom's monopoly and prompted Russia to conclude its own gas deal with Turkmenistan. It also opened the way for the China National Petroleum Corporation to enter into a production-sharing agreement (PSA) to develop the Turkmen gas fields feeding the pipeline, Turkmenistan's only PS to date.[15]

Chinese activities in the energy sector in Kazakhstan, Turkmenistan and Uzbekistan have broken Gazprom's domination of Central Asia. The evolving Chinese-Kazakh pipeline structure will be linked with Iran along the Caspian Sea, and the Chinese pipeline from Turkmenistan is also being extended across the border to Iran. This will; not only reduce China's dependence on energy shipped by sea but will advance the development of Xinjiang. China is also in the process of exploiting the rich hydropower potential of Kyrgyzstan and Tajikistan and is looking to Kazakhstan to construct electric power stations and then send China electricity through the power grids.[16] China also controls the headwaters of the two main rivers that supply water to Kazakhstan. For now, however, China comes third behind Russia and Iran in its level of investments in Tajik hydropower.[17]

In its inroads into the Central Asian economy of Central Asia, China puts money on the table with important conditions. Under the aegis of SCO it has announced $900 million worth of loans to Central Asian countries, all of them contingent on buying Chinese goods and services. The Central Asian Republics remain wary of their big neighbor. They would like to benefit from engaging with China but would not like to become too dependent on it. Kazakh leaders worry that their country might become an 'economic protectorate' of China. Even in their military cooperation Kazakhs favor Russia rather than China.[18]

Despite the overwhelming presence of the Americans and NATO in Afghanistan, China's metallurgical group won a $3.5 billion bid to develop Afghanistan's Aynak copper field. This contract also includes construction of a $500 million electrical plant and railways from Tajikistan. Revenues from the project would meet more than half of the current annual state budget. This is part of the Chinese policy of spending more whatever is necessary when its strategic interests are involved – the bids by other competitors were all around $ 2 billion.[19] The Pentagon is not favorably disposed to this decision of the Afghan government, even though it may contribute to the stabilization effort.[20] The security and stability of Afghanistan remain critical factors in the effort to connect Central Asia with South Asia, along with the obvious economic gains.

Other Powers

Turkey, Iran, Pakistan   have also been engaging the CAR to pursue their interests.

Turkey's strategic interests include enhancing its economic and security relations with the Central Asian states to exploit the common linkages based on pan-Turkic identity and gaining access to its rich hydro carbon reserves. Turkey offers itself as an energy conduit for exports to Europe. As a sign of greater interest in forging ties with Turkic countries, Turkey organized a meeting in October 2009 in Azerbaijan; the Kazakh and Kyrgyz presidents attended along with a representative from Turkmenistan. The attendees agreed to set up a Turkic-speaking Countries Cooperation Council that is envisaged to be similar to the CIS, the Council or Europe, or the Arab League. Turkey plays a significant and U.S.-supported role in trade and cultural affairs in Central Asia among the region's mainly Turkic peoples. It was the only country that criticized China's handling of Uyghurs' unrest in Xingjiang last year.

Iran as a neighbour of CAR has a significant role to play in Caspian politics. The agreement on exploitation of Caspian Sea's oil and gas reserves is stuck because of the differing views on delineation of Caspian Sea borders. Recently Iran has started receiving enhanced quantity of gas from Turkmenistan and the capacity of piped gas to Iran will be increased to 20 million cubic meters from next year. Iran also has cultural and ethnic ties with Tajiks and has invested in the hydropower sector of Tajikistan. Further, its views on developing situation in Afghanistan and its likely adverse impact on Central Asian countries are closely aligned with those of CARs. For India, Iran is a gateway to Central Asia as the route to Central Asia is blocked due to instability in Afghanistan and as well as obtuse policies of Pakistan in not allowing overland transit. The Northern Transit Corridor passing through holds prospects for enhanced trade between South Asia and Central Asia and even beyond to the mutual benefit of the countries in the region.

Pakistan had sought to extend the notion of its strategic depth from Afghanistan to central Asia when it saw strategic vacuum in the decades of 90's after the collapse of Soviet Union. It relied on the common factor of religion to extend its influence. Along with Turkey and Iran it was a founding member of the Economic Cooperation Organisation which includes the five Central Asian countries also. However, the ECO has not taken off in a big way because of many contextual factors.

India's Interests and Profile in Central Asia

India's cultural and civilization links, its liberal and secular fabric, its pluralistic society and other elements of India's soft power are India's strengths for improving its profile in Central Asia. India considers Central Asia as its strategic neighborhood and has been endeavoring to develop economic and trade relations which, to a large extent, are being hampered by the lack of a direct route to the region. India's motivations in this direction are propelled by the rapid growth of its economy with rising demand for energy imports and other natural resources. India therefore is looking at Central Asian hydrocarbon reserves to diversify its gas and oil imports.

The driving force behind India's accelerating engagement with Central Asia is economics. India has the ability to help build CAR's capacities in the areas of information technology, science and technology, knowledge industry and soft power. Furthermore, India prefers the stability of the current regimes and peaceful reform rather than the promotion of any aggressive democratic practices. India's engagement with Central Asia leads with trade, health, technology and transport and it is directly relevant to ordinary people in Central Asia and Afghanistan. Therefore, India is considered as a friendly partner by Central Asian states and a country which can play a balancing role in the fierce power play taking place in Central Asia.

Further, CARs and India shares the goals of anti-terrorism, security and stability in Central Asia along with the curtailment of drug trafficking in the region. India has been cooperating on the issues of security both at bilateral and multilateral levels. It has Joint Working Group (JWG) on Combating International Terrorism with Uzbekistan[21] and a JWG with Tajikistan on Counter-terrorism and a JWG on international terrorism and other types of crimes with Kyrgyzstan. These JWGs have been having regular meetings to address threats arising from instability and fundamentalism in the region. At multilateral level India as an observer has been supporting the objectives of SCO which seek to ensure stability in the region, combat terrorism and extremist view points and is keen to play constructive and active role in SCO. India is also a member of Conference on Interaction and Confidence Building Measures in Asia (CICA) - a Kazakh sponsored initiative of sixteen Asian nations that includes CARs (less Turkmenistan). Many member states seem to view CICA as a useful instrument to pursue bilateral relations with individual states. For Kazakhstan CICA has been an expression of its multi-vector foreign policy as also an attempt to seek a role for itself in the conflict situations in the region. The compatibility of security interests between India and Kazakhstan also finds reflection in the signing of Declaration of Strategic Partnership in 2009.

CARs attempts at securing multiple outlets for its energy surpluses rhyme well with India's growing requirements of energy. Attendance of June 2006, August 2007 and August 2008 SCO summit meetings by India's Petroleum and Natural Gas Minister, Mr. Murli Deora, signifies the importance which India attaches to its energy needs. SCO's summit of 2009 in Russia was attended by our Prime Minister signifying the importance attached to this multilateral structure. India has also been keen to invest in hydro-power sector in Kyrgyzstan and Tajikistan and transport the surplus energy through a power grid extending to India via Afghanistan and Pakistan. India has also constructed a power grid line from Uzbek border to Kabul as part of its developmental aid programme.

India considers Iran as its gateway to Central Asia because of Pakistan's obtuse policies of denying it access to Afghanistan and consequently to Central Asia, which has deleterious effects on promoting intra-regional economic activity and development of trade. Thus, India has been developing a transport corridor from Chah Bahar in Iran to Afghanistan, with eventual linkages to Central Asia. However, the Taliban (with the backing of Pakistan) had carried out attacks on Indian engineers working on the project to discourage its construction.

Concluding Observations

While U.S. influence has already peaked in Central Asia, both Russia and China are cementing their political, military and economic relationship with Central Asian nations. Meanwhile, India has been endeavouring to improve its profile in the region in order to exploit its energy reserves and to establish a mutually beneficial security and economic relationship. Central Asian nations, while exploiting the competition between different players for their own perceived national interests have many conflicts among themselves and are still in the process of moving towards regional harmony. Political processes are yet to mature and the threat of terrorism remains real, especially because of the unstable situation in Afghanistan with the resurgence of the Taliban.

There are complex strategic equations evolving at both the global and regional levels with each nation attempting to pursue its national objectives. There are calls on India to join one bandwagon or another in an arena where the end game is yet to be played out. Russia is already emerging as an influential and powerful actor in Central Asia. China is also fiercely pursuing its interests in the region, and has been gaining ground. However, Russia remains a partner of choice for India because of its defence industrial base, its oil and gas resources and above all its historical and friendly relations with India. India's efforts in intensifying its engagement with Central Asia are stymied because of lack of a direct route. Development and completion of North-South Transport corridor with the help of all the nations involved, therefore, assumes added significance.

Endnotes

[1] Full text of U.S. 'Silk Road Strategy Act 2006' available at http://www.govtrack.us/congress/billtext.xpd?bill=s109-2749: The Act notes that the United States has come to view democratization of the countries in the region as essential to enhanced security. Besides Central Asian states and Afghanistan it includes Azerbaijan, Armenia and Georgia as part of Central Asia and the South Caucasus. After severe criticism of Uzbekistan regime's reaction to Andijon violence in may 2005 and as a consequence eviction of the U.S. troops from the military base there; the U.S. has recognized the virtues of being more pragmatic in its policies towards the Central Asian states. The modified Act observes: 'While these revolutions (the coloured revolutions) resulted in the ouster of corrupt and ineffective regimes by largely peaceful protest movements, the long-term interests of security, stability, good governance, and economic growth are better served by evolutionary democratization.'

[2] Strobe Talbott, 'A Farewell to Flashman: American Policy in the Caucasus and Central Asia,' July 21, 1997, http://www.state.gov/www/regions/nis/970721talbott.html

[3] For a detailed treatment of the subject see Fiona Hill, ' A Not-So-Grand Strategy: U.S. Policy in the Caucasus and Central Asia Since 1991', February 2001 published by Brookings Institution available at http://www.brookings.edu/articles/2001/02foreignpolicy_hill.aspx? rssid=hillf. Also see Murat Laumulin, 'U.S. Strategy and Policy in Central Asia', Central Asia and Caucasus Journal of Social and Political Studies, No. 4(46), 2007 available at www.ca-.org/2007/journal_eng/cac-04/05.html

[4] John CK Daly, 'The Battle for Central Asia', ISN Security Watch, Washington DC, June 11, 2007, also available at http://www.res.ethz.chnews/sw/details.cfm?ID=17723 &nav1= 1&nav2=2&nav3=3

[5] Stephen Mulvey, 'EU dreams of Central Asian Gas', BBC Online, March 27, 2007 available at http://news.bbc.co.uk/2/hi/europe/6500943.stm

[6] See NATO Parliamentary Subcommittee on Democracy and Governance Report 'Democracy and Security in Central Asia: what policy for NATO and EU?' March 20, 2008, available at http://www.nato-pa.int/Default.asp?SHORTCUT=1462. The report observes: 'It is undeniable that Kazakhstan has established a stable political system, one which in many regards appears strikingly more open and competitive than those of certain of its neighbours. Thus, the decision of the Ministerial Council of the OSCE to grant the presidency of the organization to Kazakhstan in 2010 recognizes the genuine efforts of the Kazakh authorities.'

[7] In an interview with Euronews TV channel on 03 September 2008, Dmitry Medvedev outlined five principles he would follow in Russia's foreign policy:

'...The fifth principle is that Russia, like any other state, has certain regions it will pay particular attention to. These are regions of our privileged interests. We are going to have special, cordial, long-term relations with the states in these regions.'

[8] For detailed analysis see Erica Marat, 'CSTO Summit Disappoints Russia, Unites central Asia', Eurasia Daily Monitor, September 12, 2008, Volume 5, Number 175 available at http://www.jamestown.org/edm/article.php?article_id =2373371

[9] For instance see Sebastien Peyrouse, 'Sino-Kazakh Relations: A Nascent Strategic Partnership', China brief, Volume VII, Issue 21, November 7, 2008 available at http://www.jamestown.org/terrorism/news/uploads/cb_008_21.pdf

[10] Also see Michael Mihalka, 'Not Much of a Game: Security Dynamics in Central Asia', China Eurasia Forum Quarterly, Volume 5, No. 2 (2007), pp.21-39.

[11] Konstantin Syroezhkin, 'China in Central Asia: From Trade to Strategic Partnership', Central Asia and Caucasus Journal of Social and Poloitical Studies, No. 2007 available at http://www.ca-c.org/online/2007/journal_eng/cac-03/ 04.shtml Also see Ablat Khojaev, ' China's Central Asia Policy' (Based on Chinese Sources) in the same issue of the journal.

[12] F. William Engdahl, 'China lays down gauntlet in energy war,' Asia Times, December 21 2005, www.atimes.com/atimes/China/GL21Ad01.html

[13] 'CITIC Group to buy Kazakhstan oil assets,' China Daily, October 26 2006, www.chinadaily.com.cn/china/2006-10/26/content_717784.htm

[14] See MK Bhadrakumar, 'Russia sets the pace in energy race,' Asia Times, September 23, 2006, www.atimes.com/atimes/Central_Asia/HI23Ag02.html

[15] Chemen Durdiyeova, 'Berdimuahammedov Launches Turkmenistan-China Gas Pipeline project', CACI Analyst, September 20, 2007 available at http:// www.cacianalyst.org/?q=node/4701

[16] For details of China's mounting presence in Central Asia's electric power scene see Sebastein Peyrouse, 'The Hydroelectric Sector in Central Asia and the Growing Role of China', China and Eurasia Forum Quarterly, Volume 5, No. 2 (2007), pp.131-148.

[17] Ibid.

[18] Sebastien Peyrouse, 'Sino-Kazakh relations: A Nascent Strategic Partnership', China Brief, Volume VII, Issue 21, November 7, 2008 available at http:// www.jamestown.org/terrorism/news/uploads/cb_008_21.pdf

[19] Nicklas Norling, 'The emerging China-Afghanistan relationship', CACI Analyst, May 14, 2008 available at http://www.cacianalyst.org/?q=node/4858

[20] Ibid.

[21] See "Joint Statement by Republic of India and Republic of Uzbekistan," April 26 2006,Tashkent, Uzbekistan available at Ministry of External Affairs, Government of India website Joint Declarations and Statements at http://meaindia.nic.in/ jshome.htm

RUSSIA AND CENTRAL ASIA

Dr. Alexander Lukin

It is very important to assess how Russia sees this region of Central Asia and how Russia and other countries can cooperate with India in this region. Of course Russia has special interest in Central Asia. Generally speaking Russian influence has become significantly smaller as compared to earlier times but it is still an influential country. Territorially speaking as compared to the Soviet Union, Russia moved to the East. It lost some territories in the west therefore its relations with the Eastern and Southern neighbours especially the Central Asian countries have become more important. Russia looks to maintain the significant influence it has in Eurasia. But is it good or bad? Any influence is good for something unless you are an empire. Russia is no longer an empire like the Soviet Union. It is certainly not an ideological empire trying to tell everyone what to do and impose their own model of development. From this point of view the only empire left is the United States because the US knows what everybody should do, even the smallest country in Africa. Even China is not an empire from this point of view because they do not impose their mode of development to other countries, though they like their model of development very much. From this ideological point of view Russia is not a rival state and even China is not a rival of the US in Central Asia.

Another ideology doing round in Central Asia is that of radical Islamism. It does not represent a country. As Mr Putin said when he was the president, 'Russia has no monopoly over Central Asia and this was not a slogan but recognition of the reality'. In this part of the world the political influence of the United States is growing, the economic influence of European Union is growing faster and for some countries even more. The influence of China both economic and political is also growing. Today Beijing is an important economic partner of Kyrgyzstan, but Russia is still the first. The Chinese are the second largest trading partners of Tajikistan and the main importer for both these countries. It is the third largest partner of Kazakhstan and seventh of Turkmenistan but it is the third largest importer.

As mentioned earlier the influence of EU is also growing. For instance last year the author was invited to be part of an economic forum meeting in Venice to speak on the Russian perspective. Who could imagine ten years ago an Italian-Kazakhstan economic conference taking place in Venice. One also found out that bilateral agreements were there not only between countries but also between region to region. The fact that Russia is trying to maintain and hopes to maintain its influence is due to several reasons. First of all Russia is not trying to make these nations as part of Russia. This is absolutely impossible and from this point of view Russia is no more an imperialist country. But of course it tries to pursue its national interest in this region and there is nothing special about it. Russia is behaving like a former part of the Soviet Union and treading cautiously than many other powers. Russia is very cautious about moving troops anywhere unlike France which often sends its troops to Africa. It was rightly said that during the crisis in Kyrgyzstan when the Kyrgyz government asked for Russian or CSTO troops to be sent to Kyrgyzstan, after serious discussions in Russia it was decided against it. This was so because Russia can be again seen as an imperialist power or it could suffer or there might be casualties. Russia believes in the sovereignty of these countries and tries to persuade these governments to solve their problems by themselves.

There are other interests of Russia. Firstly, the security threats which come from this part of this region. Security threats to Russia come from south i.e. Afghanistan possibly via Central Asia. It is well known that if something goes wrong in Afghanistan it will influence the stability of Central Asian friends because of the porous borders. There is even no custom authority between Russia and Kazakhstan after Kazakhstan joined the Custom Union. Of course, it is important for Russia that Afghanistan and CARs maintain their political stability. The main threats that come to Russia from south is of course terrorism which stimulates separatism and religious extremism and also drug trafficking because according to official estimates 90 per cent of the drugs that is consumed in Russia comes from Afghanistan.

Second interest of Russia in Central Asia is primarily economic interest. As putting in place of the custom union shows, many people of these countries and Russia want to live in some kind of union without knowing what shape the union might take. But of course economically Russia would like to cooperate very closely. Still some of the countries of Central Asia are very much dependent on the Russian economy. It is also in common interest to cooperate economically. And even if this union takes some political form along with economic cooperation it would be something like the EU.

The third interest is the common cultural roots which are still very strong. When one visits any of these countries one finds people who studied with Russians in the same university and they speak the Russian language. In Kyrgyzstan there are schools in the Russian language. These countries think on many issues as Russians do. Russia is not against these countries; they are sovereign but Russians like the fact that they are spiritually very close.

Then there is the problem of Russian citizens, Russian speakers, the fate of the language there is different from country to country and it is not necessary to be specific about it.

Further, maintaining stability is very important for this region. Russia is ready to cooperate with everybody and one does not subscribe to the theories that say that great chess game is being played in Central Asia. That all the powers in Central Asia should necessarily work against each other. In fact the interests of Russia, China, USA, and EU and of course India coincide with each other. There is a need to point out three main basic interests.

First, maintaining political stability is important because nobody wants a politically unstable Central Asia.

Second is keeping in power secular regimes because political instability may lead to radical Islamism coming to power which would be very bad for everybody.

Third is economic development because fast economic development and solid economic basis could be a good political platform for maintaining political stability. Of course there should be economic competition in this part of the world but economic competition should not be mixed up with political rivalry. The supporters of the chess game theory and anything like that point out that Gazprom and some Chinese companies try to create some kind of political conflict. It can easily be recalled that the so called economic wars are very common between good political friends and allies. For instance, sometime back in Canada there was a talk about some kind of potato war between Canada and the US. But it did not lead to any political rivalry. There was a banana war between Britain and the EU a decade ago. Thus, it is normal that specific companies compete with each other and it is only natural that they do so. Sometimes the big companies and governments support this and if general political relations are stable then it should not lead to any kind of political differences.

Russia is already cooperating with China on all these lines in central Asia within SCO in the three main directions which is political, security, economic and cultural cooperation. Russia strongly supports India becoming a full member of the SCO. This support was formally expressed in the joint declaration between India and Russia in 2009 during the visit of Indian Prime Minister to Moscow. Of course everything is decided by consensus in the SCO. Not everyone is happy with the idea. Our Chinese friends are the unhappy ones. But Russia is trying to persuade them because Russia thinks that India will play a very positive role in SCO and most likely Russia at the summit that will take place in Astana this year will support the membership of India. Possibly, Russia will support Pakistan's membership also because Pakistan had applied earlier and Russia should give something to Chinese friends.

Why is the interest of India towards this region so great? There are several reasons. India can play a positive role and it has a secular government.

It has a very positive history of economic development and the model of Indian development is different from the Chinese model of development or other countries. So it would be very good for some countries to study it. The economic crisis has shown that India was more ready for the crisis because of the model of economic development than China for example. There are many historical ties that Central Asia and India share. What is important is that India is a democracy and it does not indulge in lecturing anyone on the merits/demerits of democracy. The fact that India will be a part of SCO would provide an example for all the members of SCO. India can also play an important role in solving the Afghan problem. It is well known that India has invested more than a billion dollars in investments. India is the sixth largest donor and what is important is that there are two ideas that are being put forward in solving the problem. Some people say that talks with some parts of moderate Taliban should be done. Others like our Central Asian friends say that there is nothing called the moderate Taliban and it is completely unacceptable. And the position of India would be closer to the second position because Taliban is more of a Pashtun force and India may not like the future dispensation to be oriented only under Pashtun forces in Afghanistan. And its position would be closer to Tajikistan. Therefore, India could play an important and active role. Overall India can play a very active and positive role in Central Asia and Russia is ready to support it in whatever manner it can.

THE ROLE OF CHINA IN CENTRAL ASIA

Amb. TC A Rangachari

There is a need to take a look at the internal situation in China to understand China's role in Central Asia after the breakup of the Soviet Union and the emergence of the Central Asian states. In those initial years, the Chinese took a backseat.

In 1989, China was faced with a major crisis following the happenings at the Tiananmen Square that led to the purge of the General Secretary of the Communist Party of China at that time. The disintegration of Soviet Union came in 1991. That is the time when China was engaged in a huge internal debate on how the problem of economic freedom versus political modernization could be dealt with and the direction, or the way forward, in view of the collapse of the Glasnost and Perestroika way. Teng Hsiao-Ping had then undertaken a tour of the south and pushed ahead with economic reforms process. Thus, the view was that China must have much more economic reforms, much more of modernization, much more of attracting investment and so on; therefore political freedom must be on a slower footing.

This had nothing to do with Central Asia per se. The preoccupation that China had with its own internal developments left little time to devote to Central Asia. At the same time one must also look at the state of economic development. Current perception that China was a powerful neighbour and resource-hungry was not yet the case when the Central Asian states became independent in 1991. It is worth recalling that China had set for itself a goal to double the 1980 GDP by 2000. Actually they achieved that goal in 1995 and in 1995 they set themselves the goal that they would double their 1995

GDP by 2000 which also they did. So they ended up quadrupling the 1980 GDP by 2000. But in this process the focus was so much on internal developmental issues. China, at that time, was not 'resource hungry' which it became post 2006-07. So the approach to Central Asia then was governed by different considerations. Perhaps one anecdote might indicate the kind of attitude that China had towards Central Asia then. In 1996, when the then Chinese President Jiang Zemin visited Central Asia, in one of the discussion with a Central Asian President, he asked what the total population in Central Asia was. He was given a figure of a particular country which was less than that of Shanghai. He commented that everybody must then know each other! This was the kind of attitude. They were so small in number that they would know all each other just as one would if one lived in Shanghai. It sort of typified the attitude that China had at that time.

Possibly the Chinese approach towards Central Asia can be divided into three phases. The first phase is from 1991 to about 1996-97 where the focus was on domestic issues and therefore not much trade and economic relations could develop with the Central Asian countries. The border of the erstwhile Soviet Union and China was so impregnable that they did not have even border posts at that time. At that time, much of the trade was done between the bordering Xinjiang and Soviet Union; much of the border trade was in the hands of the Uighurs. Then comes the second phase which is a bit of a consolidation of the first phase which lasted till about 2001-02 and this is the phase when China was doing two things. One is out of concern about terrorism and the smuggling of arms and drug trafficking. The trade itself shifted from the Uyghur's to the Hans. Secondly, China was putting a lot of pressure on the Central Asian states arising from fears about separatism to clamp down on whatever local pockets of influence or organizational set ups that the Uyghur's had so that they would not be a problem within China. The third phase was from 2002-03 onwards when China started looking into the future and what was happening in the rest of the world and that was the time when China became resource hungry. The Chinese in the course of 20 years have followed both bilateral and multilateral strategies.

What are China's dominant concerns? Peace and stability with development and prevention of terrorism, fundamentalism, drug trafficking and so on. These are objectives that India, too, would have vis a vis Central Asia. These would also be Russian objectives. In that way it can be said that there is a consensus in regard to the way in which the major neighbouring countries of Central Asia are looking into what should be the future development of Central Asia.

What is the Chinese view? We might look at the speech of President Hu Jintao and his six points. The first point is that there should be peace and solidarity. Not only should there be strategic dialogue and policy coordination, China and Central Asia should closely work with each other and have common interests of sovereignty, development and so on. This is similar to the kind of stand that the European Union is taking towards its own member states: develop the same position and speak in one voice on major international and regional issues. So a kind of regional integration in which all the countries of the region including China would have a similar, if not identical, approach or views.

Second, there should be economic cooperation at a regional level. Clearly, this is something which suits China. There is economic cooperation given the fact that China is a much larger economy and is in a position to push development in Central Asia. Evidently, this would be also beneficial to China.

Third, China is looking at not only how it benefits itself but also how it benefits Central Asia by talking in terms of Human Development Index. Hu Jintao spoke about joint research in agricultural development and cooperation to resource areas.

Fourth, member states should clearly define basic principles, priorities and project implementation and deepen cooperation in the prevention of diseases, epidemics, public health, people's livelihood, education and so on. This is not only what benefits China but also Central Asia.

Fifthly, his reference to internal governance is very interesting. Member states should develop a legal system, rule of law. They should create decision making mechanisms which will serve the needs of the people and so on.

Sixth, he spoke of cooperation across the board in variety of fields like security, trade, energy, transport, and customs and so on.

And in return for all these China will pledge to adhere to all the multilateral and bilateral agreement it has entered into and also to assist Central Asian republics in achieving these objectives.

This is the way the Chinese are delivering. They are not simply saying what should be done but they are also actively following up on it. The Chinese pledged $2 billion to the SCO and in regard to individual countries, $4 billion to Turkmenistan, $3 billion to Kazakhstan, and $1 billion to Tajikistan in regards to infrastructural developments, electricity, and rail road. Perhaps the most telling of all is (cooperation in the oil and gas sectors and other areas is not included here as it has already been mentioned elsewhere) that the China-Central Asia trade figure is almost touching $50 billion with the trade balance in favour of China by $6 billion. In contrast, the two-way trade between India and Central Asia stands at $ 212 million. This is a 2009 figure and there might be an increase but even so the market in Central Asia is dominated by China. India has not been able to do so. India does have a similarity of objectives with regard to Central Asia but has been unable to give it a concrete form.

The physical constraints between Central Asia and India and China are not very dissimilar. The 1800 kilometers long pipeline that is being laid for supplying gas to China is going to pass through extremely difficult terrain including mountains etc. India does not have similar kind of geographical contiguity with Central Asia. Central Asia and China have that advantage in building pipelines and other linkages. The Chinese are putting money and technology and making an effort. When the pipeline starts feeding China, its resource needs would be significantly met. It doesn't stop at oil and gas but also precious metals. There is perhaps another dimension which needs to be looked into. A couple of years back when there was a major flood, a significant amount of minerals which the Chinese are in need of like Tungsten, Molybdenum etc was destroyed. There was a need and China started investing in Central Asia in these commodities. More importantly there is Uranium. By 2020 estimates say China would be producing 30 billion MW of electricity. An interesting fact is that, this capacity would be 4 per cent of total global nuclear power production. This is in the course of next ten years. Uranium is something which China would be importing in a major way from Kazakhstan.

Not only have the Chinese done deals at the Central government level, they have also done it through enterprises and also allowed provinces to make deals, including in the Muslim provinces. So there are agreements being signed by Xinjiang. One of the officials of the commercial department has said that they need to restructure their export, food markets and products and explore new markets in the Middle East, South Asia and Central Asia. By 2050 the region would foster 20 export oriented regional centers of Muslim products. (It is not clear what Muslim products means) including processed food and farm produce.

China has concerns in regard to terrorism, Islamic fundamentalism which might affect the Muslim population in China. The Chinese are also looking at opportunities in some way to undermine the effect by building up linkages with countries in Middle East, Central Asia, South East Asia so that the Muslim population is not only seen as part of the population but also having opportunity in economic inter-course and other forms of linkages other than religion.

The other point which may be of interest is that there is a huge amount of minerals Tungsten, Molybdenum, gold, silver, Mercury, Uranium etc. Many of these (Indians must take a look at it and study it) are found in Tibet. With the railway line now having been established and power becoming more accessible for the Tibet region, China would be able to exploit the same. This has been a major constraint in the Tibetan region for mining purposes apart from other environmental considerations. But one estimate from Chinese sources suggests Tibet might be able to yield mineral resources valued at a trillion RMB. To the extent China is not able to fulfill its requirements and to the extent Central Asia can fulfill its needs, China will be interested in developing Tibet. There is another point i.e. Nepal. For India's requirements of power, one possible source is Nepal. India has not been able to do much. There is a Mahakaali Treaty of 1996 and even the Detailed Project Report has still not been prepared 15 years down the line.

Is there a possibility of China developing the power sector in Nepal for developmental purposes in Tibet?

In conclusion, it can be said that basically, countries like Russia, India have interests similar to China. In addition to that, Chinese have possibly some baggage which makes the Central Asian states a little more wary towards China than Russia or India. In case of India, it is not contiguous and not much reason to worry. For example in Uzbekistan there was a Chinese proposal to lease farmlands and there were protests against them. Interestingly some scholars say, if the proposal had come from Russia the reaction might not have been that averse. This is the baggage that the China has to carry which needs to be dealt with over a period of time. But ten years down the line the profile that China has today, the scene might be different. A lot of money has been given to the Central Asian states by China in the form of loans. The Sri Lankan Finance Minister was in India a few months ago and while talking to the author observed that the Chinese have given them a huge amount of money, approximately $30 million as loans. India has given far more money to Sri Lanka than China and much of it as grants. The difference is that when the Chinese give money they deliver the project also. But India on the other hand gives the money as grants but the projects fail to fructify.

Ten years down the line given the political consolidation of China domestically there is the real prospect of it emerging as number one (they are number two now in terms of economy). There is a strong chance of their becoming a strong political competitor. Second, they have a strong presence given the amount of money they have put in Central Asia. That presence might well work to the exclusion of others. This can be only prevented if others have a similar kind of relationship or a relationship which is not marginal. Third, as far as Central Asia is concerned, their point of view is that whatever assistance comes from China is without any conditions of a political nature. For their own future development their commitment to values like democracy and freedom makes Central Asian states to look at India, Russia, and European Union. They need to consider whether it makes sense for their own development, political stability to develop closer relations with India and in what way it can be done so that even if India is not able to match China's reach and influence lacking the deep pockets, at least to an extent India will be a balancing factor there.

PROBLEMS OF REGIONAL AND GLOBAL SECURITY: KAZAKHSTAN'S VISION

Dr. Lerov Tarakov

As is well known, twenty years of independent development of the New Independent States of Central Asia - the creation of the attributes of statehood, development of political and economic systems, the establishment of the Nation - every element of the state building is inseparably linked with the search for the optimal model to ensure national safety. Our countries, as the former republics of Soviet Union, have faced in 1991 a threefold call.

First, in the Union security problems of the unified country were incurred by the Unified Center, therefore the new independent states turn out to be, without exaggeration, novice in global system of the international safety and are yet to create regional.

Secondly, the disintegration of Soviet Union and the elimination from the international military-political arena of the socialist camp inevitably caused serious dynamic political-military situation near the southern borders of the newly independent republics.

And, thirdly, the escalation and globalization of new threats and challenges to humanity, such as international terrorism and extremism has occurred in a greater degree after the disintegration of Soviet Union, and from the pervasive effect of these phenomena, our countries had to look for quick search of recipes of protection also without experience of conducting an independent policy of national security.

However, the open foreign policy has helped Kazakhstan to overcome these serious problems, a sincere aspiration to make its contribution to ensure international security and certainly to help the world community.

What are the basic approaches and achievements of Kazakhstan along this way?

Firstly, Kazakhstan has been actively involved in improving the global system of international security. As is well known, Kazakhstan was the first of the nuclear states of the world to end nuclear testing permanently at the Semipalatinsk nuclear test site even when the country was still a union republic.Within a year and a half, independent Kazakhstan voluntarily renounced the world's fourth largest nuclear missile arsenal including 1,150 warheads. Since that time, Kazakhstan is one of the most active and initiative members of the global nuclear non-proliferation movement, and August 29, 1991, the day our country abandoned nuclear weapons, has gained the status of internationally celebrated anniversary as per UN decision. These steps by Kazakhstan paved the way for a nuclear weapon-free world, and the subsequent successful developments proved that the most reliable guarantee of security are dialogue and peaceful confidential cooperation with other countries, rather than huge stocks of the most powerful weapons.

Having made such a significant contribution to the international security system, Kazakhstan reliably ensured its own safety, having received formal guarantees of security and territorial integrity from the five recognized nuclear powers.

Secondly, Kazakhstan has taken active part in international and regional organizations whose activities are directly related to the issues concerning security and trust-building in Central Asia. Kazakhstan, one of the first independent states of the former Soviet Union became a member of the Organization for Security and Cooperation in Europe. In 2010, Kazakhstan, the first of the post Soviet republics, has achieved the OSCE Chairmanship and by the statements of some European leaders and heads of OSCE institutions, Kazakhstan has proved itself as one of the most active and initiating Presidents in the history of this respected international organization. Thanks to Kazakhstan the international negotiations and consultations the situation in Nagorno-Karabakh and Pridnestrovie, have considerably improved.   Kazakhstan as OSCE chairman, by personal example has demonstrated commitment to humanitarian methods of the International Assistance in post-war reconstruction of Afghanistan by providing $ 50 million to train Afghan youth to peace professions in Kazakhstani universities.

The culmination of Kazakhstan's chairmanship in the OSCE was in December 2010 at the Astana Summit. Prior to that, such meetings were not held for 11 years. The summit, at which, after such a long time, the Astana Declaration has been accepted, is also entirely as a result of the initiative and persistence of Kazakhstan.

At present, in 2011, Kazakhstan is the chairman of a major international structure, the Organization of Islamic Conference, and remains a member of the troika of the OSCE, and is seeking to use the potential of both international organizations to find ways of convergence and the expansion of dialogue and trust on a line "the East – the West", the Islamic and Christian world.

This idea, incidentally, was the basis of the Conference on Interaction and Confidence-Building Measures in Asia (CICA), a project sponsored by the Kazakh President Nursultan Nazarbayev. With the idea of creation of an Asian analogue of the OSCE Kazakh leader acted in 1992 at the 47th session of UN General Assembly. To date, the CICA has been transformed into a stable factor in world politics, and Kazakhstan highly appreciates the fact that India, Russian Federation and our neighbours in the region are active participants of CICA. Despite the fact that the CICA is not an organization, but a forum, its relevance is growing from year to year. Discussion of issues concerning peace, security and stability in the Asian continent and to develop common approaches to this, standards of conduct, to develop and implement the principles of peaceful coexistence and mutually beneficial cooperation between States, regardless of their political and ideological orientation that takes on the modern stage of crucial importance. The political and economic potential of the CICA, their ability to influence global and regional processes make this council potentially one of the most important forums in the world. In June 2002, Almaty hosted the first summit of CICA, which was attended by the presidents of Kazakhstan, Russia,

China, Pakistan, Turkey, Mongolia, Kyrgyzstan, Tajikistan and Afghanistan, the prime ministers of Azerbaijan and India, authorized officials of Iran, Egypt, Palestine and Israel, state representatives of United States observers, Indonesia, Malaysia, Japan, Thailand, Vietnam, Ukraine and the Republic of Korea, as well as leadership organizations, the OSCE observers, the UN and Arab League. During the Summit the representatives signed the Almaty Act - the founding document - and the Declaration on Eliminating Terrorism and Promoting Dialogue among Civilizations. Also the task of creation and the beginning of the CICA Secretariat, was placed in front of the State heads.

Uniqueness of the Almaty Summit of 2002 consisted in the participating leaders of the countries who were at that time in a state of deterioration in bilateral conflict: India and Pakistan, Palestine and Israel. Thus, the CICA confirmed its purpose and became an open forum for discussion in order to find settlement to the problems and conflicts in the region.

Thirdly, Kazakh objective has been to secure the country's boundaries and direct cooperation with the military institutions of regional security.

In the past, it was our region, and to be precise, the Kazakh-Chinese border that was the most potentially explosive part of the region. In Soviet times, for this reason the largest and technically equipped Central Asian Military District with the headquarters in Alma-Ata was located.

Kazakhstan was one of the initiators of multilateral meeting to reduce tensions in the area, which soon turned into a so-called "Shanghai Five", and then in the Shanghai Cooperation Organization, in which now India takes an active part. The countries in this region have decided to solve the seemingly insurmountable issues of disputed territories, and developed a strong potential for regional economic cooperation.

Kazakhstan was one of the initiators and today is an active member of the Collective Security Treaty Organization (CSTO). Of course giving priority to the modernization of the armed forces, the country finds it necessary to rely on the general military technical potential of strategic partners and allies. We have common interests in regional stability and meeting security threats and challenges to the region.

There is not only the penetration of extremist groups, but also drug trafficking, illegal migration, environmental problems which can be solved only by united efforts. But along with the constant participation in military exercises under the Collective Security Treaty Organization, Kazakhstan pays a great importance to cooperation with NATO within the framework "Partnership for Peace", with the international antiterrorist coalition, to ensure peace and order in Afghanistan. Kazakhstan is committed to multi-vector policy in economic integration and foreign policy matters, political and military cooperation.

Fourthly, the economic component of ensuring security guarantees. It is important to note that hundreds of foreign companies since the early years of independence have taken an active part in the working out of Kazakh hydro carbon deposits and other natural resources, strengthening the country's banking system and other businesses. This allowed not only to attract a record quantity of investments, which over 20 years amounted to about $ 100 billion, but also provided a new status as a country that has become an integral part of a global system of world economic development, and accordingly, has aroused immense international economic interest. Stability and security in Kazakhstan became part of the vital interests of world powers, the states - leaders of economic development, international financial institutions, and multinational corporations.

Nevertheless, the top priority for the economic development of the country is to overcome the commodity orientation of the economy and the implementation of the strategy of industrial innovative development of the country, for the period until 2020. Today the basic attention in Kazakhstan is given to the search of new technologies, and among foreign investors, not to those who wish to pump oil, gas and metals, but to the companies bearing new manufacturing and other modern and innovative technologies.

And finally the fifth and the most important point that deserves mention. It is obvious that the main condition of stability has to exist. The main condition for us is the people of Kazakhstan.

At one time our country was among the most dangerous zones of the risk of occurrence of inter-ethnic conflicts; then Kazakhstan had every chance to become the arena of civil war. The complex structure of the population after the collapse of the Soviet Union was the most painful legacy and the most serious test for the newly independent state. The problem was not only that of nation building, the Kazakhs at that point of time did not have majority. It was, in my opinion a massive psychological installation of the population, which to a greater extent than in other republics identified themselves as "Soviet people". After all, Kazakhstan was the site of mass migration on ethnic or political grounds. Kazakhstan was also the place of realisation of many Soviet Union projects - the construction of the Baikonur cosmodrome, the Semipalatinsk nuclear test site, the industrial giant projects such as the Karaganda Metallurgical Combine, a massive development of virgin and fallow lands.

Kazakhstan was the place of service for soldiers and officers of the country's largest military district. At one time I was deputy director of the Centre for Analysis and Strategic investigations of the Administration of the President, the Director of the Institute of Strategic Studies under the president. And in reality, in spite of a correct and optimal long-term national development strategy until 2030, the main subject of research and systems of internal political decisions, which were adopted on their basis, were precisely the problem of civilian self-identification of a Kazakh. For Kazakhstan the number one issue is not economic growth, not the creation of attributes of independent statehood and nation building as such. Today this complex issue is almost resolved. The vast majority of the population of the country sees themselves as citizens of an independent Kazakhstan and in their aspirations among the priorities is to strengthen the independence and the preservation of political stability. Kazakhstan citizens have radically changed their attitude to the state Kazakh language, which has moved away from the open-aversion in the initial years of independence to the status of the formative language of interstate communication.

For a country which is inhabited by about a hundred ethnic groups, to build a model of ethnic harmony and cooperation, having the interests of many countries of the world is a huge achievement.

Today the Kazakh Nation is a reality; it is guarantor of stability and conflict-free development, the guarantor of the economic progress of the country under the President of Kazakhstan Nursultan Nazarbayev, leader of the nation inspite of criticism from some nations. Nazarbayev proclaimed the principle of "economy first, then politics" and qualified as commitment authoritarian methods of leadership in the country. And, nevertheless, pro-democratic procedures in the country will never be violated; Nazarbayev won the election solely due to its own highest authority.

At the same time, in many countries today there are discussions about globalization and threat of international terrorism and extremism. They are to determine what should be the priority: time-tested democratic institutions that are not able to ensure the safety of the population, or the authoritarian regimes that control the situation and ensure peace and security of citizens. Such a discussion had taken place invisibly in our country. Perhaps it was the implementation of the initiative of holding a referendum, which resulted in the current president's term to be extended until 2020. Even at the stage of collecting signatures five million people, virtually a third of the population of the country, voted in favour. Nevertheless, President Nazarbayev was opposed to the decision, for it meant an extraordinary presidential election two years prior to the expiration of his lawful authority. In 2012, Kazakhstan will elect a new parliament.

Under the amendments to the Constitution adopted at the initiative of Nazarbayev, in the new composition of the supreme legislative body of the country there would at least be two political parties. We have no doubt that the elections on April 3, Nursultan Nazarbayev will win (he did win by a massive mandate) and in the parliamentary elections - his party "Nur Otan" would be the victor. And, nevertheless, the president's decision suggests that, in his view, the development of democratic institutions in society remains a priority for public policy, and, consequently, the systems and processes would ensure long term stability and security and development.

RELEVANCE OF CENTRAL EURASIA FOR INDIA: GEOPOLITICAL AND ECONOMIC PERSPECTIVES

Nivedita Das Kundu

Introduction

In recent years, after the disintegration of the Soviet Union the relatively new geopolitical term 'Central Eurasia', has gained popularity. The term Central Eurasia is normally applied to Azerbaijan, Armenia, Georgia, Kazakhstan, Kyrgyzstan, Tajikistan, Turkmenistan, and Uzbekistan, which are treated as a single geopolitical area. However, the logic suggests that if the physical dimensions of the continent's parts are put aside, then the geographic Eurasia as a continent consists of two parts of the world that is 'Europe' and 'Asia'. Traditionally, Central Eurasia as a geographic concept is related to the territory between the Bosporus in the west and the Xinjiang-Uighur autonomous region in the east and from the Kazakh steppes in the north to Afghanistan in the south. There is even wider interpretation of Central Eurasia, which also includes the Black Sea region.[1] The geographic Central Eurasia almost completely covers geographic Central Asia and the Caucasus.

Central Eurasia consists of mostly Turkic-speaking people they are mainly Tatars, Bashkorts, Azeris, Turkmens, Kyrgyz, Kazakhs, Uyghurs. They all share the heritage of common Turkic language. Their language includes not just the lexicon and grammar but also texts, proverbs idioms and sometimes-even part of oral epics, such as the 'Alpamish' derived from a linguistically transmitted common Turkic heritage. Influence of Iranic linguo-cultural factor is the second important determinant here. There is a direct representation by the languages and cultures of Iran (Persian), Tajikistan (Tajik), and Afghanistan (Dari), all these belong to the significant classical Persian literature and language.[2] All these have exerted a great influence on the culture and civilizations of the region.

The heritage of Arabic language is also quite prominent here. The words from Arabic in the Iranic and Turkic languages of the region constitute from 50 to 60 percent of their vocabularies. Arabic heritage contributed greatly to all areas of culture in the region. They are all inseparable from the Iranic and the Turkic heritage starting from the writing systems and calendars of the area. It was only in the 20th century that the Arabic writings and calendars of Central Asia were replaced with the Russian-derived ones.[3] All these signify that there is a unique combination of determinants characterizing Central Eurasia. Geopolitical as well as the economic factors are the ways and the means, but the linguo-cultural factors are the content for the explanatory narrative and the focal point for the people sharing them.

In Central Eurasia different global as well as regional players practice active politics. The significance of this region increased mainly due to its geo-strategic location natural resources and rich cultural heritage which became noticeable mainly after the collapse of the Soviet Union and when these states became independent sovereign states. It is also due the Islamic terrorist activities emanating from the region that received international attention, which increased immensely after 9/11 terrorist attack and at the same time increased US (United States) attention towards the region.[4] Of late, Central Eurasia is occupying more and more central place in the international power politics. While dealing with Central Eurasia, it is pertinent to see what relevance it bears to the reality of power politics that is witnessed today. These states that are the members of the Common Wealth of Independent States (CIS) today are at varying stages of political or economic development. Some are vibrant democracies whereas others are centralized totalitarian regimes.

Driven by India's security and increasing energy needs, India emerged with a high profile in Central Eurasian region because of its long standing special relationship with the erstwhile Soviet Union and its links with Central Eurasia in terms of security and trade. India also tried to become a major factor in shaping and organizing the Central Eurasian region. States of Central Eurasia also showed keenness to develop close relationship with India due to India's economic growth and geopolitical influence.

The Objective of this article is to focus on the relevance of 'Central Eurasia' and its significance in the regional/international power politics and economics. The general discourse is that the region is important mainly due to its geo-strategic location, natural resources and rich cultural heritage. While dealing with this region's relevance for India and examining its geopolitical and economic perspective the major question that comes up is that, can India play a significant role in the region? What factors are working in India's favour in the region? What are the constrains? To what extend can India be seen as a Central Eurasian Player? What strategy can India devise to engage these countries meaningfully and effectively? The argument given in this article is that Central Eurasia is occupying a central place in the international and regional politics and is a factor for connecting Western and Eastern civilization, in spite of having distinct character from Russia or Asia or even from the Islamic World. In this article an attempt has been made to signify specific factors of the region and also determine the future perspectives by building few future scenarios. The article also provides some policy recommendations for India to improve relation with the region.

Two Distinct Parts of Central Eurasia

Two Distinct Parts of Central Eurasia is Caucasus & Central Asia. The contemporary geopolitical interpretation of the term 'the Caucasus' came-up when Russia conquered the region. It is also known as 'the Trans-Caucasus/South Caucasus that is, the part of the region found beyond the main Caucasian Range if viewed from Russia and 'the Northern Caucasus,' the territory to the north of the Trans-Caucasus and the mountain range.[5] The southern limits of the Caucasus were always identified by the Russian Empire's southern state border in the Caucasus. The border change was amply illustrated by the case of Kars of the late 19th century, when the Russian Empire detached it by force from the Ottoman Empire and it came to be known as part of the Caucasus. The entire territory of the North Caucasus, which consists of the piedmont and mountainous areas, comprises of part of the Russian Federation (RF). The piedmont area comprises of the following RF region, the Krasnodar and Stavropol territories, the Astrakhan and Rostov regions and the Republic of Kalmykia. The mountainous areas are the Republics of Adigey, Daghestan, Ingushetia, Kabardino-Balkaria, Karachaevo-Cherkessia, North Ossetia-Alania and Chechnya.[6]

In Soviet times the Central Asian region was called *Sredniaia Azia* (Middle Asia). *Sredniaia Azia* includes Kyrgyzstan, Tajikistan, Turkmenistan, Uzbekistan and Kazakhstan. Western scholars mostly use the term 'Central Asia,' while some Russians have not yet dropped the old term 'Middle Asia.' Another term, 'Greater Central Asia', is of more or less recent coinage.[7] Recently this term has been given more exact geopolitical specification and applied to the five former Soviet Republics including Afghanistan.

In the early twentieth century Britain's geopolitical theorist Halford J. Mackinder called Central Eurasia the Eurasian 'Heartland' to specify the region's geopolitical and geo-strategic importance in global politics. Mackinder was of the opinion that the one, who would control this region, would also control the whole world. Indeed, with the end of Cold War and disintegration of the Soviet Union, Central Eurasia has developed as an important geo-strategic and geo-economic region in world politics.[8] Central Eurasia, however, suffers from localized conflicts as well as economic distress. Ethnic tensions continue in many of these states, making the region susceptible to instability and threatening its political and economic development. Its location between, Russia, China, Iran, Turkey, and Afghanistan make the region a focal point for foreign powers as well as potential conflict between them.[9] The US, EU, China, Japan, Pakistan, Saudi Arabia, and Israel are all interested in the region. It can thus be said that here a new 'Great Game' is underway.

Unlike the Great Game of the nineteenth century, which was played out between the British Empire and the Czarist Russia, the post-Cold War Great Game involves not only states but also non-state actors, international organizations, transnational oil corporations (TNOCs) etc. Active in the region in military security terms is the US and NATO. NATO also runs military programmes in Central Eurasian states in the context of the Partnership for Peace Programme (PfP). The Organization for Security and Cooperation in Europe (OSCE) is also active in the region. Another significant multilateral organization coming up in the region in a big way is the Shanghai Cooperation Organisation (SCO). This can be a possible counter-balance in the region with the western organizations. The SCO set up in August 1996, including Russia, China, Kazakhstan, Kyrgyzstan, Tajikistan, and Uzbekistan as main members of the organization now expanded its agenda.[10] The agenda of the SCO is based mainly on the economic cooperation, but now also working towards curbing drugs trafficking and terrorist activities in the region focusing on the security concerns of the region. The Russian factor is still very strong in the Central Eurasian States politico-economic as well as in the energy sectors. Today lot of study is going on to understand the problems and prospects of this region including the three South Caucasian States (Azerbaijan, Armenia, and Georgia) and the five Central Asian States (Kazakhstan, Kyrgyzstan, Tajikistan, Turkmenistan, and Uzbekistan).

Geopolitics of Oil and Gas

The Central Eurasian region's oil and gas reserves could be a major contribution to socio-economic development and transition of the region. The newly Caspian littoral states (Azerbaijan, Kazakhstan, and Turkmenistan) together with Russia and Iran have one of the world's largest oil and gas reserves, which makes them significant to global markets.

Estimates of proven and possible oil reserves across the whole Caspian area, excluding Russia and Iran, run-up to 190 billion barrels of oil. Its proven gas reserves are estimated at 196 trillion cubic feet. The Trans-Afghanistan Pipeline (Turkmenistan-Afghanistan-Pakistan-India) is a proposed natural gas pipeline being developed by the Asian Development Bank.[11] This pipeline (TAPI) will transport Caspian Sea's natural gas from Turkmenistan through Afghanistan into Pakistan and then to India. The Indian government has approved Inter-Governmental Agreement and Gas Pipeline Framework Agreement for TAPI pipeline project at a summit meeting of the four participating nations at Ashgabat to import natural gas through Turkmenistan-

Maps Showing BTC & TAPI

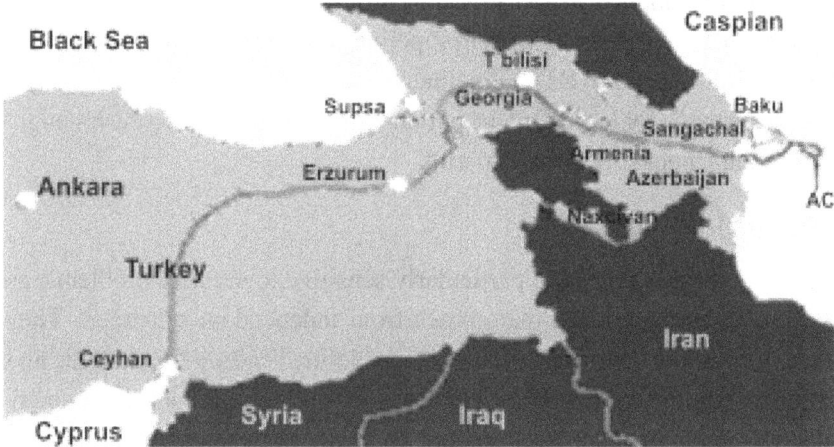

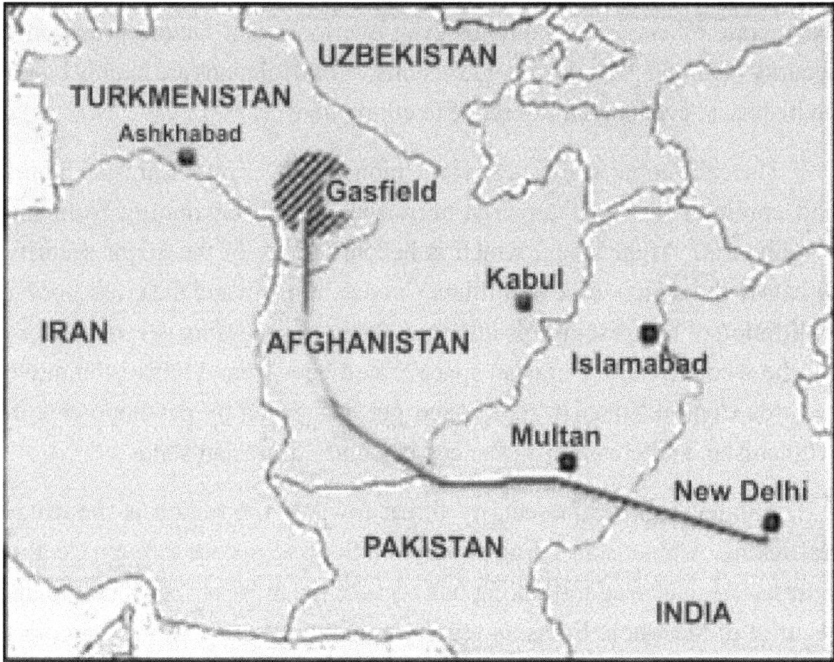

The proposed TAPI gas pipeline

Afghanistan-Pakistan-India pipeline on December 11, 2010. Turkmenistan will supply gas from its South Yoloten-Osman field and state-owned gas utility GAIL India has entered into a Gas Sales and Purchase Agreement (GSPA) with Turkmenistan's national oil firm Turkmengaz during the Summit in Ashgabat.[12] Another significant Pipeline connection of the region is the Baku-Tibilisi-Ceyhan (BTC) Pipeline; these pipelines can become a major energy resource for India. But the political situation in these countries might make their smooth operation difficult.

Security Concerns

Central Eurasian states are particularly sensitive to security problems, as they lack the experience that comes from independent statehood. They have not had the opportunity to develop a defined culture for strategic and security planning or for policy engineering. Furthermore, all these newly independent states feel insecure and quite uncertain about their security interests and priorities. They tend to underestimate certain security threats, exaggerate others and sometimes even overlook vital factors in national security planning.[13] Their strategic visions and calculations are mainly based on historical events with reference to ethnic lines.

Since the collapse of the Soviet Union, all the Central Eurasian States had common threat of terrorist activities mainly emanating from the neighbouring Afghanistan, which is becoming one of the major security threats to the region. Rise of militancy and extremism and the cross-border infiltration of terrorist groups into their territories, causing severe concern for the whole Central Eurasian space.[14] Refugees from Afghanistan move towards Central Eurasian region and get influenced by developments in Afghanistan and create disturbances in Central Eurasian states.

Another significant security threat towards the region is the drugs trafficking. Afghanistan's drug production flows to Europe through Central Eurasia. Afghan drug trafficking has become the most serious threat to the security of the whole Eurasian region including Russia. Afghan narcotics kills' 30,000 people in Russia every year, twice as many as the Soviet Union lost during its decade-long military intervention in Afghanistan. The action plan from Russia called for joint SCO-Afghan operations.[15] As most of the

Central Eurasian States are full members of SCO, it is expected that the joint operation can curb drug trafficking, organized crime, combat laundering of drug money and improve border controls.

India and Central Eurasia

India's relation with Central Eurasia is very strong mainly because of its civilization links. India has deep interest in the region as it lies in its extended neighbourhood and also due to its security concerns and energy requirements. India maintains relatively high profile in the region because of its long-standing special relationship with the erstwhile Soviet Union and its links with Central Eurasia in terms of age-old trade and economic relations through silk route. The study of Central Eurasia has also grown over the past few years in India, including their nationalism policy, about their civil society organizations and about urban development in these states. India has been active in Central Eurasia, although China was quicker off the mark in developing close relationship with post-Soviet Central Eurasia than India.[16] However, all visits to the region by senior Indian Politician's have been treated as significant occasions. India has strong diplomatic presence in the region. Significant and deep cultural contacts between them have also existed for past many years.

➢ *India-Central Asia*

Central Asia is an important region for India with its vital geo-strategic location. The five landlocked republics of Central Asia – Uzbekistan, Kazakhstan, Kyrgyzstan, Tajikistan and Turkmenistan are in India's neighbourhood or extended neighbourhood. The region not only connects Asia to Europe, but also rich in natural resources. It occupies a special place in India's foreign policy priorities. Its importance to India today is not merely civilisational, but also linked to geo-political and economic issues.[17] India's attempt has always been to increase political, cultural and economic ties with the Central Asian Republics (CARs).

Since 1991, India-CAR relations have come a long way. Though numerous political and economic changes have taken place in the recent past in these states but the relationship between India and CAR has gone beyond the historical and cultural ties to a strong political and security cooperation. There are still significant common interest ties on which India and CAR can accelerate future cooperation. India-CAR relations are aimed to counter common threats to their security, as both face the menace of religious extremism. The fight against terrorism is one major area of cooperation. Both CAR-India shares the view that the problem of drug trafficking and threat of weapons of mass destruction (WMD) are to be addressed jointly. On the situation in Afghanistan both hold similar views. India and the States of CAR have signed number of agreements to improve their relationship and cooperate in economic and energy sectors.[18] Both India and CAR have similar approaches towards major international and regional issues. There have been emergences of new strategic equation and security realignments in the region.

India is also taking an initiative to provide satellite based tele-education and tele-medicine connectivity between India and CAR which would be a demonstration of cutting edge technological and human resource cooperation between them. One of the CAR states Uzbekistan would become an important connecting point in the transport corridor, the route connecting India with Central Asia via Mumbai-Chah Bahar-Zaranj-Delaran-Heart-Naibabad-Khairaton-Termez and further has high potential for success.[19]

India's approach to secure a niche for itself in Central Asian hydrocarbons have so far been unsuccessful. New Delhi had earlier tried to secure a share in the Kurmangazy field of Kazakhstan, but lost to China. However, it is hoped that India's present energy diplomacy would mark a breakthrough and will help ONGC Videsh and the Gas Authority of India Limited (GAIL) to put their plans of investment in CAR's on the fast track.[20] As far as increasing the cooperation on nuclear energy is concerned it is going to increase. Among five Central Asian States, Uzbekistan is reported to have vast quantities of uranium and India is examining the option of buying uranium from Uzbekistan for its nuclear energy production requirements.

All CAR States have affirmed its support to India's wish to become a permanent member of the extended United Nations Security Council

(UNSC). After the events of 11 September 2001, India has also started building military technical cooperation with this region. India is engaged with the States of CAR in intelligence sharing, sharing of joint military experience and providing training and assistance to Central Asian forces. Both India and Central Asia have economic complementarities in terms of natural resources; human resources and markets, which if exploited can broaden cooperation. Opportunities for joint ventures in banking, insurance, agriculture, information technology and in pharmaceuticals also exist. The Indian pharmaceutical industry has done well in all the states of CAR. Today, it accounts for nearly a quarter of the imports into the region. Indian industrialists have also registered an impressive presence in the steel and construction sectors there.[21] India is exploiting its expertise in the construction of small and medium-sized hydroelectric plants mainly in Kyrgyzstan and Tajikistan, which have substantial hydropower potential.

With Central Asian energy reserves being estimated at 2.7 per cent of world oil reserves (between 13 and 15 billion barrels) and 7 per cent of natural gas reserves (around 270 to 360 trillion cubic feet, mainly in two big fields Kashag and Tangis), the region has a potential to become future energy hub for India. The main hydrocarbon deposits are in Kazakhstan, Turkmenistan and Uzbekistan. These Central Asian states with energy potential have agreed to cooperate with India in the fields of oil and natural gas exploration and production. On 26 April 2006, India's GAIL and Ministry of Petroleum signed an MOU to conduct oil and gas exploration in Uzbekistan. Uzbekistan has also agreed to allocate geological territory to Indian companies to explore its hydrocarbon resources. The work is in progress between GAIL and *Uzbekneftogas* to build facilities in Uzbekistan to produce LPG (liquefied petroleum gas).

In the field of defence, India acquired six Ilyushin-78 in-flight refuelling aircraft from Uzbekistan. Indian aircrafts are being regularly serviced at the Chekalov aircraft plant in Tashkent in Uzbekistan.[22] Indian experts have also been involved in repairing military aircrafts in Tajikistan.

India and Central Asian States together are discussing to develop the human resource potential in the region. India has shown its desire to build major software development centre and light motor vehicles manufacturing sector in Central Asia. India being observer in Shanghai Cooperation Organization (SCO) has opened up further opportunities for cooperation with the States of CAR in areas like in security, communication and for economic integration. There has been an articulated policy of India to integrate Central Asia with India and consider an observer status for the States of CAR in South Asian Association for Regional Cooperation (SAARC).[23] India's membership in the Economic Cooperation Organization (ECO), which is also expected to develop soon, could also strengthen India's economic relationship with the CARs.

The overall outlook on the region suggests that for India there is an enormous scope and potential to engage in meaningful and fruitful politico-economic cooperation with five States of CAR. Tourism, diplomacy, defence, education, food processing, and products related to small-scale industries offer considerable potential for cooperation. The region could be used as a ground for joint ventures for producing goods and commodities for export to the wider world.

➤ *India-South Caucasus*

Friendly relationships between India and South Caucasus have existed for more than four thousand years. Affinities of culture, language and mythology brought these two regions closer. In the South Caucasus State of Armenia from 149 B.C. till A.D. 301 there existed a Hindu colony. As far back as the fifth century, Armenian traders regularly traded in Indian muslin, spices, precious stones and herbs. Many Armenians who became citizens of India were traders, government servants and academics. Some Armenians were even involved in India's independence movement and even served in the Indian army. Armenians were mostly resident of Chennai, Mumbai, Kolkata and Surat but currently there are hardly hundred Armenians in India, mostly in Kolkata. In Chennai, the first Armenian Constitution was written.[24] Today, the main concern of the Armenian Church Committee of Kolkata is to preserve the Armenian heritage and properties such as the Armenian College and Philanthropic Academy. India and Armenia are both keen to cooperate with each other in politico-security and economic spheres.

India's relationship with Azerbaijan is also very old. The *Atesgah* monument near Baku, with Sanskrit and Gurmukhi wall inscriptions, is a surviving proof of the ancient relationship between India and Azerbaijan. Trade was carried on between the two countries over the Silk Route. Master craftsmen from Tabriz, principal city of Iranian Azerbaijan were involved in the construction of the Taj Mahal. India and Azerbaijan established diplomatic relationship on February 1992.

Much of the trade of Indian items with Azerbaijan is carried out through UAE, which does not get reflected in the trade statistics. However, many Indian pharmaceutical companies are successfully competing with their European companies for the Azerbaijani market. Bharat Heavy Electricals Limited (BHEL) has executed a project for *Azenergy,* a government undertaking, for the supply and installation of power generators for the Mingechevir Power Plant in Azerbaijan. Aluminium Ore and Concentrate from Gujarat has supplied raw material to the aluminium plants in Ganja and Sumgait, which has contributed largely to the quantum jump in India's exports to Azerbaijan. During the Soviet period, the educational institutions in Azerbaijan were a favourite destination for Indian students. Currently there are over 500 Indian students in Azerbaijan mainly pursuing medical and technical studies. Indians make their presence felt in various sectors in Azerbaijan even today.[25] If the oil and gas industry in Azerbaijan takes off as a global energy supplier in the near future, this development can be of immense benefit for India.

Bilateral relationship between India and Georgia also goes back to several centuries. Georgia has consistently supported India's position on Jammu and Kashmir and India's candidature to the UN Security Council. Both sides have emphasized the need to combat international terrorism and separatism. Georgia also supports India's draft Comprehensive Convention on International Terrorism (CCIT). Georgia's unstable political situation has slowed down the growth in trade and economic cooperation between the two countries. India's main exports to Georgia are pharmaceuticals and consumer durables. Imports comprise metals like aluminium, copper and ferrous. Indian construction company Punj Lloyd was a major sub-contractor in 2004-05 for the construction of Georgian part of the Baku-Tbilisi-Ceyhan (BTC) oil pipeline. Indian automobile company Mahindra & Mahindra's MUV 'Bolero' is assembled at the Kutaisi Auto Plant in Georgia and doing good business there. Mahindra's 'Scorpio' also did good business in Georgia. India's expertise and experience could be useful to Georgia in the small and medium size industries such as in light engineering, IT, agriculture, e.g. in silkworm rearing, tea, high-yield wheat varieties and in dry land farming.[26] There is also a huge scope to cooperate in science and technology and in the health sector.

In recent conflict between Georgia and Russia where two breakaway territories of Georgia, South Ossetia and Abkhazia declared independence on 26th August 2008 and Russia supported this move, India's official viewpoint was that:

"India has a long-standing and consistent policy on the issue of recognition. Recognition is normally accorded on the basis of a country having a defined territory, a duly constituted government in charge, which is accepted by the people and which has effective control over an area of governance. It has been India's consistent position that the sovereignty and territorial integrity of all countries should be fully respected by all states".[27] However, in Georgia's case India was upset by the sudden escalation of the conflict and loss of human lives and hope for an early restoration of normalcy in the region.

Future Scenarios (2021)

Scenarios for Central Eurasia have been developed here to widen perspectives and explore uncertain aspects of the future of the region. Scenarios also help to seize new opportunities. Particularly, the issues like the shift from resource dependence to economic diversification; economic reforms and formation of effective governance could help bringing in various changes in the systems during next decade. The ranges of such possible scenarios are many. However, in this article only five scenarios have been mentioned.

- **Scenario One**

➤ By 2021, resource extraction will remain as an important part of Central Eurasia's economy. Good economic policies could lead to inflow of foreign direct investment outside the energy sector while any failure to diversify Central Eurasia's economy could well lead to the 'petro-state phenomenon,' leading to huge income inequality, capital flight and social tensions.

- **Scenario Two**

➤ Central Eurasian states are likely to be challenged by the twin pressures of growing population and a lack of arable land and water resources. The economic and demographic challenges can negatively impact the environment, compounding the current degradation caused by the high rates of 'dirty' resource extraction. Also, states with the limited supplies of natural resources would face challenges to develop effective service industries.

- **Scenario Three**

➤ Ethnic unrest mostly arising due to xenophobia and economic difficulties would cause disturbance in the region. Particularly susceptible are the northern Caucasus including Chechnya, Dagestan and Ingushetia, may prove insoluble and could persist in one form or another till 2021 which could affect the bordering states of South Caucasus causing severe civil unrest.

- **Scenario Four**

➤ West will continue to pursue self-centered foreign policy objectives in the region. This also could give rise to the aggressive nationalist politicians (due to anti-Western rhetoric) creating more tension with the west.

- **Scenario Five**

➤ Central Eurasia's relations with China would deepen. This could happen due to Chinese economic investments in the region. China in collusion with Russia will counterbalance the US interests in the region.

Keeping in mind above mentioned scenarios following recommendations have been made for India:

Recommendations for India

1) Work towards improving relations with the Central Eurasian region in politico-economic and security sectors through regular interaction at the higher decision making level.

2) Work closely with the three CAR's bordering Afghanistan (Uzbekistan, Tajikistan and Kazakhstan) to curb security threats emanating from Afghanistan.

3) Try to revive the silk route traditions to improve trade and economic cooperation with these states.

4) Try to develop close contacts with the multilateral organizations currently active in the region.

5) Formulate strong energy policy to intervene in this regions energy sectors as this region has got the potential to provide India energy security.

6) Try to bury difference with Beijing in Central Asia to form a powerful alignment in the region.

7) Look for ways to assist them in areas of IT and S&T sector, which could help their economic profile to grow beyond natural resources.

8) Revive India's strong civilizational linkages along with the religious connections (like Buddhism) with the Caspian Sea region.

9) Look for ways to utilize India's soft power to get closer to the region.

10) Look for ways to increase people to people contacts and information sharing.

Endnotes

1 *Central Eurasian Studies Review*, available at http://www.cesr-cess.org/ CESR_contribution.html   accessed on 16th February 2011.

2 Richard Lugar, "Energy Security: Cause for Cooperation or Competition"? 90th Anniversary Leadership Series, The Brooking Institution, 13 march 2006, http:/ /www.brookings.edu/comm/events/20060313.pdf. also see Pabst, Adrian, *Central Eurasia in the Emerging Global Balance of Power*, American foreign Policy Interest, Volume 31, Number 3, May 2009, pp. 166-176.

3 Shahram Akbarzadeh, *Uzbekistan and the United States*, Palgrave Macmillan, New York, 2005,pp1-7.

4 Firdous T., "India and Central Asia", in M.A.Kaw and A.A. Banday (eds.) *Central Asia Introspection*, Crown Press, Srinagar, 2006,pp.321-322.

5 Yekaterina Kuznetsova, " The Near Abroad: Increasingly far away from Russia ", Russia in Global Affairs, Vol.3, No.1, January-March, 2005,p.27.

6 Bolshaia Sovetskaia Entsiklopedia, Moscow: Sovetskaia Entsiklopediia, 1977, p.255.

7 Nacelenia Rossia, Edzegodniyie Demographicheskie Doklad, Center Demographicheskie Chelavieka, Moscow, 1993, pp 15-20.

8. Tomohiko Uyama, ed. *Empire, Islam and Politics in Central Eurasia*, Slavic Eurasian Studies, No. 14. Sapporo, Hokkaido University, 2007, 376 pp

9 Faultline of Conflict in Central Asia and the South Caucasus, RAND Document, RAND Publications, 2003.

10 Svante E. Cornell, "Security Threats and Challenges in Caucasus after 9/11", in Ariel Cohen ed, Eursaia in Balance: The US and the Regional Power Shift, Aldershot: Ashgae Publishing Ltd, 2005, pp.44.

11 Anita Singh, "India's Relations with Russia and Central Asia", *International Affairs,*71(1), January 1995, pp. 69

12 Daily News Analyses, "Government approves signing pact for TAPI gas pipeline project", December 11, 2010.

13 Nationalism and Ethnic Conflicts in Transcaucasia in Comparative Perspective,"www.geocities.com. also see Zurab Davitashvilki, "The Ethno Political Situation in the Caucasus and the Problem of Oil in Transportation", http://ourworld.compuseve.com

14 Afghanistan & regional security http://www.globalsecurity.org/military/world/ afghanistan/opium.htm, accessed on 17th February 2011

15 Sengupta Kim, Afhganistan: Russia steps in to help NATO, in The Independent World News, 27th October 2010.

[16] M.S. Roy, "India's Interest in Central Asia", *Strategic Analysis*, Vol.34, (12), March 2001, pp. 2273–89.

[17] "India-Central Asia Economic Relations", A Report of RIS/CII Seminar RIS-DP # 94/2005, May 2005.

[18] "India looking for energy supplies in Central Asia ", 13 September 2006, available at http://www.asianews.it/index.php?art=7200&l=en

[19] S.Blank,"India: TheNewCentralAsianPlayer",available at www.eurasianet.org/departments/insight/articles/eav062606a.shtml.

[20] Naira Mkrtchyan, "Armenians in India and Indians in Armenia,"in S. Paramjit Sahai (ed.), India-Eurasia: The Way Ahead, Chandigarh: CRRID, 2008, pp.203–205

[21] Naira Shovgaryan, "Cultural Links between Armenia and India", in S. Paramjit Sahai (ed.), *India-Eurasia: The Way Ahead*, Chandigarh: CRRID, 2008, pp.258–260

[22]Azerbaijan, Report of Embassy of India, available at http://meaindia.nic.in/foreignrelation/azerbaijan.htm, 2007.

[23] Zhang Deguang, "Generalising Experience, Deepening Cooperation, Leading the SCO towards New Great Achievements', available at www.sectsco.org., accessed on 15th February 2011

[24] Ibid, Naira Mkrtchyan

[25] Sadiqoglu Afet, Azerbaijan-Hindustan Relations, Nurlan, Baku, 2009, pp5-8.

[26] Ibid Sadiqoglu Afet,.E-mail. dr.niveditadaskundu@gmail.com

[27] Eurasian Division Report, MEA, 2009.

SECURITY SITUATION IN AFGHANISTAN AND CENTRAL ASIA

Dr. Davood Moradian

In assessing the current situation in Afghanistan and the way forward it is often the case of speaking of the challenges and alternative course of action to avoid disaster. In my view another way to look forward to this question is to ask what should be the end state of Afghanistan and what are the principles that will make Afghanistan and its international partners to realize the vision and what particular role the neighbours of Afghanistan should assume especially Pakistan.

This paper would be focussing mainly on the regional dimension of the Afghan crisis. Looking at what is going on right now in Kabul. Afghanistan is natural land bridge culturally, strategically and in many other ways a connector, an integrator and a crossroad and roundabout for the region and wider international communities. There is a need to understand in the recent geo-strategic identity and inclination of Afghanistan. Since the establishment of Afghanistan we have seen two main geo-strategic identities and foreign policy orientation. The first one was expansionism where Afghanistan was the centre of a regional empire. The second identity was an isolated identity where Afghanistan became a buffer state and later acquired a neutral identity. The last stage was when Afghanistan became a battleground for competing and conflicting interests of warriors. The new Afghanistan as the connector working for cooperation and regional integration is built upon our early history of expansion, isolation and empowerment.

In the words of President Karzai, Afghanistan wants to become more than cross-roads of civilizations. Afghans believe that no country can or should monopolize the internal affairs or feel excluded. Afghanistan is determined to follow a multilateral foreign policy which means specifying different roles and expectations from the neighbours, the region, the Islamic nations and the western world but only to complement the order and maintain cordial relations rather than competing with them. The Afghan crisis is a trilateral one comprising of local, regional and global drivers and causes. Therefore any conflict resolution for Afghanistan should aim to garner cooperation and understanding between and among the three principal actors. In order to have a better understanding of Afghanistan's relations with its neighbours there is a need to address this question by utilising our principle moral and legal framework. There could be six principles that need to be adhered to.

The first principle which is a minimalist one is the principle of reciprocity. Afghanistan and its neighbours need to come out with a contract which would specify each party's responsibility and expectation. The two keywords would be responsibility and respectability. Our neighbours rightly expect to see a responsible Afghanistan which does not export problems or challenges. In return the neighbours should supply us respectability which means treating Afghanistan as a sovereign, independent multi ethnic country. There will be no responsible Kabul as long as it is not granted respectability.

The second principle is the principle of accountability which applies equally to all stakeholders. Some of our international partners and neighbours cannot wish to find a way out by contributing to Afghanistan's misery. From the soviet invasion to the support that were given to some of the despised and radical groups to the continuance support of Taliban and other terrorists groups.

The third principle is the principle of responsibility and rejection of fatalist and opportunistic behaviour. This principle calls upon us not to remain passive and reactive to the developments in Afghanistan. Specifically, those who are afraid of the Taliban remaining cannot contain what Pakistan or the US can or should do for us. Afghanistan needs to have its own plan and scenario. The counter Taliban forces are playing the role that Pakistan has charted for Afghans. But there is a need to find an Afghan-owned scenario for the counter Taliban strategy.

The fourth principle is the principle of regional cooperation. Unfortunately South Asia and Central Asia belong to the less developed and less connected regions in terms of connectivity and integration. Our enormous human and natural resources would be further enriched if and only if we incorporate regional cooperation into our domestic and international relations. We must synergize our domestic, regional and international policies. Some say we see regional cooperation as a fantasy or academic project or in contradiction with our national interest.

The fifth principle is the principle of complementarity. It is well recognised that the Afghan conflict is multi-dimensional one. Afghanistan and its neighbours and wider international community need to develop a complementary policy and strategy to utilize and synergize our respective competency and expertise. For instance, the development of Afghan national police; the EU is in charge of training and equipping Afghan National police. But unfortunately because we are not following complementary policies and there is a situation that EU does everything when it comes to sustaining the police and what Afghan government have proposed to the European partner is about the division of labour in the region. Particularly India is well placed to provide training for Afghan police because the challenges for policing in Afghanistan are similar to what is happening in India. Thus, while Europe can provide the funding and specialised training India can undertake the balance aspects of training Afghan National Police. In many sectors in Afghanistan articulation and enforcing of complementary policies has not been possible. That is one of the main reasons why there are problems in Afghanistan.

The last principle is the principle of solidarity. Decades of persistent underdevelopment and authoritarian regimes and three decades of violence has made Afghanistan one of the most wounded and destroyed nations in recent history. The principle of solidarity calls all members of the international community to extend every possible help to alleviate the suffering of the needy members. The example is the European Union. Since its inception the EU has followed a persistent solidarity policy to help less fortunate members and neighbours. While acknowledging and appreciating the wide amount of support Afghanistan has received from its neighbours in the last three decades we believe that our more resourceful and powerful neighbours like India can afford to be more generous. As again like the model of EU our neighbours will benefit from it.

The relation between Pakistan and Afghanistan is the most important for us. Afghanistan needs a stabilised and cooperative Pakistan. However the international community has so far failed in the task of civilising Pakistan. Appeasement seems to be the only strategy. There are three models in the relationship between Afghanistan and Pakistan. The first is the positive and strategic partnership. The second model is the normal and good neighbour relations. The third is the negative strategic relation model. Our current relation with Pakistan feature many attributes of the negative strategic relations model. This means the fundamental clash of interest between Pakistan and Afghanistan and deep mutual mistrust. Neither Afghanistan nor Pakistan nor the region can afford to have negative relations and there is a need to change the dynamics of this relationship.

Naturally, it is difficult to jump directly from current negative strategic relations to a positive one at one go. There is a need first to try to normalise our relations with Pakistan which means becoming good and normal neighbours. In order to achieve this end state most countries need to engage in multilateral relations apart from bilateral relations. Negotiations and confidence building measures should play a part. Thus there has been a number of confidence and trust building measures through Afghanistan-Pakistan -NATO, Afghanistan – Pakistan –UN, Afghanistan- Pakistan-Turkey. These have failed yet there is a need to resort to different sources and mechanisms to continue with the mediation efforts. There is no clarity or consensus about the real issue in the bilateral relations between Pakistan and Afghanistan. Mediation and negotiation efforts should enable Afghanistan and Pakistan to understand their respective position and concerns. In addition to that confidence building and mediation efforts with Pakistan have become another component of concern and priority. Only a resilient Afghanistan can command the respect of a hegemonic Pakistan. There are challenges on multiple fronts in Afghanistan. Yet, there is an air of optimism about the realization of the vision of peaceful and stable Afghanistan. However, realization of this vision would be expedited if all the necessary components are put into place.

ROLE AND STAKES OF CARs IN AFGHANISTAN AND APPROACHES TO A REGIONAL SOLUTION: AN UZBEK PERSPECTIVE

Dr. Laziz Tursunov

Introduction

The conflict in Afghanistan has long been and remains a key issue of strategic importance for Uzbekistan. Tashkent consistently calls for serious attention to this problem during all international and regional forums. This topic still continues to be at the centre of consideration in this paper.

The dynamics of the situational development for the last period of time is evident. In spite of huge efforts and measures taken by the Afghan government and coalition forces for peace-keeping in Afghanistan, the situation, unfortunately, is worsening. While the preferred strategy of coalition forces is not yielding the expected results, the unfortunate state of the people of Afghanistan has been deteriorating with every coming day of the war, complicating the solution of the problem itself.

The gravity of the situation in Afghanistan is demonstrated by the simple fact that last year has been the bloodiest in the US-led coalition's nine-year war against Taliban forces, with civilian casualties at an all-time high. Afghanistan Rights Monitor reported that almost 2,500 Afghan civilians were killed and more that 3,000 were injured. Even Red Cross recently called humanitarian condition in Afghanistan worst in last three decades.

Similarly, Pentagon's official data indicate, that Taliban small-arms attacks against the US-led troops in Afghanistan have almost doubled in less than a year.

In contrast the insurgent and other militant groups continue to have a strong influence and position in up to 70 per cent of Afghan territory, vowing to drive all "occupiers and aggressors" from the country. Extremely worrying trend is spreading insecurity and violence towards northern Afghanistan. Militants are expanding their presence in once relatively stable and secure provinces like Kunduz, Faryab and Baghlan and using these as a launch pad for cross-border infiltration into Central Asia. Some observers point out that it's almost impossible for foreigners or representative of the Afghan government even to take a car from Kabul to Mazar-e-Sharif or to Kunduz. Only NGO's can possibly go with a letter from the Taliban.

Another reason for much concern for Uzbekistan is growing militarization in Afghanistan and the region as a whole. According to some data, there is abundance of arms, i.e. approximately 10 million units of rifles and machine guns remain in Afghanistan. This is an extremely over sufficient quantity of ammunition available in this country to keep fuelling the war. As the senior writer for New York Times Chris Chivers has exactly put it in his article in 'Foreign Affairs', "more than two decades after the end of the Soviet war in Afghanistan, there has never been a successful, comprehensive military small-arms disarmament program in the country; instead, more guns keep flowing in"[1].

Overall, it is now widely accepted that there can hardly be a military solution to the conflict in Afghanistan. Uzbekistan emphasized this thesis in April 2008 at a meeting of EAPC/NATO in Bucharest and other international forums, while today it is the subject of discussion by leaders of many nations. At present high level officials in the West acknowledge the fact that there is no military solution to Afghan conflict. They began to realize that it is impossible to pacify Afghanistan using military means exclusively.

Afghanistan is not a country that you can easily impose, especially by force of arms. Our great ancestors, for instance Zahiriddin Muhammad Babur, were pretty familiar with the unique nature of Afghan people and their historical resistance for independence. Today everyone knows the unfortunate experience cost of which great powers paid for the occupation of Afghanistan as British Empire in the 19th Century and the Soviet Union in the last Century.

Some historical lessons are also helpful even today. For instance, Louis Dupree, the premier historian of Afghanistan, points out that four factors contributed to the British failure: the foreign troops presence in Afghan territory, the placing of unpopular Emir on the throne, the harsh acts of the British-supported Afghans against their local enemies, and the reduction of the subsidies paid to tribal chiefs by British political agents[2]. The British repeated these mistakes in the second Afghan War (1878-81), as did the Soviets a century later; and therefore reflecting on these examples would be helpful for international coalition.

Coming back to the present time, the start date July 2011 announced by Obama for withdrawing U.S. troops from Afghanistan creates uncertainty for all forces involved in the Afghan settlement and above all the Central Asian states. Moreover, it remains unclear what will happen in Afghanistan, how effective the new U.S. strategy will be, and what further action Washington and NATO will take to support Kabul.

With the uncertainty posed by the planned beginning of the withdrawal of U.S. troops from Afghanistan, it is critically important to seek for alternative ways of establishing peace and stability in Afghanistan. There is no other option here since the further intensification of conflict, escalation of tension in this country will create more serious challenges to regional stability and global security as well.

One of those means, would be creation of a mechanism – a multilateral format to ensure that security and stability be maintained in Central Asia and other regions contiguous to Afghanistan.

As is well known, Uzbekistan's viewpoint was formulated in the concept of establishing under auspices of the United Nations a Contact group on Afghanistan, called "6+3", and presented by President Karimov back in 2008[3].

The idea is to create a platform where the issues of the Afghan settlement could be discussed on a multilateral basis involving the six immediate neighbors - China, Pakistan, Iran, Turkmenistan, Uzbekistan and Tajikistan—along with Russia, the United States and NATO.

The essence of the Uzbek initiative is based on the recognition that internal Afghan affairs must be resolved by the Afghan people with assistance from countries whose security interests include bringing an end to the war and promoting stability in Afghanistan.

In this sense, the central objective of "6+3" contact group is to propose to the confronting parties a Program of Secession of Hostilities in Afghanistan, common principles of possible settlement of the Afghan problem, promoting dialogue and negotiating process between conflicting parties, to ensure security and provide required guarantees taking into account the interests of all the parties to the conflict.

There is an urgent need for a political settlement involving ordinary Afghans and all – without exception – warring parties, ethnic and religious groups into settlement process. As long as various Afghan warring factions and forces don't solve their fundamental disagreements and do not reach consensus, any stability in Afghanistan will be short-lived and the threat of Afghanistan spiraling into chaos will exist, with consequent predictable and negative implications for regional security.

In the meantime, considering that Afghans ultimately will live with the outcome of any settlement, Afghan people should determine themselves the exact conditions of establishing peace in this country with assistance of its neighbors. In other words, any political initiative, which lacks Afghans' confidence, support and acceptance, most importantly neglecting aspirations of Afghans may even exacerbate the violence. For this reason we truly believe that to make collective decisions without any consideration for Afghanistan's interest and its neighbors would be totally futile.

And, most importantly, the proposed Contact Group should be formed and work under the aegis of the United Nations. Only this organization has the necessary authority and capacity to ensure the negotiation process in

Afghanistan. All other international and regional organizations do not possess required legitimacy and authority.

Uzbekistan's efforts to strengthen regional security are not limited by its desire to foster a multilateral dialogue. It puts special emphasis on measures to assist Afghanistan's economic development—the direction in which Uzbekistan sees the possible union of the interests of key countries that have influence in the region. Uzbekistan itself, for instance, delivers electricity to Afghanistan, conveys cargo through its transport communications to the northern Afghan provinces, and hopes to expand bilateral trade. Among recent major projects is the construction of the railway line 75-km long Hairaton to Mazar-i-Sharif worth nearly $170 million, which was completed last year. This is a breakthrough project for Afghanistan, one that significantly increases the supply of goods from almost all the adjoining countries. It also creates a large number of jobs that, in turn, contribute to the economic development of the Northern provinces and their integration into the Central Asian market.

Support of development projects is entirely in line with the strategic position of Uzbekistan, which had long believed that the economic revival of Afghanistan must form the fundamental basis for the country's stability and security. That's the reason why we strongly believe that in resolving the Afghan problem, foremost emphasis must be placed on rendering economic assistance, implementing socially oriented, infrastructural and humanitarian projects, addressing unemployment and tackling the huge poverty and misery.

Regretfully, nine years after 2001, billions of dollars have been spent, still the situation in Afghanistan has not radically changed yet, especially in terms of decreasing the level of poverty and unemployment.

Hence, international community should increase its help in the reconstruction and development, transport-communications and social infrastructure projects in this country, providing employment, addressing the most acute problems of poverty. Each person in Afghanistan must witness the results of these positive transformations in his own example, in the example of his whole family.

In addition, we must not forget that Afghanistan is a Muslim country, where the unfounded attacks and biased attitude in Western countries towards Islam in most cases create absolutely intolerable situations and tensions. Cartoons of the Prophet Mohammed, demonstrative actions to burn Muslims holy book "Koran" and other Islam phobic manifestations in the West invariably cause a backlash in Afghanistan and reinforce the tensions in this country.

That's why it is necessary to put all effort to provide respectful attitude and consideration to the historical, ethnic and demographic characteristics of Afghanistan, centuries-old customs, traditional and religious values of multinational and multi-confessional Afghan people.

Conclusion

There is no need to prove that without resolving the problems of Afghanistan, where the war is going on for 30 years, it is impossible to talk about peace and stability in Central Asia. Hence, in Uzbekistan it is clearly realized that peace and stability in Afghanistan is a decisive factor of security which opens up broad opportunities to resolve the vitally important problems of sustainable social and economic development of an entire Central Asian region.

Endnotes

[1] Chivers C.J. "Small Arms, Big Problems: The Fallout of the Global Gun Trade" Foreign Affairs. New York: Jan/Feb 2011. Vol. 90, Iss.1;

[2] Bearden Milton. "Afghanistan, Graveyard of Empires". Foreign Affairs. New York: Nov/Dec 2001. Vol. 80, Iss.6

[3] Address by President Islam Karimov at the NATO/EAPC Summit. www.uza.uz

CONFLICT RESOLUTION IN AFGHANISTAN: A REGIONAL APPROACH

¹**Gurmeet Kanwal and Samarjit Ghosh**²

An Army brigade commander in Afghanistan recently put his finger squarely on the problem, using the military term "tactical " to refer to "battlefield" and "strategic" to refer to the grand purpose of the fighting. Tactical is how you fight; strategic is why you fight. "We've made a lot of progress... a lot of tactical gains," said Col. Dan Williams, who commands the 4th Infantry Division's Combat Aviation Brigade. The question is, has that had a strategic... effect?"³

Strategic Stalemate

The present situation in Afghanistan is best described as a strategic stalemate. While the United States and its NATO-ISAF allies are not exactly losing the fight against the Taliban, they have failed to achieve their objectives of eliminating the al-Qaeda, defeating the Taliban and ensuring that the afghan government is able to prevent the Taliban from returning to power by force. The US and its allies are now looking for a face saving exit strategy, which some Western commentators have described uncharitably as "declare victory and run".

A review of the war strategy in Afghanistan was completed by the Obama administration in December 2010. The publicly released version of the report claimed major gains against the al Qaeda and the Taliban, particularly in the core areas under their control for long, including the Helmand and Kandahar provinces. However, the report acknowledged that the gains were fragile and could be undone unless the Pakistan army acted against the Taliban operating from safe havens in the NWFP and FATA with equal vigour.

Addressing the media at the White House, President Obama said the US "will continue to insist to Pakistani leaders that terrorist safe havens within their borders must be dealt with." The American civilian and military leadership has been trying to convince Pakistan for some time now that eliminating safe havens for terrorists is as much in its own interest as in the interest of lasting peace and stability in Afghanistan. The criticality of Pakistan in achieving overall success almost certainly means that a major increase in US drone strikes against terrorists in the NWFP and FATA can be expected even though substantive ground operations across the Durand Line remain unlikely.

Though the review report claimed substantial progress in training and equipping the Afghan National Army, this is not borne out by the ANA's performance in operations and its ability to independently take over responsibility for operational control of an allotted area. Despite the uneven progress and the fragility of the gains, the report concluded that the drawdown of troops scheduled to begin in July 2011 could go ahead as planned almost a year ago when a surge of 30,000 troops was announced. Meanwhile, military operations will continue to be supplemented by a mix of development and diplomacy.

The broad goal of the US-NATO-ISAF war strategy in Afghanistan is to ensure that Afghanistan acquires the stability that is necessary to be able to control its territory so as to prevent the Taliban and al Qaeda combine from operating successfully from its soil against the US and its allies and to reduce the risk of a return to civil war. The American aim in Af-Pak is to prevent the border regions from being used as breeding grounds for fundamentalist terrorism and as launch pads for terror strikes on the US and its allies.

According to a Council for Foreign Relations (CFR) task force report the US objective in Pakistan is, "To degrade and defeat terrorist groups that threaten American interests from its territory and to prevent turmoil that would imperil the Pakistan state and risk the security of Pakistan's nuclear programme." The US also seeks to prevail on Pakistan to stop providing support to the Afghan Taliban, the Haqqani Shoora, Gulbudin Hekmatyar's Hizb-e-Islami and Pakistani terrorist organisations like the LeT and JeM.

President Obama cannot afford to lose a war on his watch and yet hope to win re-election in 2012. The US exit strategy will be based on a phased drawdown with not more than 10,000 troops being withdrawn each year till an "equilibrium that is manageable" is achieved. The US and NATO troops are still thin on the ground while the Taliban has shown a marked degree of resurgence. Negotiations with the so-called 'moderate' Taliban have also failed to acquire gravitas.

For several years the US-led ISAF pursued a three-pronged military strategy in Afghanistan: security, governance and development. The massive interventions in Helmand and Kandahar achieved little other than to diversify and diffuse the insurgency. New initiatives, such as the Afghan Peace and Reintegration Program (APRP), have resulted in a few hundred surrenders but not enough to undermine the manpower available to the Taliban. Village Stability Operations (the formation of irregular forces) are exacerbating tensions in the North and may be contributing to a below-the-radar process of factional remobilisation. The international community has high hopes in 2011 as it would make ISAF's quest for withdrawal [between 2011 and 2014] more feasible.

Marjah was supposed to be a test case for the success and relative superiority of ISAF tactics, in collaboration with Afghan forces. However, the 'victory' over the Taliban and related insurgent forces was short-lived. As soon as the presence of ISAF and the Afghan forces was thinned down in order to address and clear other areas, the Taliban sneaked back in and resumed control over the countryside and another full-scale offensive had to be launched. Even after 10 months, the area which was formerly completely held by the Taliban has only some semblance of the Afghan government's presence, both in terms of security and infrastructure. Similar offensives targeting other Taliban-controlled areas have met a similar fate. In fact, despite the urgent need to clear Kandahar, it has not been possible for ISAF to begin an offensive there.

Regional Dimension: Lip Service

"The reconstruction of fractured states and societies or combating insurgencies effectively always requires goodwill, support, and constructive engagement of neighbouring states."[4]

The Bonn Agreement in 2001 increased the international community's commitments towards Afghanistan beyond what had been envisaged at the beginning of the intervention. It envisaged the re-creation of the state of Afghanistan, and made provisions for a role for the international community to play in it, under the helm of the United Nations.[5] It was envisaged that a regional approach towards Afghanistan would be the most effective in the long run. The point has been reinforced in the international community's deliberations on Afghanistan's reconstruction during the past nine years, in the Kabul Declaration [2002],[6] the London Conference [2006],[7] the Paris Conference [2008],[8] the conference at The Hague [2009],[9] and the 2010 conferences at Istanbul,[10] London[11] and Kabul.[12] President Barack Obama had mentioned it specifically in his Af-Pak policy review in March 2009, when he stated, "Together with the United Nations, we will forge a new Contact Group for Afghanistan and Pakistan that brings together all who should have a stake in the security of the region – our NATO allies and other partners, but also the Central Asian states, the Gulf nations and Iran; Russia, India and China. None of these nations benefit from a base for al Qaeda terrorists, and a region that descends into chaos. All have a stake in the promise of lasting peace and security and development."[13] However, beyond a redefinition of the strategy targeting this region as 'Af-Pak', the regional approach soon fell by the wayside.[14]

Neither the international community, nor the Afghans themselves, ever devised a comprehensive plan detailing the reconstruction of the nation's economic and social institutions. In fact, the Coalition's policy of managing the relations between Afghanistan and its neighbours has always been from issue to issue, and has never been developed into a cogent regional framework.[15] As a result, when it actually began, the policies of the international and the regional actors differed. While there is no denying that all of Afghanistan's neighbours would benefit from its stability,[16] they remain unsure, not without cause, of the international community's commitment. Until they are satisfied of it, they will develop their singular policies, oriented to protecting their own interests.

The cooperation of the governments of regional actors is essential for sustainable reconstruction of any sort, as international actors, notwithstanding the extent of their involvement, will eventually leave, and rightly so – for it would not be acceptable to anyone – Afghan or otherwise – if one were to discuss the possibility of permanent garrisons within Afghanistan. The reconstruction efforts required in Afghanistan would entail not only the repair and extension of infrastructure and economy, but also the reconstruction of the institutions that form a state. And it is this requirement that makes the Afghan government hesitant of involving any of its neighbours in such an intimate part of its establishment. For reasons of poverty, geopolitical isolation and geographical barriers, Afghanistan has always been in a somewhat unfortunate position, at the mercy of its more powerful neighbours. Regional cooperation in this situation becomes viable only if the countries involved in lending assistance utilise the opportunity for openness and collaboration more than the ability and desire to exert control. The implementation of a regional approach in Afghanistan has to go beyond a simple redefinition of the region as 'Af-Pak'. Given the history of negative regional influences, envisioning a positive, constructive, regional relationship may seem like a utopian ideal. Notwithstanding the same, it is the state of affairs that is required, for the challenges Afghanistan needs to confront will require cooperation from the countries in and of the region.

Past histories with regional actors and Afghanistan are crucial to an understanding of current dynamics and future possibilities of regional engagement in Afghanistan. However, it bears keeping in mind that while incidents of the past may well be relevant, they may not necessarily be binding on current perceptions within Afghanistan, nor on policy decisions being taken, either by Afghanistan or by the United States.

Geographically, Afghanistan is located at the intersection of Southern Asia, Central Asia and West Asia and, as a consequence, a number of regional and extra-regional actors (both countries and organisations) have an important role to play in shaping the current narrative. And while there is disagreement over which of the regional security complexes has more stake in it, there is none over the fact that the stability of each one of them is influenced by instability in Afghanistan.

Central Asian Republics (CARs): Stake and Role

The CARs are an anomalous entity in the Afghanistan situation. Given their proximity, there is no doubt regarding their involvement and stake in Afghanistan. However, their history and political situations prevent them from being the ideal partners for reconstruction efforts. Formerly of the Soviet Union, none of them are conventionally strong and stable nations. However, it is very important to them to be able to present a face of being so, for the rich resources they have at their disposal make them a tempting target for any strong nation to exploit.

The CARs are perpetually beleaguered with power shortages, lack of employment opportunities and the overall remnants of an ineffective system of Soviet social welfare that existed twenty years ago. The conditions of extreme poverty and lawlessness that are present on the border regions between some of the CARs and Afghanistan are priming the populace within for the growth of militancy, an eventuality that their various governments are eager to avoid. Thus, they see the reconstruction involvement in Afghanistan as a golden opportunity for themselves and are trying to engage with various members of the international community already involved in Afghanistan.

Engagement between the CARs and Afghanistan is specifically needed in the area of energy, which is a concern for the whole region. Energy supplies in Central Asia would be sufficient for Afghanistan to be secure, as far as electricity and water are concerned, and given its location, it could also earn transit income. Tajikistan and Kyrgyzstan, in that sense, have great potential as far as the export of electricity is concerned.[17] However, there are obstacles in the path of full engagement. For one, the CARs differ amongst themselves on how they would like their resources to be used. Uzbekistan, for instance, would rather secure water resources for its cotton sector and would allot export as a secondary priority. Tajikistan and Kyrgyzstan are more interested in developing their electricity potential for themselves than for other parties. While it is clear that regional trade would offer excellent prospects for all actors involved, they haven't proven to be effective enough just yet. Agreements between CARs and Iran or China have a much better track record.[18]

However, there have been positive developments as far as regional engagement is concerned. The Northern Distribution Network, which was initially utilised only as a conduit for the transportation of non-military supplies and materials, has now been retrofitted to be equipped for the transport of weapons and other assorted military hardware, designated for the Coalition forces in Afghanistan. To this intent, the United States has put in place lethal transit agreements with Uzbekistan, Kazakhstan and Kyrgyzstan.[19]

The CARs also provide an access route from the north into Afghanistan. Should the land route through Pakistan become untenable, temporarily or over a long duration, there will be no option but to rely primarily on the northern route for sustaining the presence of troops and providing essential supplies to Afghanistan.

The Way Ahead

The interlocutions of the international community over the past decade have exhibited a clear recognition that a regional approach towards Afghanistan is essential towards a more comprehensive management of the conflict situation in Afghanistan. However, there has been a [perhaps unconscious] reluctance on their part to resolve the exact details, shape and framework of such a regional approach. One particular factor which has played into this circumstance is that such an approach is unlikely to be straightforward, and there may be an understandable reticence on the part of the international community not to complicate a situation that is already so complex. However, such difficulties cannot be allowed to confound the possibility of further resolution and need to be firmly grappled with.

In terms of the CARs, as noted previously, their stake in the stability of Afghanistan is non-negotiable, especially for the countries which share borders with Afghanistan [Turkmenistan, Uzbekistan and Tajikistan, respectively], whether it is in terms of drug trafficking or the transmission of radical extremism. However, in terms of involvement, they are understandably likely to toe the Russian line on a strategy of regional engagement. And unlike most of the other regional actors discussed, they do not possess abilities of any significant nature to bring to bear on Afghanistan [though Uzbekistan and Tajikistan do have more of a stake, especially in terms of the people in the border regions]. Therefore, while it is necessary that they should be involved in every regional discourse, it should be understood that their involvement would be oriented towards facilitative action, not initiative-based action.

But there is much that they can contribute, in terms of the former, i.e. facilitative action. Their potential in so far as a transit route is concerned is already being explored, and in some cases, is already in operation, along the new Northern Distribution Network. In the recent past, Uzbekistan, Tajikistan and Kyrgyzstan had rented airfields to NATO, although only Kyrgyzstan's are still in use [the French contingent of the ISAF does continue to make use of the Dushanbe commercial airfield in Tajikistan]. These avenues can be restored in terms of regional involvement, in terms of the transportation and facilitation of both men and materials, of a lethal and non-lethal nature. Kazakhstan is the only Central Asian nation which sends foreign assistance money to Afghanistan, and has even contemplated sending a detachment of engineers to join the ISAF forces. A similar involvement, in terms of civilian and military [human] assistance may be encouraged on the part of the other CARs as well, under the umbrella of a cohesive regional approach.

Regional Involvement – pros and cons

- Viable stakeholders will be involved, making for a more cohesive approach.

- Anti-West sentiments will be reduced.

- WHAM tactics would be utilised in place of air-strike/ heavy tactics.

- Turkey, a regional power in the making and an Islamic-majority country, may play a leading role.

- US may not support Iranian involvement.

- Indian and Pakistani troops may be both involved, to each other's displeasure, as also that of the United States.

- US may want China to be involved, but it remains to be seen if they wish to be involved.

- US and Russia are coming closer together on Afghanistan, and while US may want Russian troops to be involved, (Russian) history may restrain them from once again getting embroiled in Afghanistan.

- It may make sense for the Central Asian countries to supply troops; but their acquiescence will depend on the Russian perspective. Also, ethnic clashes may make the involvement of their troops unfeasible.

The use of words such as 'success' and 'solution' are often counter-productive, when used in the context of the conflict in Afghanistan. It would not be worthwhile to imagine that an involvement of nine years, regardless of its varying level of coherence, could bring an 'end' to a conflict situation which has been ongoing for over twice that much time. 'Progress', in that sense, while slow, has been there, and the end-state which the international community should, and indeed does, seek to arrive at, even if it may not state as much in a documented manner, is a state of Afghanistan which is at peace with itself, and not ruled by others.

Conclusion

From the Indian perspective, Afghanistan lies on the strategic crossroads to Iran, West Asia, the Caucasus and the Central Asian Republics and its regional neighbours have important geo-political and energy security interests in the area. The foremost concern is that the US and its NATO-ISAF allies will begin their deadline-mandated exit before putting in place a strong international force to continue their work. The apprehension is that the Taliban will defeat the weak and poorly trained Afghan National Army, take over Kabul and once again begin to practice their peculiar brand of Jihad and cultural bigotry. Even Iran and China are wary of the return of Wahabi Islam to Afghanistan. Another key regional objective particularly that of India, is to prevent the re-emergence of safe havens for terrorist groups operating from Afghanistan.

The Indian approach is not tactical but long-term. India has invested over US$ 1 billion and immense time and effort in the post-2001 reconstruction of Afghanistan, but has been completely marginalised in discussions for the resolution of the ongoing conflict due to Pakistan's sensibilities, indeed paranoia. It is in India's long-term interest to seek a regional solution to the Afghan conflict with the help of the CARs, China, Iran and Russia. This would involve putting together a regional force, preferably under a UN flag, to provide a stable environment for governance and development till the Afghan National Army can take over.

Endnotes

1&2 The authors are Director and Associate Fellow, Centre for Land Warfare Studies CLAWS), New Delhi, respectively.

3 David Wood, "The Afghanistan War: Tactical Victories, Strategic Stalemate?"Politics Daily, 13 February 2011, http://www.politicsdaily.com/2011/02/13/the-afghanistan-war-tactical-victories-strategic-stalemate/, accessed on 13 February 2011.

4 Rasul Bakhsh Rais, Recovering the Frontier State: War, Ethnicity, and State in Afghanistan (Lanham, MD: Lexington Books, 2008), p. 177.

5 "Agreement on provisional arrangements in Afghanistan pending the re-

establishment of permanent government institutions," United Nations, http://www.un.org/News/dh/latest/afghan/afghan-agree.htm, accessed on 20 November 2009.

6 "The Kabul Declaration on Good Neighbourly Relations," 22 December 2002, http://www.diplomatie.gouv.fr/fr/IMG/pdf/3_-_Kabul_declaration_ dez02.pdf, accessed on 20 July 2010.

7 NATO/ISAF, "The Afghanistan Compact: Building on Success – The London Conference on Afghanistan," 01 February 2006, http://www.nato.int/isaf/docu/epub/pdf/afghanistan_compact.pdf, accessed on 20 July 2010.

8 Rebecca Roberts, "Reflections on the Paris Declaration and Aid Effectiveness in Afghanistan," AREU Discussion Paper, April 2009.

9 Reuters, "FACTBOX-Hague conference on Afghanistan," 30 March 2009, http://in.reuters.com/article/idINLU23712920090330, accessed on 20 July 2010.

10 Ministry of Foreign Affairs, Turkey, "Istanbul Statement on Friendship and Cooperation in the "Heart of Asia","26 January 2010, http://www.mfa.gov.tr/istanbul-statement-on-friendship-and-cooperation-in-the-_heart-of-asia_.en.mfa, accessed on 28 January 2010

11 Foreign and Commonwealth Office, UK, "Afghanistan – The London Conference," 28 January 2010, http://centralcontent.fco.gov.uk/central-content/afghanistan-hmg/resources/pdf/conference/Communique-final, accessed on 31 January 2010

12 Ministry of Foreign Affairs, Kabul, "Kabul – International Conference on Afghanistan," 20 July 2010, http://www.mfa.gov.af/Final%20English%20Communique%20-%20Kabul%20%20%20International% 20Conference %20on%20Afghanistan%20-%2020%20July%202010.pdf, accessed on 25 July 2010.

13 "Transcript: Obama Announces New Afghanistan, Pakistan Strategies," CQ Transcripts Wire, 27 March 2009, http://www.washingtonpost.com/wp-dyn/content/article/2009/03/27/AR2009032700891.html, accessed on 16 November 2009

14 A caveat – the discussion of a regional approach was not the primary intent of most of the international conferences, being as they were donor assistance-oriented events. However, the importance of the same was discussed on repeated occasions, but often without the necessary follow-up.

15 "Afghanistan's other neighbours: Iran, Central Asia and China," Conference Report – American Institute of Afghanistan Studies, March 2009, http://www.humansecuritygateway.com/documents   AIAS_   Afghanistans OthersNeighbors_Iran_CentralAsia_China.pdf, accessed on 16 November 2009.

[16] Each of Afghanistan's neighbours – Pakistan, India, China, Russia, Iran – is threatened by one or the other aspects originating from Afghanistan, more so than the world is by the emergence of it as a base for international terrorism. Pakistan, by the Al Qaeda; India by jihadism and terror groups; China by fundamentalist Shiite jihadist in Xinjiang; Russia by unrest in the Muslim south; Iran by the fundamentalist Sunni Taliban. Henry Kissinger, "Deployments and diplomacy," Newsweek, 12 October 2009

[17] Robert Matthews and Fionnuala Ni Eigeartaigh, "The Afghanistan Crisis: Regional and International Dimensions," FRIDE/NOREF Conference Report, March 2009, http://www.fride.org/descarga/CR10_Afghanistan_Crisis_Regional_Eng_sep09.pdf, p. 10, accessed on 20 November 2009, p. 12.

[18] Ibid.

[19] Deidre Tynan, "Afghanistan: Central Asian states now allowing military cargo bound for US, NATO forces," Eurasia Net, 31 October 2009, http://www.eurasianet.org/departments/insightb/articles/eav101309.shtml, 20 November 2009.

A PERSPECTIVE ON AFGHANISTAN'S LIKELY ALTERNATIVE FUTURES AND ITS REGIONAL DIMENSIONS

Arun Sahgal

Introduction

The scenario in Afghanistan remains mired by contradictions and political gamesmanship, even as there is no discernable improvement in the situation. At one level, US and ISAF forces have been able to enhance their operational space through tactical victories however this is carrying little convictions with political elites at home who have little faith in the victory as the war on terror enters second decade. In so far as Afghanistan per se is concerned it has been through somewhat flawed presidential and parliamentary elections, but what is important is that people continue to repose faith in democracy and what can be seen is the rooting of the idea of freedom, democracy and free society, despite corruption or poor delivery of governance in parts where the writ of the Afghanistan government runs. There are in fact two Afghanistan's; one seeking freedom and democracy and above all release from tribal systems to become a dynamic modern state responsible for its own destiny, and the other are tribal leaders, Maliks and Jagirdars, rooted to the past who are loathe to losing control over the masses and are able to preserve their foot soldiers only through dole and coercion. The ideological content appears to be giving way to fight for survival not so much of the masses but the leaders. It is in above scenario reconciliation and reintegration of disgruntled cadres begins to make sense.

Within the above backdrop, year 2010 could be described as the year of multiple initiatives at peacemaking in and for Afghanistan, with multiple actors seeking to seize the initiative. This has been primarily motivated by the clock of ISAF engagement beginning to tick given the growing public pressure back home. Even as the counter insurgency operations continue unabated and according to senior Afghan Officials and observers are making credible gains, the Afghan government appears to have given full flip to reconciliation strategy over the year, and appears to be concentrated on two processes – with the Afghan Taliban and other armed groups inside the country, and with Pakistan and to a lesser extent Iran on the cross-border insurgency. Ideally the two tracks should be in parallel and in tandem, but they do not as yet appear to be so.

Within Pakistan there is general support for the Afghan reintegration policy, but no consensus on the reconciliation policy that is being pursued by the Afghanistan Government. Indeed the whole notion of reintegration and reconciliation appears to have polarized both state and society. Some Pakistani political leaders and many amongst policy analysts and civil society argue that distinctions between Afghan, Pakistani and Punjabi Taliban cannot be made because their relations are fluid; they state, further, that it is the Taliban ideology that must be defeated. These views are deeply opposed by many in the military and polity, especially the religious parties. An inevitable polarization, which is most marked in civilian Pakistan, intensified over the year 2010, with political and civil society leaders taking strong positions, even at the risk of their own lives in a worsening security situation. There have been more casualties from terrorist attacks in Pakistan in 2010 than in Afghanistan. The fact that these are domestic rather than cross-border is cold comfort, but it also acts as a brutal reminder of the policy challenges in Pakistan.

In effect, Afghanistan is faced with trying to work on two discrete peacemaking fronts: inside Afghanistan and between Afghanistan and Pakistan. While most analysts would agree that there is a better chance of success on each front if they can be separated, the two however overlap, as they naturally must considering the Pashtun population in both countries. Natural as the overlap is, it raises threat perceptions amongst the other communities in Afghanistan, and creates a security dilemma that can only be addressed through bridge-building.

Evolving Contours and Perspectives of Situation in Afghanistan

Period between now and 2014 will be critical for the stability of Afghanistan. Given the current nature of reconciliation and reintegration efforts, Afghanistan is likely to remain unstable in the near to medium term, even as efforts are made by competing interests to bring about rapprochement.

Ground Situation

In terms of ground situation by all indications as mentioned earlier surge appears to be working with ISAF and Afghan forces in joint operations widening their control to country side both in Kandhar and Helmand provinces as also in the north east. Nonetheless despite tactical victories; 'clear-hold-build' policy of protecting population centres can be said to be at best partially successful. The scenario is further exacerbated by open borders, local support for variety of reasons and open collaboration between Afghan Taliban, TTP and Al Qaeda. Above will in the interim efforts at reconciliation and reintegration, as a consequence of which sustainable stability in East and Southern Afghanistan appears distant.

Prevailing scenario as it moves closer to 2013 United States elections is likely to create basic military dilemma for the United States, with regard to the dominating strategies to be pursued in Afghanistan; between counter insurgency (CI) or counter terrorism (CT). As per inputs from Afghanistan and discussion with US academics and others, pentagon is keen to pursue CI strategy in the backdrop of recent successes and greater participation of Afghan National Army (ANA), this thinking is also being shaped by the perspective that US forces cannot simply quit and run whatever be the fig leaf. On the other hand growing political costs of going nowhere campaign in the minds of state Department and political leadership of the United States and NATO, CT focused on Al Qaida backed by some sort of deal with Taliban is a far better strategy that will bring closure to the strategic albatross. There is however universal acceptance that whatever be the strategy, United States must maintain long terms presence in the region for larger geopolitical factors that include Central Asia and developments in Pakistan and of course the China factor.

Then there is the question of defining success which remains a nebulous concept at best. Would disrupting and dismantling Al Qaeda in Afghanistan and Pakistan be adequate, is it possible to do that without addressing Taliban given its organic links with Al Qaeda? Further, is elimination of Al Qaeda which according to many reports has not been very effective lately, be the only definition of success? A more limited approach was more likely to impact negatively the goals of overall strategy which among others lays stress on improving Afghan government's capabilities for governance and sustained development including accelerating the efforts for developing Afghan security forces.

While internal debate on strategy continues there are discernable efforts being made by the ISAF to make northern distribution network more effective which essentially means supporting and consolidation of the remaining elements of the Northern Alliance as also evolving a working relationship with Russia, Tajikistan and Uzbekistan dictated by the convergence of interests?

State of Governance

Although Afghanistan has come a long way from the Taliban controlled regressive state, nonetheless people's expectations having been aroused by the glitz of Kabul and other provincial capitals and the foreign workers, they are demanding more facilities and better deliverables. On the other hand endemic corruption is plaguing much of the government machinery, especially the police and judiciary, both of which affect the everyday life of the common man. This has undermined credibility of the elected government and its ability along with security forces to bring peace and stability. Thus the success of the coalition Forces operations is closely linked to empowering local and district governments and providing Afghan's not only in the cities but in making provincial and district governments more functional. This can only happen if the writ of Afghan Government was to run across the country, which is clearly not the case. Scenario is further accentuated by flawed elections and dwindling credibility of Karzai. Therefore given the prevailing circumstances governance and democratic dividend in the near term, there can at best be incremental with teous balance between stability and instability. Lack of political structures, institutions, sharpening ethnic divide, and intangible peace dividends, is exacerbating the peace and development process. Absence of political parties that could keep the government in check and put pressure on transparency is another factor for the governance deficit. What is heartening however is that socio economic factors and development dividend is giving people hope and restraining them from joining the ranks of Taliban. In fact future of the next generation and increasing stakes in democracy and fruits of development are reasons of hope.

Taliban

In so far as Taliban is concerned, today they are no doubt on the defensive but certainly not defeated. In fact they can be said to be in the phase of consolidation. While figures of their presence and control vary South and East remain strong bastions of Taliban resistance where it literally runs a parallel government. Attacks throughout Afghanistan continue; the use of IED's, suicide bombings and hit and run tactics being the most favored methods. IED's alone have accounted for an astounding 75 per cent of the total US and NATO troop casualties, while the use of hit and run urban guerrilla tactics remains the second factor. Most of these attacks are directed against security forces.

Reasons for Taliban Resurgence

(a) **Corruption**. First, is endemic corruption plaguing much of the government machinery, especially the police and judiciary which has helped build up a degree of local support which stems more out of the Taliban's ability to fill in the governance vacuum as opposed to ideological support for their cause.

(b) **Collateral Damage**. Second is growing civilian casualties as a collateral damage as a result of heavy use of kinetic power this has resulted in, swelling the ranks of the Taliban to avenge personal loss.

(c) **Failure of Nation Building Efforts.** Third, is the failure of the international community to deliver on its pledge of a better future for Afghans; an empirical indicator of this lack of commitment to 'nation building' is reflected in the paltry levels of per capita investment that stood at a mere US$57. This figure appears even more dismal when compared to other major areas of US intervention such as US$100 in Bosnia or US$679 in Kosovo. Moreover, even of the aid that did trickle in, some 86 per cent of it is estimated to be 'phantom aid,' spent on goods and services from the US as opposed to being spent on developing indigenous capacities. Not surprisingly this has led to an increasing sense of frustration.

(d) **Narco Trafficking.** Fourth, the deepening nexus between Narco trafficking and the Taliban has provided a sound financial pillar for the insurgency. Insurgency is the strongest in the provinces where levels of drug cultivation are high. Drug trafficking has helped finance not just arms purchases but also sustain swelling ranks of the Taliban militia who are paid a monthly salary ranging from US$200 to $300, a princely amount compared to the paltry US$120 paid to an Afghan National Army (ANA) recruit. Moreover, with an estimated 14 million Afghans who are dependent on poppy cultivation with little more viable alternatives, international policy of zero tolerance towards poppy cultivation has only fuelled resentment.

(e) **Culture.** Fifth and important is the cultural factor. The Taliban have fruitfully exploited the *Pushtunwalli* code of honor, practiced amongst Pashtun tribes, to their advantage. The Taliban have in particular used the concept of *badla* or revenge to swell ranks of their foot soldiers following large scale civilian deaths resulting from coalition forces bombing campaigns. Second, the concept of *Melmastia* or hospitality, which must be offered to all visitors and under this a Pashtun can seek asylum in the house of another Pashtun regardless of their previous relationship. The use of *Melmastia* to obtain food and shelter has immensely facilitated the movement of the Taliban militia throughout the Pashtun belt.

(f) **Misperception about Taliban Aims and Objectives.** The insurgency has largely been perceived as a localised problem which could be solved by isolating local groups and defeating them. The fact that Taliban are focused on the rebuilding an *Islamic Emirate*, has not been fully appreciated. That Taliban are capable of strategic planning and coordinated action to adapt to any moves or counter moves by coalition forces too has been often overlooked. Taliban has also exploited ethnic tensions, the rejection of foreign forces by the Afghan people. As a result Taliban has been able to consolidate their hold in the Pashtun dominated areas of South and East, by isolating the Coalition forces, marginalizing the local Afghan administration, and establishing a parallel administration. In recent months, a more professional Taliban had succeeded in making significant inroads by recruiting from non-Pashtun communities.

(g) Taliban have the ability to mobilize large number of fighters through innovative use of field radios and cell phones. Using modern communication systems they are able to coordinate complex attacks, and are becoming more sophisticated in the use of IEDs. Their intelligence is good, providing advance knowledge of the moves of coalition forces.

(h) Taliban are also getting increasingly successful in the perception management through relatively sophisticated propaganda apparatus, employing radio, video, and night letters. Taliban is also exploiting internet websites to chronicle the advance of the jihad. The propaganda is invariably built around widely perceived corruption in the Afghan government, lack of basic services and reconstruction apart from exploiting collateral damage through wanton coalition attacks.

(i) Taliban is also effectively exploiting the open Afghan–Pakistani border and continues to maintain sanctuaries and bases in Pakistani Tribal areas and to dominate almost all major logistics routes coming into Afghanistan. As a result the FATA, especially North and South Waziristan, remains largely impenetrable allowing Taliban a measure of strategic depth in the sanctuaries of FATA.

The reason of somewhat elaborate analysis of Taliban resurgence is to highlight its operational efficiency, effective command and control and ability to counter both strike and psychological power of the ISAF. What this implies is that unless Taliban is denied its launch bases and local support through focussed and sustained application of military power, area domination and good governance Coalition forces are unlikely to stem the tide of their resurgence and growing influence. Taliban thus can be expected to continue its policy of selective engagements and attacks to undermine attempts at stabilization.

Afghan Security Forces (ASF)

Multi ethnic Afghan Security Forces will be an important factor in the future security and political stability of Afghanistan. Although in training, equipment and operations it has taken giant strides, nonetheless it remains a tactical force capable of undertaking at best company and in exceptional cases battalion sized operations. What is important is that in the absence of heavy support weapons and air power they will continue to need US and coalition forces support. It will take anything from another 5-10 years for this force to become a regular army. This means sustaining nearly three billion dollars yearly budgets over the next decade and half, where is this money going to come from? The current projected strength for the ANA, by December 2011, is 134,000; but Afghan officers say they're planning for a force of 200,000, while the Western press often cites 240,000 as the final figure. The number 400,000 is mentioned as the combined strength of the security forces — an army of 240,000 soldiers and a police force with 160,000 men. Under the circumstances it remains questionable whether the ANA and ANP that constitute ASF would be able to fill the force ratio gap in order to create a winning CT strategy for the ISAF.

Second and more important perspective linked to the Afghan future is the political space that this Army is likely to create in a future scenario. Presently it is closely linked to coalition forces as they are providing funding and training support; in the scenario of US withdrawal such a support would end creating a question mark on its future. On the other hand a strong and well trained apolitical ANA loyal to the government of the day will be an important factor in future stabilisation scenario in Afghanistan. Thus loyalty and political leanings of this multi ethnic Afghan Army is an important factor, notably the reintegration process must not be allowed to undermine this. An issue that will require constant watch will be the political leanings and cohesion of its command element.

Pakistan: Growing Salience and Posturing for Strategic Depth

Salience of Pakistan in resolution of Afghan imbroglio can be gauged by the fact that America has accepted Pakistan as a power-broker as was evident from Richard Holbrooke's statement on a visit to Kabul in mid-February, 2010. He opined *"Pakistan's ISI can play a role in negotiations and I support that role. - -Pakistan has an influence in this area and has a legitimate security interest."*

Further in March 2010, for the first time; Kayani chaired a meeting of federal ministers at General Headquarters Rawalpindi to set the agenda for the US – Pakistan Strategic Dialogue a confabulation in which he was the central player despite the presence of the Pakistani Premier, providing vivid reflection of who is in the driver's seat in Pakistan.

Trend of Pakistan military losing its internal credibility has been reversed in 2010 and are being further consolidated by successes gained in operations against TTP in Swat and South Waziristan. Offensive against militants in Bajaur and Orkazai is continuing. Despite pressure from the US, Pakistani Army has yet not fully accepted the US request to expand these to North Waziristan. In fact in a dialogue with Pakistani interlocutors it was clear that they were not going to start these any time soon. Pakistani dilemma; in the prevailing circumstances is how much to support failing US Afghan enterprise and its impact on already growing back lash within Pakistani heartland. Lurking fear in Pakistan is that the plot in Af – Pak could get out of control, drawing it into major LIC commitment, and open wounds of ethnic fault-lines. Above prevents full cooperation, make military cut deals, and continue to support its strategic assets. This will heighten the conflict of interest between US and Pak.

As a result, Pakistan Army has not touched Mullah Omar and its *Quetta*

Shura, Hikmetyar and Haqqani groups. But then even the US too has not carried out any drone attacks against *Quetta Shura*. Nonetheless the backlash from TTP in the shape of militant attacks on Pakistan government's symbols of power is continuing. Pakistani military importantly considers Afghan Taliban as strategic assets and appear confident that they have the ability to manipulate them to shape favourable outcome of conflict in Afghanistan. Pakistani perspective appears to have been bought by the US and allies. From Indian perspective this is a huge development that will allow Pakistan to shape future discourse with a regime in Kabul which would be beholden to Pakistan (read Pakistan military) and its world view.

Having assumed a key role as the arbitrator of Afghan destiny, Pakistan has already started to flex its muscles. Pakistani Army Chief Gen Kayani, fresh from attending NATO military commanders meeting in Brussels in end January 2010 averred that "Pakistan wants a 'peaceful, friendly and stable' Afghanistan; strategic depth isn't about 'controlling' Afghanistan but about ensuring Pakistan doesn't have a long-term security problem on its Western border; India's role in Afghanistan is 'unhelpful'; and more importantly Pakistan wants Afghan state institutions, including the Army and the Police force, to be fashioned in a manner that they don't pose a threat to our strategic interests". Evidently, it is not merely a declaration; unless Pakistan has a certain degree of control over Kabul it cannot promote the Kayani doctrine modeled on Zia doctrine premised on 'from Indus to Oxus (Amu Darya) should be the sphere of Pakistani influence'.

It would thus be apparent that Western Coalition focused on their immediate interests has allowed Pakistan to shape the future discourse in a manner that does not augur well for strategic stability in the region and may end up undermining all that has been achieved in nearly decade of struggle against terrorism. It is hardly important whether the policy of divide and rule now being attempted by UK and NATO supported by the US will work, what is important from Indian perspective is that despite having excellent relationship with Afghan Government and undertaking sterling development projects India is being sidelined.

Role of Regional Actors

Emerging trends indicate that despite declarations of involving regional stakeholders as one of the planks of the US Af-Pak strategy, nothing very much has been done by the US to move towards this goal. General Petraeus, commander of US Central Command too has stated that those seeking to help Afghanistan and Pakistan need to widen the aperture even farther to encompass at least the Central Asian states, India, Iran and even Russia and China. Despite these observations and policy ideations formation of regional Contact Group has not materialized.

Cooperation with Iran remains stymied because of its nuclear ambitions and the American claims that it is following a dual track approach. Even though Iran would not like to see a Taliban Sunni government in place in Kabul, yet it would also like to see an early departure of Americans from Afghanistan seen as a destabilizing influence from their perch in Afghanistan and Pakistan. There was a time when the route from Chahbahar port to Afghanistan was under consideration as an alternative logistics supply route for coalition forces but the emerging internal and external dynamics in the region have prevented that option to be exercised, despite the increasing relevance of Northern Distribution Network. Attempts by the Shanghai Cooperation Organization (SCO) to improve its salience in Afghanistan are not viewed positively by the US and its NATO allies.

China is comfortable in dealing with Afghanistan from a distance even while it is concerned with the likely negative fallout of radicalism and extremism spilling out of Afghanistan and affecting Muslim majority region of Xingjian. On balance it would tend to continue endorsing Pakistan's policies in Afghanistan with an understanding that Pakistan would protect its interests even when the coalition troops pull out. During Karzai's visit to China in March, 2010 Beijing chose to focus on increased economic investments and support to Afghanistan and a very limited help in the shape of training Afghan military personnel (about 19 or so) in China.

Moreover, the US and its leadership has increasingly become receptive to Pakistan's refrain of reducing the Indian footprint for its cooperation with the U.S. as the discussion carried out earlier has pointed out. General

McChrystal was one of the fore runners in this field when he pointed out that India's improved signature even though in the developmental field was a cause for Pakistan to take a counter action. Thus he showed an implicit understanding if Pakistan was to take offensive actions against Indian interests in Afghanistan. The, harsh reality is that Pakistan is becoming central player to the exclusion of other regional actors. This trend is unlikely to lead to a scenario where Afghanistan can be envisioned as a peaceful and stable country in the near to mid-term.

Dilemma's Faced by Main Actors

Above perspective analysis was aimed at highlighting the obtaining scenario and to highlight dilemma's faced by main actors in the Afghan imbroglio.

United States: Geopolitical compulsions

Burden of Af – Pak, is increasing political, and economic costs in an essentially failing enterprise which is sapping the political will and if reports in US media are indicators the morale of tactical leadership. For the US pull out is not an easy option without creating conditions that are looked upon by the world as a sort of victory or in the least favourable status quo. As a result United States will try and look for number of operations rather than tactical victories which essentially means significant control over southern and eastern Afghanistan, effectively blocking entry routes from FATA and above all inducing sustained support from increasingly radicalised Pakistan if the current blasphemy debate is an indication. In addition it will have to weigh consequences of loss of strategic space in Afghanistan, given its linkages to Central, East and West Asia. Incrementally a situation is emerging *wherein US will need to take support of regional actors, including Russia.* However intransigence over Iran will remain a dilemma. Above is likely to induce tactical shift in the United States Strategy salient aspects of which include;

- Will need to take a call on optimum strategic approach which entails resolving the dilemma between; civilians preferred CT strategy aimed at targeting at Al Qaida, accommodation of moderate Taliban, and gradual pull out. Military hurt by reverses in Iraq and the stigma of

Vietnam believes winning and drawing down as part of broader CI strategy is doable. What course to adopt and the end state remain engaged or orchestrated withdraw and on what terms remains a dilemma?

- In case perceptions point toward *possible mission collapse* – political and military assessment, on timing for withdrawal, together with implications of Taliban and by corollary Al Qaeda victory and its consequential global effects on War on Terror.

- Impact of the pull out on United States 'Greater Central Asia' policy and energy interests particularly in the context of growing Chinese influence and its rising stakes. Main issue is can a favourable regional architecture which compliments American interest be woven?

- Above is also subsumed in political time constraint. In another 12 months Obama will have to start his campaign for second term; imperatives of success will hang heavily on his head – he must show success, even if he wants to pull out.

- Lack of cushion of time could result in discarding restraint upping the ante of operations against Taliban and Pakistan which could create a serious situation with the potential of destabilising the entire region.

- Developments in Pakistan inextricably linked to the decision dilemma. Taliban will never be beaten or brought to negotiating table as long as Af-Pak border is not sealed. Growing Chinese assertiveness and emergence of Sino – Pak nexus could have detrimental impact on the region. Situation complicated with ISAF laying down time lines for pull out. Role of regional players becoming increasingly salient.

Pakistan and Imperatives of its Afghan Policy

The major decision dilemma faced by Pakistan primarily relates to post withdrawal scenario these include;

- Consequences of US withdrawal and Taliban victory. What does rise of fundamentalist forces and growing radicalism that will accompany it, mean for the internal cohesion and security of Pakistan?

- Can resurgent Taliban backed by extremist ideology be contained, particularly in the event of partial success or failure of military operations in FATA, what are the consequences of failure? What are the consequences of this on internal cohesion?

- Implication of the breach of buffer zone East of Indus by fundamentalists and their entry into Pakistani heartland, together with their political and security implications. Can such a scenario lay the foundation for the possible balkanization of Pakistani state?

- Possibility of clash between radical forces and moderates of the civil society, particularly in the context of deteriorating internal situation marked by continued acts of terrorism and declining economy?

- Can China be the strategic crutch against US domination, cost benefit analysis of open collusion with China, at the cost of relationship with the US? What will be the impact of above developments *on its bargaining power with India?*

- Last and even more importantly implications of internal developments on the security of nuclear weapons.

Afghanistan's Dilemma

Afghanistan in the run up to 2014 too faces number of decision dilemma's some of which include the following;

- Ability of the Afghan Security Forces post withdrawal of the ISAF to with stand Taliban attempts to capture power. What will be the effective Modus Vivendi where Coalition forces provide close combat support and mentor while ANA undertakes CI operations.

- Second and even more importantly has the Afghan civil society developed adequate stakes in peace and development to challenge Taliban. What are the terms of reconciliation are these acceptable both politically and broader social terms. Basically is new Afghanistan willing to compromise with tribal culture? If so on what terms?

- Ability of northern warlords supported by Russia and Central Asian countries to mount a challenge on Taliban and likely consequences of such a standoff? Similarly, can the current two tier dialogue process bring accommodation between Taliban and existing political forces?

- Perception of strategic depth for Pakistan and its implications and consequences. Implications of making Durand Line the international border?

India's Dilemma

From Indian perspective the developing scenario in Afghanistan also places a number of dilemmas, chief among these include the following;

- Was Taliban to gain influence and stage a comeback - what will be the consequences of a radicalized Afghanistan for India and regional security?

- Implications of Pakistan emerging as a radicalized state. How to deal with scenario wherein it seizes to be a buffer state against advancing tide of Islamic fundamentalism.

- Implication of Pakistan acquiring strategic depth, through expanding influence in Afghanistan, what does it mean for Indian interests, given the close Sino – Pak collusion. How should India protect its interests?

- What can India do to stabilize Afghanistan – at what stage Indian national interest will dictate more active involvement.

- Can India take a lead in formulating or putting together regional response to deal with post US/ISAF scenario?

- How will India react to loss of nuclear weapons?

Afghanistan's Alternative Futures

Above discourse vividly highlights that the most important driver of Afghanistan's future is the manner in which the Af-Pak strategy shapes on the ground and how various actors relate to the decision dilemmas outlined above. The implementation of current Af – Pak strategy or the nuanced changes that are brought about in run up to 2014 will depend upon its implementation on the ground which itself is bedevilled by many factors of friction. Simply put there are too many moving parts in the shape of actors with competing interests including allies and adversaries that militate against execution of the articulated strategy. Critical uncertainties of emerging strategic scenario would be the degree of success achieved by the US in its goals after defining its Af-Pak strategy objectives clearly and ability of Taliban to sustain the offensive against coalition forces which would in turn be determined by Pakistan's attitude as also Pakistani military success in FATA region.

Long-term commitment of the US to 'invest and endure' rather than looking for an early exit, improved governance, strengthening ANA and ANP, increased engagement of the regional actors, additional contributions by NATO/ISAF/international community, bringing Pakistan in line with the U.S. and its allies goals in Afghanistan rather than allowing Pakistan to shape the discourse and reversing Taliban resurgence would be the key elements of the success

In light of the above three scenarios are plausible depending upon the degree of virulence of the key determinants and a combination of the driving factors and trends as discussed earlier. These scenarios are outlined below.

Scenario: Defecto Balkanization

- This scenario outlines a clear shift in strategy wherein ISAF and US forces begin to concentrate in bringing stability to Northern and Western Afghanistan, together with reconciliation efforts to bring moderate Taliban on board.

- Above strategy is circumscribed by simultaneously launching concerted operations against Taliban, using overwhelming kinetic power but ensuring least possible collateral damage. Above results in a 'push' factor which forces cross border movement of Taliban to take shelter in relatively secure FATA, resulting in large scale refugee movement to Pakistan. The whole idea is to create what can be termed as a "Pashtun phenomenon" aimed at pressurising Pakistan to act or face consequences.

- To deal with inevitable retaliation; coalition and ASF bolster areas around Kabul together with the Afghan government becoming more responsive, transparent together with a discernable effort toward sustainable development. A concerted effort is made at delivering governance benefit.

- ANA acts as a lead player in CI operations, supported by ISAF. Increasingly both Afghan's at home and international community see Afghans becoming stakeholders in own security and governance.

- Above actions together with calibrated cross border strikes and collusion with Pakistani military by Coalition forces could pressurize Pakistan military to undertake pro active operations in North and South Waziristan for the fear of blow back effect from the TTP?

- As military operations on both sides of Durand divide meet success Taliban resistance begin to reduce making them amenable to peace overtures.

Scenario: Pakistan Brokered Peace

- Pakistan as 'means toward an end theory' manages to position a friendly pro Taliban dispensation in Kabul. Such a scenario allows Pak to control access to Central Asia, payoffs of which are greater economic integration in terms of allowing development of TAPI, and *'Mekran'* Coast as a industrial cum strategic hub. Connectivity makes it a cost effective option for China.

- In such a scenario India is effectively contained in Pakistan's backyard. Allowing Pak to be a dominant player in a "friendly" Afghanistan. However it will be naiveté to expect Afghans will allow uncontested strategic depth to Pakistan. An adverse consequence of such a scenario will be much sharpened standoff with ANA. It is here the importance of well trained and apolitical ANA becomes critical for the stability of Afghanistan.

- The new dispensation brings the region more under the influence of Political Islam, with all its attendant ramifications. An important side effect will be that any faltering by Pakistan in calibrating its response to the Taliban may well result in an Islamic Inferno within Afghanistan with flames touching Pakistan as well.

Scenario: Regional Influence

- India and other regional stake holders become concerned with emergence of Afghan - Pakistan - Taliban alliance as the fulcrum for deciding Afghan destiny. To prevent such a scenario from emerging, regional stake holders reach out to second generation Pashtun leadership and former Northern Alliance (NA) leadership with tacit backing of Karzai government and the United States and Russian support.

- Brings to forth an opportunity for a degree of ethnic reconciliation and elusive stability. NA revival appears on cards and both Iran and Central Asia see in this an opportunity to make common cause in stability of Afghanistan.

- China too acquiesces to protect its investments and agrees along with Iran and India to invest in stability of Afghanistan. As a sop offer Chah Bhar as an alternative trade and pipeline route to Central Asia.

Conclusion

Afghanistan's future remains largely dependent on the US strategies; developments in Pakistan and manner in which reconciliation between moderates and radicals are structured. The Af-Pak strategy has gravitated towards a counter insurgency dominant approach yet the degree of success which the US-NATO combine can achieve remains unpredictable.

Laying down timeline for drawdown of forces has engendered dynamics with every competitor attempting to claim his own strategic space. Pakistan military establishment is convinced that western forces lack commitment and resolve for a sustained fight and therefore it is waiting to claim its strategic depth in Afghanistan after their eventual withdrawal which could be sooner than later.

Over reliance on Pakistan to pull the US and NATO's chestnuts out of the Afghan fire have resulted in the Americans throwing good money after the money gone bad in terms of military and other aid given to Pakistan. Further, Pakistan itself is reeling under multiple terror attacks as a blowback from its failed policies of supporting jihadi terror groups. While Pakistan establishment thinks that it can control Taliban after the departure of western coalition, Taliban is more likely to act autonomously throwing more challenges to Pakistan, region and the international community.

It is time for India to consider options other than only soft option of development assistance to Afghanistan. Regional consensus with Iran, Russia, talking to China as also opening backchannels to Pakistan and establishing contacts with important domestic players in Afghanistan is imperative. Guarding against increasing radicalization in Pakistan would be another important step. India should also become pro active in defining its core strategic interests in Afghanistan i.e. it should never be allowed to become a haven of terrorists which would embark on a regional or global jihad.

CENTRAL ASIA: CHALLENGES OF NON-TRADITIONAL THREATS

Prof. Nirmala Joshi

The post cold war witnessed a phenomenal rise in non-traditional threats such as religious extremism, international terrorism and aggressive nationalism. These are potentially dangerous forces and have the capacity to tear nations apart as it happened in Yugoslavia. Today these concerns have moved to the centre stage of international security. The world community is grappling with these forces in Afghanistan for the last ten years. In turn these forces have given rise to negative tendencies such as narco trafficking, smuggling of small weapons and organized crime, which sustains extremism and terrorism to an extent. What has added to the viciousness and brutality is their access to global communication, mobility and availability of advanced technology. Today terrorist groups have a transnational reach, and are no longer bound to geographical locations. This is a global reach as was evident by the 9/11 devastating events. The defeat of the Soviet Union at the hands of the Mujahideens in Afghanistan instilled in the forces of extremism and terrorism a sense of triumph, a confidence in their ability to defeat a super power. Consequently, under the Taliban rule Afghanistan emerged as the epicenter of terrorism. Extremism began to make inroads into the post Soviet space and Central Asia was no exception.

The unexpected independence and the on-going fratricidal war among the various Mujahideen groups for power in Afghanistan impacted on the Central Asian States (CAS) complicating their security environment. The immediate concern of the CAS was for the stability of the Fergana Valley, the heart of Central Asia. The Fergana Valley straddles three states, namely Kyrgyzstan, Tajikistan and Uzbekistan. In the Fergana Valley Islam had always flourished, though it had an underground existence during the Soviet period. But the Islam that existed was militant in nature. Tajikistan and Uzbekistan share borders with Afghanistan. In fact it is a tradition among the Tajiks who cross the Tajik- Afghan border and vice-versa. In due course extremist groups and organizations sprang up in Central Asia particularly in the Fergana Valley. External impulses were largely responsible for this rise. The defeat of the Taliban has severally impacted on these groups and some of them have sought sanctuary in the border lands between Afghanistan and Pakistan. However, religious extremism has an existence in Central Asia and what shape these groups will assume after 2011 would depend on the stability of Afghanistan and the Afghan ability to effectively contain this danger.

Inextricably linked with terrorism and extremism is the growth of drug production in Afghanistan and its trafficking leading to organized crime. It is a well known fact that a drug profit is one of the sources of finance that sustains religious extremism and terrorism in the Central Asian region. In the context of trafficking, Central Asia is one of the major routes through which this contraband passes. Turkmenistan which shares a border with Afghanistan has also emerged as one of the transit routes. Unless the problem of narco trafficking is resolved it may be difficult to defeat and destroy extremism and dismantle the terrorist infrastructure. Importantly, narco trafficking is posing a serious challenge to the Central Asian governments because of increasing violence at the societal level.

The challenges of religious extremism and terrorism are serious in nature more so as the CAS are not adequately equipped to confront them. As a consequence they are relying on religional as well as efforts by all the stakeholders in defeating and destroying terrorism and its infrastructure. The CAS have supported all such efforts.

From the Indian perspective Central Asia is considered as part of its extended/strategic neighborhood. Indian concern is that the rise of non-traditional threats in Central Asia and its neighborhood have the potential to destabilize the fledging states of Central Asia. Indian interests lie in seeing that the secular and modern ethos of the CAS is not disrupted by forces of religious extremism.

Growth of Religious Extremism and Terrorism

After the break up of Soviet Union in 1991 there was a revival of religion all over the Soviet Space. Such a revival was partly a response to the brutal suppression of religion during Soviet period, and partly a manifestation of peoples' cultural identity, an identity that was different from the Soviet one. It is also plausible that many may have felt the need for an ideological anchor. The result was that in this phase of revival mosques, madrassahs sprang up. People began to observe religious practices with fervour. Over 5000 mosques were built in Uzbekistan, while 1500 sprang up in Kyrgyzstan in the last decade of the Twentieth century. Similar hectic building activity was witnessed in Kazakhstan and Tajikistan.

The beginning of the civil war in Tajikistan in September 1992 signalled a new phase in the growth of religious extremism especially its rapid rise in the Fergana Valley. The Tajik Opposition sought refuge in northern Afghanistan. Here all help and co-operation was extended to them by Ahmed Shah Masoud in terms of safe sanctuary, training in ideology as well as combat activity arms and equipment and financial support. What is of importance is that Tajik Opposition gained vast experience in political and military struggles and were able to establish contact with other Islamic movements and organizations. It is estimated that nearly 100,000 opposition members relocated to Afghanistan between 1992 and 1997. The civil war was possibly a power struggle and it was the radical Islamist across the border who painted the Tajik crises in a religious colour. According to E Mamitova, a research scholar from Tajikistan "… till today Islam has not played a consolidating role and it is regional, clan and tribal interests, and not some common faith that plays a great role in all, without exception, the states of Central Asia". Nevertheless the threat of radical Islam in Central Asia is real and should not be underestimated. The rise of Taliban and their ability to hold on to power ushered in the phase of militant Islam in Central Asia. The question of security and stability in Central Asia assumed tremendous significance not only for the countries concerned, but for other nations in the region including India.

Taliban's impact on the Fergana Valley was visible in the rising profile of the Islamic Movement of Uzbekistan (IMU) a party that was formed during the militant phase of Islam in Central Asia. During the Tajik civil war the IMU fought alongside the Tajik Opposition. The objective of IMU was jihad against the Karimov government. It believed that the fall of the Karimov government would have a ripple effect on the other states of Central Asia. In this objective the IMU received full support from the Taliban regime in Afghanistan. In fact there is a persistent view that the IMU was an affiliate of the Al Qaeda. In due course the IMU became a conduit for drugs and arms smuggling through Uzbek territory. In pursuance of its objective the IMU carried out several incursions in Uzbekistan and Kyrgyzstan and even dared an attempt to assassinate President Karimov in 1999. During the War on Terror the IMU fought alongside the Taliban. It also suffered reversed as its leader Juma Namangani was killed and its ranks decimated. The IMU has an existence in the Fergana Valley. It is difficult to estimate its membership. A faction of IMU led by Tohir Yuldashev, who is no more, is presently based in the Federally Administered Tribal Areas (FATA) in Pakistan. Whether in the Fergana Valley or the FATA region, the IMU is active; albeit its activity is considerably reduced.

The second prominent extremist organization is the Hizb-ut-Tahrir (HuT) Party of Islamic Liberation having a presence in Central Asia. Incidentally, the HuT is not a home grown product and has been active in the Middle East. After the breakup of the Soviet Union, it established its presence in the Uzbek part of the Fergana Valley. The aim of HuT is to create a Caliphate from Mongolia to the shores of the Caspian Sea. Reports suggest that the Party received support from the Taliban. The Party, however, believes, in propaganda and a group of three or four activities distribute literature and educate the people about the Party's aims. However, this is not to suggest that the Party was averse to the use of force. During the War on Terror it did fight on the side of the Taliban. The Party continues its existence and is active. However, all the CAS have banned IMU, HuT and other extremist groups.

There are other groups and splinter ones such as Al Bayat (large presence in Tajikistan), Lashkarlari, Islamic Movement of Turkistan,

Akramiya, Islamic Renaissance Party of Tajikistan, Lali Badkshan Hizb-ut Nusrat, a splinter group which broke away from HuT on the issue of violent means. These groups are based mostly in the Fergana Valley. Similarly there are such groups in Tajikistan, the Alash Party in Kazakhstan. At this juncture it is difficult to determine whether they receive external support, nevertheless their presence cannot be discounted.

The war on terror has however adversely affected Tajikistan; Firstly refugees have been flocking to Tajikistan. Traditionally the Tajik-Afghan border was an open one and therefore a cross-border exchange of people was common in the past. The policing of the border is presently not effective, and therefore the porous border has encouraged people's movement to and from Afghanistan. According to the United Nations (UN) High Commissioner for Refugees more than 3000 Afghans have fled to Tajikistan since January 2008 imposing an additional burden on the fragile economy of the country. Secondly, the continuing uncertainty in Afghanistan could have two possible repercussions on Tajikistan. The surge in Western troop's levels with decisive military action has been driving militants to Tajikistan. The highly mountainous character of Tajikistan provides an excellent hideout to terrorists from across the border. For instance a group led by Abdullo Rakhimov returned to Tajikistan from his hide out in Pakistan bringing with him 100 militants to the Rasht Valley, 150 km east of Dushanbe.

Reports suggest that Al Qaeda has established a presence in the eastern province of Gorno-Badkshan. The Tajik authorities are equally concerned about students studying in madrassahs in Iran and the FATA region. Zubaidulo Zubaidov, the Tajik Ambassador to Pakistan said "… the majority of such students have entered the country illegally mostly through Afghanistan and Iran. It's an alarming situation that the majority of them study in underground madrassahs — in so called religious schools that have no license to operate. When you speak to these young men you quickly notice that their views of their own country and society have completely changed".

Another factor is that by offering its territory as an alternate transport route for supplies to the coalition forces, Tajikistan has incurred the ire of the insurgents. Rashid Abdullo, an independent analyst in Dushanbe maintains that by allowing the US military use of roads to transport non lethal supplies to Afghanistan as an alternative route, the Taliban has warned of reprisals. Such a possibility appears real because of close links that exist between terrorists and increasingly violent drug trafficking groups. Tajikistan is the crucial link in the Northern Distribution Network of the coalition forces and it is also the gateway to the Fergana Valley.

Inextricably linked with the issue of extremism and terrorism is drug production and it's trafficking. Today it is a major concern of all the CAS. Since the last decade there has been a tremendous increase in its production. In 2007 Afghanistan produced a record 8,200 metric tons of opium, twice the total amount of 2005 and accounting for 93 per cent of the world's entire heroin. As mentioned narco profits are a vital source of finance for the terrorists and to sustain insurgency. Linked with the issue of trafficking is the appearance of criminal groups and it is their network that oversees the safe passage of narcotics through Afghanistan and the Central Asian route to markets in Europe and Russia. A negative fallout of narco trafficking is the growing number of addiction in Central Asia. In his recent book "The Critical Decade" President Nursultan Nazarbayev has mentioned that there are over 45,000 known addicts in Kazakhstan. Unless this problem is resolved, it may be difficult to completely defeat extremism in Central Asia. What is required is sufficient resources training and equipment for the law enforcement agencies. Of equal importance is better border controls and management and uniformity of customs and regimes.

Hence we find that extremism and terrorism has a presence in Central Asia particularly in the Fergana Valley, although it is a low key one. As a Russian scholar Aleksei Malashenko opines "Although Islamists in that region (Central Asia) are not capable of rocking a society independently they nevertheless have an excellent chance of becoming part of any crisis". If the extremists and terrorists are active in the Fergana Valley it is because it is one such crisis areas in Central Asia. The Fergana Valley denotes agriculture and population. The density of population is high and agriculture is unable to provide adequate sustenance to the people. Initially people from the Fergana Valley were reluctant to leave in search of livelihood, but now the trend has reversed. Traditionally the Fergana Valley was one integrated market. The artificial division of the Valley has caused tremendous dislocation of economic activity, separating producing areas with the market. So far there are no alternate markets or transport corridors to see the products. The landlocked status of Central Asia has compounded these difficulties.

In the Fergana Valley there are large ethnic minorities in the States. The borders between the States are highly complicated, complex and as yet unresolved. This often erupts into ethnic tensions. For instance for the Uzbeks to travel to Shahimardan a border area as well as a fertile areas they have to pass through Kyrgyz territory or the Tajiks to reach areas in the Soghd province have to pass through Uzbek part of the Fergana Valley. The problem of sharing of water of the two life giving rivers of Central Asia – Amu Darya and Syr Darya — is an explosive ethnic issue. It appears to be intractable problem, but cooperation among the States could show the way forward. Often these ethnic tensions are exploited by the extremists to further their objectives and the people are an easy prey to their propaganda.

The CAS are still in the process of completing their systemic transformation. Meanwhile economic hardship, low quality of life and lack of participatory politics often drives people to extremism especially the young unemployed ones. In narco trafficking young unemployed men are carriers for this contraband. While it is true that poor economic conditions could drive people to extremism, it also cannot be ignored that these are ideological tendencies, a mindset that it is not bred in poverty alone. As succinctly pointed out by former National Security Advisor M.K Narayanan, "Today the Al Qaeda mindset, even more than the Al Qaeda network provides the most pervasive threat to Asian and international stability". Extremism is an attitude grounded in socio-psychological thinking. Similarly, the democratic option is the best one as it would widen the space for participatory politics. As observed by Muhiddin Kabiri, Chairman of the Islamic Revival Party of Tajikistan that restrictive government policies concerning religious expression are driving young people in the direction of radicalization.

Response to the Challenges

The security environment was not conducive for peace when the States gained independence. All the groups which had an underground existence surfaced within no time. On re-emerging these groups were banned for espousing religious extremist ideology, though some of them were focused on social service or cultural pursuits. In Uzbekistan the following groups operating in the Uzbek part of the Fergana Valley; Adolat or Justic the Birlik or the Unity Popular Movement and Erk or the Freedom Party were banned. In the words of President Karimov the reason for such decision was "Regardless of our will or aspirations, Uzbekistan following the disintegration of the Soviet Union has practically turned out to be a frontline state, on its external perimeter two cauldron of conflicts go on boiling, one in Afghanistan and the other in Tajikistan".

On 23rd May 1998 Tajikistan passed a law banning all political parties based on the primacy of religion. Lack of experience and inadequacies of the Central Asian governments may have led them to adopt restrictive policies on faith based political parties. The CAS turned to the Russian Federation for their security requirements. In May 1992 the CAS, except Turkmenistan, joined the Collective Security Organization which implied that the external borders of the member states were the strategic borders of the Commonwealth of Independent States (CIS). A Peace Keeping Force was stationed at the Tajik-Afghan border to keep hordes of extremism at bay. Had the extremists not been stopped at their border, they would have destabilized the Fergana Valley and subsequently the whole of Central Asia. When the war on terror was launched in 2001 the CAS supported the Western military action in Afghanistan. They offered the international coalition forces all cooperation including military bases.

Presently Kyrgyzstan, Tajikistan, and Uzbekistan have offered such military facilities to the coalition forces. Over the years, the CAS have dealt severely with extremists and terrorists. Stringent laws have been introduced, but there is no uniformity among the states on this issue. As a consequence extremists take advantage of this difference and cross borders with impunity.

By the turn of the century two security oriented regional groupings came up which included non-traditional threats as well. The Shanghai Co-operation Organisation (SCO) came up in 2001 and the Collective Security Treaty Organisation (CSTO) was formed in 2003. The SCO's security agenda expanded from tranquility on their common borders to religious extremism, terrorism and separatism. The SCO has set up a Regional Anti Terrorist Structure (RATS) at Tashkent. The focus of RATS is to "… arrange studies of regional terrorist movements and exchange information about counter terrorist policies. The RATS also coordinates exercises among SCO security forces and organizes efforts aimed at disrupting terrorist financing". The first Executive Director of RATS, V. Kasymov stated that 260 terrorist acts were prevented because of the information passed on by the center and scores of leaders of terrorist structures were identified. Recently the SCO organized a special conference on Afghanistan. In its present form the means at the disposal of the SCO are limited to achieve its objective of maintaining stability and security in Central Asia.

The CSTO is a defence alliance with the aim of bringing about greater defence integration between its members. It hopes to establish a unified defence command system under the leadership of Russia. The CSTO has initiated programmes on better security. The CSTO has a large military presence in Central Asia, a military bases in Kyrgyzstan and Tajikistan and reports suggests it is likely to acquire another base in Osh (Kyrgyzstan) located in the Fergana Valley. The CSTO has already established a Joint Rapid Reaction Force (JRRF) with more than 4000 soldiers and is developing crises management capacities. It is not known whether the JRRF has been deployed at any given time in Central Asia. Incidentally Turkmenistan is not a member of CSTO. In view of the likely decisive changes in Afghanistan, Russian forces may take over the policing of the Tajik-Afghan border.

Indian Interests

Since the CAS gained independence in 1991, India's geopolitical scenario underwent a radical change. Its interests widened considerably and lay primarily in a stable and secure Central Asia. In Indian perception the threat to Central Asian stability arose from the non-traditional threats, which were gradually assuming dangerous proportions. India's key concern at that time was the apprehension that Pakistan would seek to acquire "strategic depth" vis-à-vis India by bringing these newly emergent states within the fold of radical Islam. The strategy of seeking "strategic depth" in Afghanistan was launched by President Zia-ul-Haq of Pakistan even before the Soviet Union collapsed. The break up of the Soviet Union and the victory of the Mujahedeens in overthrowing Afghan President Najib-ullah gave a powerful impetus to the idea of strategic depth.

Indian concerns about the stability of Central Asia were not unfounded when the Tajik civil war began in 1992; rise of the Taliban and talk about "greater Afghanistan" began to circulate. In official thinking "Central Asia has emerged as a distinct geopolitical entity, stimulating global attention and interests. The region has vast untapped potential for oil, gas and strategic minerals. Engagement of the Central Asia Republics is thus an essential component of our security. The continued success of the Taliban in Afghanistan is giving rise to fundamentalist forces in the region. Further success of the Taliban is likely to affect Indian strategic interests in the Central Asia in Republics".

An additional factor that fuelled Indian apprehension was the fact that the Central Asian region was awash with small weapons. It is estimated that during the Soviet military intervention in Afghanistan the resistance fighters received arms worth US dollars 2 billion between 1979 and1989, some of which were supposedly appropriated by Pakistan's Inter Services Intelligence. An additional source was the huge stockpiles of weapons left behind by the retreating Soviet forces, which fell in the hands of the Mujahideens. Once the Tajik civil war began Russia supplied arms to the pro-government forces. Availability of arms is a factor that underpins the insurgency.

A fundamental shift occurred in India's strategic thinking by the turn of the century. India's world view broadened to include Asia and was no longer South Asia centric. Against the broadening of India's thinking, it was keen to play an active role in Central Asia. Indian involvement in Afghanistan had also begun to expand and deepen. As a consequence Central Asia and Afghanistan were perceived as one geopolitical entity and Indian engagement with the region was getting intensified. The security dimension of Indian policy was significant. The economic aspect had also acquired greater proportions. Over the years Indian demand for energy was growing at a rapid rate. India's domestic production was unable to keep pace with its rising demand. Prospects for procuring natural gas from Turkmenistan appear feasible. The transport sector is another area that holds immense promise for India. The possibility of re-establishing the ancient trade route would connect Central Asia with South Asia through Afghanistan and provide an excellent opportunity to intensify Indian engagement with Central Asia and Afghanistan. At the political level India shares the commitment of CAS to build a democratic and liberal polity with a free market economy. For India the modern and secular ethos of Central Asia need to be strengthened further. Indian interests in Central Asia are growing and acquiring a multifaceted character.

Conclusion

To conclude religious extremism has made inroads into Central Asia, though its presence at this juncture is a low key. Religious extremism and terrorism is fuelled by external impulses emanating from the Afghanistan-Pakistan borderlands. Intertwined with extremism and terrorism is the growth in illegal narco trade through Central Asia. Unless this problem is resolved it may be difficult to defeat extremism. An equally new and important dimension that could emerge is the vulnerability of Tajikistan because of its physical proximity to northern Afghanistan and Pakistan Occupied Kashmir. Possibly extremists and terrorists could re-locate themselves in the Gorno Badkshan province. Efforts by the coalition forces could be nullified, if due attention is not paid to developments in Tajikistan.

NON-TRADITIONAL THREATS TO SECURITY OF CENTRAL ASIA

Dr. Arun Mohanty

Introduction

During the last two decades following Soviet break up scholars and politicians have been talking about emergence of new threats, which push states to work out new non-traditional methods of ensuring security. Serious scholars have been stressing that threats to the security of states from other states has been declining. Terrorism, organized crime, narco-trade, ethnic conflicts, and combination of such factors such as rapid population growth or decline, environmental problems, abject poverty can lead to economic stagnation, political instability and even to collapse of the state.

For conceptual clarity, we have to define the new threat or non-traditional threat to the security of state. In the beginning of 1980s when US President Regan provided new impetus to the cold war, the traditional threats to security dominated so much that the arms race received a strong new impulse. Ironically, this was the period that witnessed a strong debate about what security is[1]. In 1983 the article titled as "Defining security once again" by Professor Richard Ulman from Princeton University set the stage for intense debate for understanding security from a new angle. Ulman stressed that the narrow definition of security under which only the military aspect is focused, distracts attention from other non-military threats, which can seriously damage national and international stability. The traditional understanding of security ignores the real possibility that some of the threats to the national security can emanate from within the state itself. He emphasized that quick exhaustion of resources, terrorist acts, environmental crisis, urban conflicts stemming from exodus of poor migrants and refugees to cities can pose potential threat to the state security.

Massive gap between the rich and the poor, abject poverty, competition among different ethnic groups to control scarce resources, acquire jobs and other economic benefits are generating lot of tension within a state system. In this connection , it is worth quoting Max. G. Manwaring who argues that, "security can no longer be considered only in terms of protecting national territory and interests against military aggressions. Rather security is being redefined more broadly to encompass stability , stability is depending on the legitimate political , economic and social development , well-being of the global community[2]."

In 1983, British scholar Berry Buzan published his epoch-making book under the title 'People, State and Fear: An Agenda for International Security' for redefining the concept of security. Buzan focuses on how individual security and state security do not coincide and even contradict each other. In other words how state itself can be a major source of threat for certain sections of people living in the given state. Buzan emphasizes the level of security issues that pose a danger to nation-states as follows:

- **Military Security** : the military security concerns with the two levels interplay of the armed offensive and defensive capability of the states , and states' perception of each other's intentions .

- **Political Security**: It concerns with the organizational stability of states, systems of government and the ideologies that give them legitimacy.

- **Economic Security**: This aspect of security concerns access to the resources, finance and market, necessary to sustain acceptable levels of welfare and state power.

- **Social Security:** This element addresses sustainability within acceptable conditions for evolution of traditional patterns of language, culture, religious and national identity and custom.

- **Environmental Security**: It examines the maintenance of the local and the planetary biosphere as the essential support system on which all other human enterprises depend.[3] After the end of cold war, within ten years of publication of the works of Buzan and Ulman, their ideas constituted the foundation for new dynamic approach to the study of security issue, which is known as human security. The concept of human security became famous as a result of "Report on development of humanity", drafted in 1994 by UNO development programme, in which an attempt was made to use 'peaceful dividend' received in connection with the end of cold war for satisfying requirements, emanating from the task of world development.[4]

Significance of new threats

Organised crime, and corruption, network of terrorism, ethnic separatism, massive migration etc have been identified as new threats to state security. These new threats have been in the increasing focus of scholars working on the issue of security. This has special relevance for the newly independent countries of Central Asia. Nevertheless, all states without any exception can be affected by non-traditional security threats. These problems have been compounded to some extend by destruction of the security system of the cold war era, based on bipolar global order. The bipolar world system simplified the problems of security by directing the attention to the issue of emergence of large-scale war fare , and at the same time limited the number of important players in the international arena ; thus easing management of global problems.

This paper makes an attempt to examine how some of the above-mentioned problems can pose a threat to the stability in Central Asian region jeopardizing the state security.

Organised crime, narco trade and money laundering

Loss of human life as result of narco-consumption has serious demographic consequences and brings profit to the people who challenge authority of the state and law. Economic resources received from organized crime and narco-trading are used for destabilizing the society, political system, economy and state governance. Their transnational network subverts territorial integrity of the country from within and outside.

It is widely believed that radical militants want to destabilize the situation in Central Asia in order to facilitate drug trafficking from Afghanistan to Russia and then to Europe. Seventy per cent of Afghan opium export passes through Central Asia, and Islamic Movement of Uzbekistan might be responsible for 75 per cent heroin and opium transiting through the area. According to Pakistan analyst Ahmed Rashid, IMU and other drug dealers had built a stock-pile of opium in Mazar and Kunduz that the ODCCP officials estimated at more than 240 tons. Quoting Tajik officials, Rashid mentions that Juma Namangani, the head of IMU and other drug traffickers had set up laboratories in Tajikistan to refine the heroin. [5]

The UN Drugs Control Programme in its 1999 report mentions that there is now substantial evidence that countries in Central Asia are being used as a transit point to transport illicit consignment of opiates and cannabis originating in Afghanistan and the chemicals used for the illicit manufacture of heroin are being transported in the opposite direction.[6]

One of the most serious problems in the sphere is that Central Asian states were not prepared for dealing with the rise of drug trafficking and drugs consumption. Collapse of Soviet Union, nascent government structures in Central Asian states, ouster of Nazibulla government in Afghanistan created a conducive situation for proliferation of drugs trade in Central Asia. Contrary to the expectation in some sections that Taliban, supposedly following true Islamic principles would ban drug production and trafficking, illicit drug production and trade rose many fold under their rule in Afghanistan.

Instead of imposing ban on drug production and trafficking, Taliban legitimized the production in an Islamic way. They justified drug production and trade by arguing that it is consumed by Kafirs in the west and not by Muslims. Taliban was scared of banning poppy cultivation as it would evoke resistance from the producers.

The problem in controlling drug trafficking can be explained by the weak institutional mechanism such as internal organization and loyalties on the part of the border guards and other law enforcement agencies to certain commanders and not to agencies , and poor personal training and even lack of basic communication equipments. Often drug traffickers are much better equipped than the border guards.

Drug trade has bolstered proliferation of corruption in Central Asian states. Corruption is rampant among law enforcement agents in all the states of Central Asia. Corruption takes place primarily as a result of the bribing of law enforcement officials by the arrested drug traders. Seized drugs are then given to circulation by law enforcement officials. In each Central Asian state, low–ranking officials are typically the primary detainees for corruption charges. Policemen and border guards are often held accountable for drug smuggling , while high ranking government officials remain immune to legal investigation.

A serious weakness in the anti-drug campaign in Central Asia is population's low level of trust in government structures. There is little confidence evident among the public in the honesty and efficiency of law enforcement system's fight against drug trafficking and organized crime. Not only are law enforcement structures criticized for rampant corruption, but they have been subject to criticism for augmenting drug trafficking and addiction in order to attain more profits from their own activities. Poor salaries, inadequate professional training and stiff hierarchies in the security structures are often cited as reasons for widespread corruption.

The weakness of Central Asia's war against drug trade is manifested in the fact often only small drug couriers are captured by law enforcement agencies. These are mostly poor people whose livelihood is entirely dependant on risky and minor drugs smuggling. Once arrested for drug smuggling , the smugglers have to pay huge amount of bribes in order to escape legal persecution or even violent treatment from law enforcement people. Drug barons and mafia kingpins, who mastermind the drug trade and receive huge profit from it rarely get caught or punished. The leaders of the drug economy can only be curtailed by the state officials, some times through informal means such as direct bullying , increase in taxation, forcible capturing of property, and imprisonment for corruption or criminal activities.

Apart from the ability of the Central Asian states to develop and implement anti-drug strategy, there exists little coordination in anti-drug campaign   at a regional level. According to experts there are some states that are interested in cooperation on joint anti-drug programmes in Central Asia. On the other hand there are states who have little or no interest in curbing drug economy through joint efforts. Tajikistan, Kazakhstan and Kyrgyzstan are known to be cooperative on the issue of combating drug trafficking. Uzbekistan and Turkmenistan are believed to be in favour of unilateral approach in combating drug trade. Uzbekistan's planting of land mines across the perimeter of state borders under dispute with Kyrgyzstan and Tajikistan   was reportedly motivated by the Uzbek security interest in preventing the crossing of drug traders and militant Islamists into the country. Since 1999 dozens of Tajik and Kyrgyz nationals have been killed and seriously injured while stepping on land mines , however few reports of land mines preventing the infiltration of illegal groups has come to light. The governments of Tajikistan and Kyrgyzstan have been requesting Tashkent to demine the border. Demining borders require huge amount of money and qualified mine pickers that Uzbekistan does not have. This is the region's most radical step towards border control for preventing drug trafficking. However this undermines   efforts   for regional cooperation and fuels distrust among the states.

Tajikistan is the most affected state by drug trading in Central Asia. Tajik officials provoked international scandals by drugs smuggling during and in the aftermath of the civil war in the country. Serious allegations exist against several top political leaders about their involvement in drug trade. In Kyrgyzstan top political figures have claimed that there are state officials with criminal ties who seek to elevate their own political power. Political leaders, particularly in the South are referred to as part of drug mafia. The drug situation is deteriorating so fast in Kyrgyzstan that some Russian scholars believe that the country is slowly but surely sliding in the direction of Afghanistan.

While contributing to rise of organized crime, drug trafficking poses a serious threat to the continuity of political regime. Corruption in law-enforcement bodies and growing involvement of the population in drug trafficking undermines the governability of the state. The colour revolutions in Kyrgyzstan and Uzbekistan are reported to be financed by drug mafia. Some times, political players involved in drug trade are interested in continuity and stability of the state because it ensures a certain hierarchy in informal relations among state structures and political figures. For example, the possibility to have a legal status of border guard or customs official can be granted only by the state. The opportunity to receive a job in law enforcement body through bribery can only be guaranteed if there is a stable institutional framework for government positions.

If the state does not take action against drug trafficking, it risks being impacted by drug money involved in the promotion of favorable parliamentary candidates or in the corruption of law enforcement organs. In this connection, some scholars would like to compare the situation in the Central Asian states with drug-affected Latin American countries such as Mexico and Columbia, where part of the ruling establishment and opposition are complicit in the existence of the drug economy. The reach of various political forces and government institutions in these states are dependent on the support of drug traders and therefore are susceptible to pressure from organized crime .[7] The experiences of both states illustrate how drug money can play a significant role in strengthening some political forces, and at the same time, undermine the cohesiveness of public officials with the state. Accusations of involvement in the drug economy can become a tool for the removal of political opponents in a system where every party might have links to the shadow economy.

Apart from undermining the state structures, the shadow economy propelled by drug delivers heavy blow to the social fabric by promoting drug use, banditry and encouraging civil disobedience. A society dominated by criminal authorities becomes increasingly lawless, as the illegal economy becomes dominant over the legal economy. The image and prestige of law enforcement bodies take a heavy beating under such a system. As in other types of illicit businesses, the involvement of drug traders in legislative and or executive structures secures the continuity of the black economy. Positions in the state structures ensures impunity and personal security to the political figures involved in the drug trade.

Drug and radical movement

There is a widespread view that collapse of communism created an ideological vacuum that is increasingly being filled by radical Islam, including in Central Asia. Drug money has been a major source for the rise and insurgence of extremist groups in Central Asia. There is strong link between the drug economy and non-state actors that challenge state authority by instigating clashes and terrorist attacks against security forces or state structures in Central Asia. Drug economy, terrorism, radical Islam, organized crime is mutually linked in general, more so in Central Asia.

The functioning of extremist religious groups has long been associated with the shadow economy, particularly with drug trafficking. The IMU armed attack on the Kyrgyz border guards on Kyrgyz –Tajik border was interpreted by some experts as an attempt to divert attention from drug trafficking routes by instigating a conflict.[8]

The drug trade is closely linked to trafficking in arms. According to Zarilbek Rysaliyev, deputy chief of the Kyrgyz general board of criminal investigation, all organized criminal groups operating in the Ferghana Valley are involved in drug trafficking and , as a consequence, are able to obtain various types of armaments. This includes   Hizb –ut –Tahrir, which was described as a more peaceful organisation, but has been maintaining its activities thanks to funding from drug trafficking. Religious motivations are important in the movement's recruitment process. However, its leaders maneuver between religion and shadow economy in order to secure continuity of the movement's existence. State officials agree that most groups that are armed and work for promoting extremism in order to change political system in Central Asian states are involved in the drug economy.

The drug economy and arms trade have merged into one. There are numerous combinations in which drugs and arms are exchanged between religious militant groups with their counterparts in the Central Asian region and Afghanistan. It is difficult to trace the processes of arms and drugs inflows because there is a lack of capacity to control national borders.

All radical religious groups mobilized around ideology towards late 1990s, became increasingly involved in drug trafficking. The IMU , formed by two young Uzbeks Tohir Uldashev and Jumaboi Khozaev (Juma Namangini) and uniting number of small Islamic organisations active in eastern Uzbekistan , began its activities in the Uzbek city of Namangan in December 1991, at a time when the Soviet Union got dissolved . Uldashev and Namangini were successful in building contacts with Islamic non-state and state organisations in Pakistan, Chechnya, Saudi Arabia, the United Arab Emirates etc and moved across state borders, recruiting members on religious basis and mobilizing funds from various sources.

The IMU's emergence as a political movement is a glaring example of how Soviet ideology was quickly replaced by religious extremism and fundamentalism. In case of IMU, religious sentiments were used as driving force to form a structure parallel to state administration. IMU reportedly expanded through out 1990s with the support of Al Qaeda. But the movement thrived thanks to drug money.

Islamic Extremism and Terrorism

Religious extremism and fundamentalism pose serious threat to the security of Central Asian states. Calls for   government based on Sharia and the Koran are supported by small but increasing minorities in most of Central Asia. Most of Central Asia's Muslims appear   to support the idea of secular government, but the influence of fundamentalists and extremist groups is on the rise. Islamic extremist threats to the regimes may   increase as economic distress fails to dissipate or widens as a result of the global economic crisis. Heavy unemployment and poverty rates among youth in the Fergana valley are widely cited by observers as making youth more vulnerable to recruitment into religious extremist organizations.[9]

Although much of the attraction to radical Islamic in Central Asia is generated by factors such as poverty and discontent, it is facilitated by groups in Afghanistan, Pakistan, Saudi Arabia and elsewhere that provide funding, education, training , and man power to the region.

The Central Asian states have imposed certain restrictions over religious freedom. Except Tajikistan, other states forbid religious parties such as the Islamic renewal party, and maintain Soviet era religious oversight bodies. The governments censor religious literature and sermons. According to some experts, the official religious control may create spiritual gap that underground radical Islamic groups seek to fill.

Uzbek officials believe that the country is increasingly vulnerable to Islamic extremism, and they have been at the forefront in combating this threat in Central Asia. It is believed that thousands of alleged Islamic extremists have been imprisoned and many mosques have been closed. Restrictions were tightened when the legislature passed a law on freedom of worship banning all unregistered faiths, censoring religious writings, and making it a crime to teach religion without a license. Public expressions of religiosity are discouraged.

Central Asian states have arrested many members of Hizb-ut Tahrir, a politically motivated Islamic movement calling for establishment of sharia, sentencing them to prison terms nevertheless this outfit seems gaining ground.

Terrorism

Terrorist actions aimed at overthrowing regimes have been of growing concern in all the Central Asian states. Although all the Central Asian states face this menace, it is particularly serious in Uzbekistan, Kyrgyzstan and Tajikistan. Radical Islam got its birth in the former Soviet Union towards the end of perestroika years. But it was not a strong force in the initial years following Soviet disintegration because of lack of social base and experience. Tajik civil war coupled with Taliban take over of power in Afghanistan and Pakistan's effort to use terrorism as instrument of its foreign policy provided the required impetus for rise of radical Islam and proliferation of Islamic brand of terrorism. Sharp decline in living standards of the people created the right environment for growth of radical Islam in Central Asia.

The 1999 February bombing in Tashkent for the first time demonstrated the striking capability of Radical Islamic forces to carry out subversive activities. Subsequently, IMU carried out number of terrorist attacks, emerging as a serious threat to state security. Apart from Taliban and al – Qaeda, this extremist outfit receives support from Pakistan's Jammat—i-Islami, Qatar Charity Society, the Saudi Islamic Salvation Front, Ikwan al Muslimin, Egypt's Muslim Brotherhood and the Saudi Assembly of Muslim Youth. The Batken incident raised the profile of the movement as an insurgent group, which subsequently spread their bases to Tajikistan and Kyrgyzstan.[10]

Terrorist activities of Islamic movement of Uzbekistan and similar groups in the region to some extent reduced by US-led coalition actions in Afghanistan, where several of the groups were based or harbored. However, some experts believe terrorist cells have been re-constituted and are expanding in Central Asia and that surviving elements of the IMU and other terrorist groups are infiltrating from Afghanistan, Pakistan and elsewhere.[11] The IMU and its break away group the Islamic Zihad Union; have become even more closely allied with international terrorist groups, particularly with al Qaeda.

Another terrorist organization which is gradually spreading its influence in Central Asia is Hizbat Tahrir al Islami (HTI). Though its strategy to spread Islamic fundamentalism in Central Asia is different from that of IMU, both the organizations share the same objective of establishing Islamic Caliphate in Central Asia. While Western sources estimate HTI's hardcore membership at 20,000, Central Asian security agencies put the figure at 60,000.

Though the US-led war in Afghanistan has forced the Taliban forces remain engaged in that country, thus containing their expansion to Central Asia, the threat from radical Islam to Central Asian security is far from over. On the other hand, US-led war in Afghanistan has helped growth of radical Islam in Central Asia. Recent trends suggest that radical Islam retains the capability to carry out serious operations in Central Asia. Rampant poverty, corruption, mal-administration, lack of democratic reforms constitute fertile ground for spread of radical Islam in the region.

Water related conflict and threat to security

Another issue that has the potential to pose serious threat to stability and security in Central Asia is water related conflict. Environmental degradation, differences over water distribution among the five states may trigger a serious conflict in the region. The shrinking of Aral Sea considered as life line of central Asia, and failure to reach a mutually acceptable agreement on water sharing between the upstream countries such as Tajikistan and Kyrgyzstan on one hand and the three downstream countries such as Turkmenistan, Uzbekistan and Kazakhstan on the other flares up tension bordering on hostility among central Asian states.

The conflict potential around water in Central Asia is so grave that experts have coined the terminology of "Hydro-war". Soviet legacy compounded with new post-Soviet realities have exacerbated the situation to such an extent that the region can be divided into two rival groups – one group from which the rivers originate and the other group through which the rivers flow. The divide between the upstream and downstream countries is so sharp that it is clearly visible in their behavior while conducting regional policy.

The root of the problem lies in the fact that while water used for irrigation and electricity production is a commercial commodity, water itself is considered as a natural and social blessing, ensuring human right for existence. Under Soviet system, the issue was resolved in a mutually beneficial basis. While there was no restriction on water-flow from upstream republics to downstream countries, the former countries were receiving energy resources from the downstream countries free. After Soviet break up the down stream countries asked money for energy supply while demanding the right to free flow of water from upstream countries that unfortunately have no hydrocarbon resources. This in return has forced the relatively poor upstream countries to regulate their hydro-resources for producing more electricity to meet their requirements.

Some agreements were signed between the regional countries for resolving the water –distribution issues in the post-Soviet period. These include Nurkusk Declaration dated 20th September, 1995 on the recognition of past agreements and normative acts regulating water resources, and the agreement on cooperation in the sphere of joint management of water resources of interstate sources signed in Alma-Ata on 18th Feb, 1992 by leaders of all five Central Asian countries. Unfortunately, the latest developments in Central Asian countries have demonstrated the inefficacy of these agreements, aggravating the situation further and making the centralized energy supply system ineffective.

The relations between Tajikistan and Kyrgyzstan on one hand and Uzbekistan on the other have really reached high tense point. So much so that experts have started talking about the possibility of a full-scale war between these countries.

Experts even talk of the dangerous possibility of South Asian countries being drawn to the perilous war.

The water dispute has added to the tensions existing because of border disputes and differences on several important issues in the region. It is likely to further destabilize the already unstable situation in Central Asia and adversely affect the security environment in the region.

It seems there is little or no hope that a solution to the vexed issue can be found on the basis of negotiations between the countries of the region without outside mediation. The international community is keen to see stable situation in Central Asia for resolving the Afghan issue. They can not afford to have a war in Central Asian territory precisely for this reason. Russia and European Union are trying to find a solution for the region on the vexed issue. However, Russian mediation does not appear to be very successful so far. European efforts to find solution also have not yielded any tangible result. EU representative special envoy for Central Asia, Peer Morale has visited the region several times and held talks with the leaders of different countries.

Here is one issue on which success can be achieved if both Russia and the West launch joint effort that would be to the benefit of both. The West and Russia can be successful in finding a solution to the issue if they jettison their geopolitical rivalry and launch sincere effort to bring all stakeholders to the negotiations table.

The jingoism demonstrated by Tajikistan while pursuing the idea of 'energy sovereignty' and Uzbekistan's effort to block trucks carrying constructions material to Tajikistan is a step towards armed conflict. Dialogue is the only to find peaceful solution to the issue and international community should leave no stone unturned to facilitate this dialogue in order to find a rational and mutually acceptable solution to the vexed issue.

Conclusion

The current situation in the sphere of security in Central Asia is complex, complicated and unstable. Notwithstanding end of 'cold war' and absence of fear about emergence of widespread war, traditional threats to security have not altogether disappeared. Sudden collapse of USSR led to unexpected emergence of sovereign states in Central Asia. These countries were not ready to solve the usual problems of running a state, not to speak of facing the challenges of nation-building and confronting new problems that arose in the sphere of maintaining security. Soviet break up led to not only emergence of new, inexperienced states but opened flood gates for new nationalism and created multitude of new non-traditional problems in the sphere of security .

The following conclusions can be made on the basis of the analysis made in the paper. First ; It is impossible to ensure long term security and stability in Central Asia as long as the states of the region can not resolve the ever-growing complicated domestic problems linked to limited potential of the state, widespread corruption, abject poverty, unprecedented rise in organized crime etc. Secondly, given domestic complexity can easily make fertile ground for trans-border problems of security such as narco trafficking, illegal migration, and terrorism. Thirdly; development of productive regional and international cooperation is required for resolving these issues, because they have created common threats, which can not be tackled unilaterally. Fourth; Centralised bodies of nation-states do not any more appear to be adequate instruments for addressing the issues of non-traditional threats to security because these new threats are less and less confined to political borders of nation-states. Finally, tackling the new threats in the sphere of security requires refusal of approaches formulated on the basis of nation states, and needs participation of sub-national and transnational groups.

Endnotes

1 Alan Russo, Netraditsioniye Ugrozi bezapasnosti rossii Ievroazii, Working Paper No -7, 1999 p.3

2 Max G. Manwaring , "The New Global security Landscape : The Raod Ahead ", Low Intensity Conflict and Law Enforcement , Vol .11 , No 2&3, winter , 2002, pp- 190-191

3 Barry Buzan , People, States and Fear : An agenda for international security studies in the Post- Cold War Era , 2nd editiion1991, Boulder , Lynne rienner,pp.19-20

4 United Nations Development Programme "Refining security : The Human Dimension", Human Development Report , Oxford :OXford Univ Press , 1994

5 Ahmed Rashid , Jihad: The Rise of Militant Islam in Central Asia , Orient Longman, Hyderabad , 2002, p-165

6 Mahendra Ved ."When Silk Routes Becomes Destructive Drug routes," Asian-Eurasian Commentary , Vol.111, No 5-7 April-December , 2000, New Delhi, p-52

7 David Jordan, Dtg Politics :Dirty Money and Democracies . Norman : University of Oklahoma Press , 1999.

8 Mikhail Gerasimov , "Religiozniye narkotrafik ", Nazavisimaya Gazetta , 3rd November, 1999

9 Ahmad Rashid , Jihad : The rise of militant Islam in Central Asia , Yale : Yale university Press , 2002

10 Odol Ruzaliyev, ," The Islamic Movement of Uzbekistan; Lines to complete the Portrait ," Central Asia and the Caucasus , 3(27), 2004 ,p-23.

11 CEDR, March 6, 2003 , Document No-217

WATER SECURITY ISSUES AND PROSPECTS FOR COOPERATION IN CENTRAL ASIA

Dr. Sanjay Kumar Pandey

It is almost a cliché to say that Central Asia is rich in natural resources. It has significant reserves of coal, natural gas, oil and water resources. The problem is that most of these resources are not evenly distributed. While most of the energy resources and the arable land are located in Kazakhstan, Uzbekistan and Turkmenistan; Kyrgyzstan and Tajikistan possess majority of freshwater resources of the region. Thus Turkmenistan and Uzbekistan possess 44 per cent and 23 per cent of natural gas deposits of Central Asia respectfully; Kazakhstan and Turkmenistan are rich in oil; besides, Kazakhstan also has large number of coalfields. On the other hand 81 percent of renewable surface water resources of the region fall within the territories of Kyrgyzstan and Tajikistan. Moreover the main rivers of the region, the Amu Darya and the Syr Darya, originate in mountain ranges of these two countries.[1] To compound the problem the five Central Asian states are located in arid and semi arid vegetation zones with poor precipitation and scarce ground water resources and hence are extremely concerned with safe water supply to meet the demands of their agricultural sector and growing population.[2] Water is an important factor in the economic and political life of the Central Asian states.

The Soviet Legacy

Many of the issues related to the present water dispute that afflict Central Asia go back to the Soviet type of economic model focussing on huge projects to extend cultivation and to build industries. The Soviet Union built a network of dams, reservoirs and irrigation canals in the mountainous areas of upstream countries (Tajikistan and Kyrgyzstan). This was because the natural conditions of upper riparian countries were better suited to higher water accumulation per unit area in comparison to the conditions of the plains of Uzbekistan, Kazakhstan, and Turkmenistan. On the other hand, the lowlands were appropriate for practicing irrigated agriculture and for growing water intensive agricultural crops (cotton, rice, and wheat).[3]

Thus under the Soviet economic model the upper riparian states of Kyrgyzstan and Tajikistan, which possessed most of the hydraulic resources and reservoirs were supplying most of the water to the lower riparian states of Uzbekistan, Kazakhstan and Turkmenistan. In fact they had to incur many losses. A significant part of the arable land and a considerable population and historical areas were inundated. This was compensated by the Soviet federal budget and by making the then Kazakh, Uzbek and Turkmen Soviet Socialist Republics (down stream) provide the upstream Kyrgyz and Tajik republics with gas and coal in the winter to allow them to generate heat and power without releasing water needed for the summer. It was a sort of give and take. With the disappearance of the single planning authority, which was estimating profits and costs for each of the riparian countries and was mitigating conflict of interest by redirecting energy and water resources through the region, the resource redistribution system broke down. The elaborate water and energy sharing agreements among the Soviet Republics of Central Asia was undermined, and the previously integrated regional water and electricity infrastructure became fragmented and suffered from lack of maintenance. With overuse and poor water management agricultural yields fell, and the water levels of the Aral Sea dropped precipitously, leaving behind a much smaller water body of what was previously one of the largest inland seas in the world.[4]

Problems in the Post Soviet Period

In the post soviet period the land-locked Central Asian countries, with their difficult climatic conditions and shared water resources, are trying to meet their food security, to increase agricultural production, to sustain energy sectors, and to protect the environment. The existing water reservoirs are strategic infrastructures for irrigation and hydropower generation. Upstream countries (Tajikistan and Kyrgyzstan) favor the reservoirs' operation for generation of hydroelectricity to meet their energy needs and to generate revenue, while downstream countries (Uzbekistan, Turkmenistan and Kazakhstan) push for irrigation use.

Apart from the above mentioned problems there are technical, operational, and biophysical issues that impact the sustainable operation and management of dams and their associated water reservoirs. These include sedimentation, improper operation, overuse of hydraulic infrastructures against designed operational regimes, and the lack of national legal and institutional frameworks for dam safety. Moreover, there is no early warning system for alerting downstream countries in the event of technical accidents or natural disasters.[5]

The future development and progress of Central Asia is greatly dependent upon the trans-boundary water management and governance. The United Nations Development Program (UNDP) estimates that the Central Asian region loses $1.7 billion per year, *i.e.*, three per cent of the region's GDP (Gross Domestic Product), due to the poor water management that lowers the agricultural yields. It further says that more than 22 million people depend, directly or indirectly, on irrigated agriculture in these countries.[6]

In recent years two interrelated developments have aggravated this difficult situation: First, the two poor upstream countries, Kyrgyzstan and Tajikistan, have decided to develop their hydro resources for export. This is opposed by the downstream countries, especially Uzbekistan, who considers this a challenge to their water security. Secondly, changes in rainfall pattern and temperatures threaten the supply of water and energy in the region. "This has created – together with rising food insecurity and the impact of the global economic crisis – the potential for a 'compound crisis' in the region in 2009 that combines humanitarian, economic and environmental threats especially for Kyrgyz Republic and Tajikistan."[7]

Bone of Contention: Rogun and Kambarata Dams

The construction of Rogun Dam, on the Vakhsh River in southern Tajikistan, upstream from the Nurek Dam, was started in 1976 during the Soviet period.

Following Tajikistan's independence in 1991, work on the dam slowed for lack of funds, and in 1993 floodwaters destroyed much of the rock fill and other work already completed.[8]

The hydropower plant, 110km (68 miles) east of the capital Dushanbe, when finished will be 335m (1,100ft) high, the tallest in the world. For the poorest country in the Central Asian region, with thousands of glaciers but no hydrocarbons, Rogun is the hope for future prosperity. To complete the first stage - producing electricity for local consumption - Tajikistan is estimated to need $800 million. The overall cost of the project is up to $4 billion. With a state budget of just over $1bn, President Emomali Rahmon has appealed to the nation to buy shares worth nearly $700 million. "Rogun is not only a source of light, but a national honour and dignity," he said. Uzbekistan strongly opposes the project and has demanded that international experts be allowed to study Rogun's seismic safety and its potential environmental impact. Analysts say Uzbekistan's real concern is that Tajikistan could potentially control the flow of water, essential for its cotton plantation. The World Bank is ready to carry out a feasibility study. But this will take up to 18 months to complete. Tajikistan believes that Uzbekistan's concerns are groundless and hopes to export electricity to neighbouring Afghanistan, Pakistan and China. The Tajik government says the dam will start producing electricity by 2012.[9]

Kyrgyzstan has launched a $200 million Kambarata 2 hydroelectric power station, located on Kyrgyzstan's Naryn River. Acting President Roza Otunbayeva took part in a ceremony to start the first unit of the hydro project, which will have a capacity of about 50 to 70 MWh. The project was abandoned in the 1990s, until it was saved by a loan from Russia. The construction has also begun on Russia's Nizhnyaya Bureya hydropower plant. The RusHydro hydropower plant will have four generating units with the total power output of 320 MW.[10] Kyrgyzstan plans to export the excess electricity generated from Kambarta 2 to southern Kazakhstan. Additionally, electricity station Kambarata-2 will store water in the Toktogul reservoir which is downstream and supply it for the irrigation of farmland in southern Kazakhstan in the lean spring season.[11] Uzbek leaders have objected to the project, saying it would reduce water flow to Uzbek territory, and negatively impact agriculture, potentially damaging the country's cotton sector, especially in summer.[12]

Both Tajikistan and Kyrgyzstan see these projects as vital for their economic and political development. They consider these as solution for their country's poverty, decrease their dependence on their larger neighbours, and generally contribute to the development of the whole region through electricity exports. Tashkent, on the other hand maintains that these projects are not cost effective and pose serious environmental risks. The Rogun dam, they maintain is located on a seismic zone and may flood its densely populated territories. Tajikistan, which imports most of its natural gas from Uzbekistan and its electricity transmission grid, also passes through Uzbek territory, views Tashkent as a direct threat to its energy security. Uzbekistan's decision to hike the price for natural gas to $240 per thousand cubic meters when Kyrgyzstan and Tajikistan were both enduring severe energy crises in the winter of 2008-2009, created apprehension in these two countries that Tashkent wants to keep its leverage over them.[13]

The dispute reflects the deep antagonism and lack of trust between the two sides. Recently EU officials have confirmed Uzbekistan's fears that "Rogun does entail high risks, warning Tajikistan that the dam replicates the past reckless Soviet industrial planning, and disregards human security." Similarly the EU condemned Russia's $1.7 billion credit to Kyrgyzstan for the construction of Kambarata-1 hydropower station and some EU officials even suggested that Bishkek should approach other countries than Russia, to improve the state of the hydropower sector in Kyrgyzstan. Dushanbe and Bishkek accuse EU of being partial and narrow minded. There are some local critics also who believe that these projects are not economically viable.[14]

Impact of global climate change

There is great deal of debate regarding the impact of global climate change on Central Asia's long term economic and ecological stability. According to some experts global warming is melting glaciers in the region at an alarming rate. As a result in the last 50 years the waters stored in the glaciers of Central Asia are estimated to have shrunk by 25 per cent and they are projected to shrink by another 25 per cent over the next 20 years. These are mere estimates, but they do reflect the broad trends that will likely see major changes in water flows of the principal rivers in the region. Greater water shortages in the long term will force Central Asian countries to use their available water much more efficiently than has been the case so far, especially in irrigation. But they will also make cooperative approaches to rational storage and allocation of scarce water resources across the region much more important if peace and prosperity in the region are to be preserved.[15]

There are two opposing views on the hydro-political future of the Syr Darya catchment. One view is that climate change is leading to increasing water scarcity in the basin and, as a consequence, to more conflict between the riparian countries. The other view is that climate change will in the short to medium term lead to increased runoff due to more glacier melt, and that increased runoff will help in filling the gap between a climate change induced reduction in precipitation and increasing demand for water. These countervailing effects will, according to this more optimistic view, prevent increases in water related disputes among the riparian countries over the next few decades. Some experts have developed a 'coupled climate change land ice hydrological model' to examine which of the two views is more plausible. They conclude that "the total contribution of glacier runoff as a fraction of total overflow in the Syr Darya catchment is rather small at the overall basin scale, but can be important in individual sub-catchments, such as those feeding into the Ferghana Valley, one of the most populated and agriculturally productive areas in the Syr Darya catchment. Increased glacier melt due to a global warming may thus help to some extent in compensating for decreasing precipitation and growing water demand in some sub-catchments." [16]

However, in view of the uncertainties in climate change projections for Central Asia and the rather low overall contribution of glacier melt to total runoff in the Syr Darya, there is very limited support for the second, more optimistic view. Therefore it would be risky to rely on a global warming induced increase in glacier melt to plug the expected supply demand gap. Instead of relying on nature and global warming to temporarily augment water availability and prevent regional water conflict, the riparian countries of the Syr Darya should arrive at an effective water allocation system. They should jointly develop new infrastructure projects, taking international help wherever needed. Scientific research could help in examining the implications of the Kambarata I and II projects taking into account climate change issues. Such studies could help in clarifying and allaying Uzbekistan's concerns about the impact of these projects on the lower riparian states. New strategies could be evolved to benefit both upstream and downstream countries.[17]

Conclusion

The fundamental problem lies in two opposing conceptions of natural resources. On one hand the lower riparian states which have most of the hydrocarbon and mineral deposits believe that they have absolute control over their natural resources and are free to determine the prices of these commodities. They also insist that according to international law and the quota system adopted in the soviet period they have a right to get water from the upper riparian states. Technically they are right and the 1992 agreement largely follows the same argument. But the upper riparian states which are very poor in natural resources, have a problem. If they don't utilise their water resources they don't have any scope for economic development and prosperity.

The solution lies in partial revival of the soviet model of an integrated development of the natural resources of the entire region in the spirit of give and take. Some of the environmentally unsound Soviet practices will have to be modified in light of new technologies and methods. Instead of self sufficiency and individual development the Central Asian states should move towards integration and benefit sharing. For this all the states should think about the common good, stability and prosperity of the whole region. They should adopt a new regional water and energy strategy based on the principles of cost sharing and compensatory schemes associated with the existing water facilities.

Some of the water intensive and wasteful agricultural practices need to be changed and new environment friendly ways and procedures should be developed and adopted. Development model based on expensive mega projects should make way for smaller cost effective and environmentally viable ventures. International agencies and external players should be involved and a multilateral approach will be the only answer to Central Asia's problems.

Endnotes

[1] http://www.ca-c.org/dataeng/05.chapter_three.shtml accessed on 29 March 2011-03-29

[2] http://www.ca-c.org/dataeng/05.chapter_three.shtml accessed on 29 March 2011-03-29

[3] Shavkat Rakhmatullaev, Frédéric Huneau, Philippe Le Coustumer, Mikael Motelica-Heino and Masharif Bakiev, "Facts and Perspectives of Water Reservoirs in Central Asia: A Special Focus on Uzbekistan", Water 2010, 2, 307-320.http://www.mdpi.com/2073-4441/2/2/307/pdf accessed on 30 March 2011.

[4] "Central Asia: long-term challenges and short-term crises"http://www.waterpowermagazine.com/story.asp?storyCode=2052456 accessed on 29 March 2011-03-29

[5] Shavkat Rakhmatullaev, Frédéric Huneau, Philippe Le Coustumer, Mikael Motelica-Heino and Masharif Bakiev, "Facts and Perspectives of Water Reservoirs in Central Asia: A Special Focus on Uzbekistan", Water 2010, 2, 307-320 http://www.mdpi.com/2073-4441/2/2/307/pdf accessed on 30 March 2011.

[6] Ibid.

[7] "Central Asia: long-term challenges and short-term crises"http://www.waterpowermagazine.com/story.asp?storyCode=2052456 accessed on 29 March 2011-03-29

[8] http://www.britannica.com/EBchecked/topic/506865/Rogun-Dam accessed on 4 April 2011.

[9] "Tajikistan Looks to Solve Energy Crisis with Huge Dam, Tuesday, 23 March 2010" http://news.bbc.co.uk/2/hi/asia-pacific/8580171.stm accessed on 4 April 2011.

[10] "Kyrgyzstan Launches Kambarata 2 Hydropower Plant at" http://www.hydroworld.com/index/display/article-display/7316705926/articles/hrhrw/hydroindustrynews/newdevelopment/2010/07/kyrgyzstan-launches.html

[11] "Construction Kambarata Hydroelectric Power Station Comes to an End" http://eng.lomerpb.com/news/december_2009/86-construction-kambarata-hydroelectric-power.html

[12] "Tensions Mount between Kyrgyzstan and Uzbekistan: Border Sector Closed"http://www.speroforum.com/a/28933/KYRGYZSTAN—UZBEKISTAN—Tensions-rising-between-Bishkek-and-Tashkent-border-sector-closed accessed on 4 April 2011.

[13] Erica Marat "Controversy Intensifying Over the Construction of Dams in Central Asia", Eurasia Daily Monitor Volume: 6 Issue: 88, at http://www.speroforum.com/a/28933/KYRGYZSTAN—UZBEKISTAN—Tensions-rising-between-Bishkek-and-Tashkent-border-sector-closed accessed on 4 April 2011.

[14] Ibid

[15] "Central Asia: long-term challenges and short-term crises" http://www.waterpowermagazine.com/story.asp?storyCode=2052456 accessed on 29 March 2011-03-29

[16] Tobias Siegfried, Thomas Bernauer, Renaud Guiennet, Scott Sellars, Andrew W. Robertson, Justin Mankin and Peter Bauer Gottwein, Coping With International Water Conflict in Central Asia: implications of Climate Change and Melting Ice in the Syr Darya Catchment, June 16, 2010, at http://climsec.prio.no/papers/siegfried_etAl_2010_2.pdf accessed on 4 April 2011.

[17] Ibid.

CONNECTING CENTRAL ASIA TO SOUTH ASIA: TRANSPORT CORRIDORS & PIPELINES

Vinod Anand

Connectivity of Central Asia to India and South Asia is an essential component of spurring intra-regional trade and economic activity. The Turkmen ambassador to India has highlighted the feasibility of TAPI project albeit with some constraints which can be overcome. In fact connectivity to Central Asia is, without any doubt, a challenge to India. This paper will also focus on the potential of South Asia as a whole to explore links between Central Asia. Central Asia is central to Eurasian land mass and has been historically important crossroads for both invaders and traders. It is both facilitator and inhibitor for external players attempting to realise their strategic ambitions. In the past trade and commerce as well social and cultural interaction took place along a number of old silk routes but in the current environment there is a critical need to introduce some modern silk routes or new silk routes. Besides deep cultural and historic ties and the war on terrorism, the countries of the region have many common concerns, such as finding outlets/sources for energy supplies, achieving prosperity through economic cooperation and moving towards enhanced security and stability. Further, central Asia has become a hub of gas and oil pipelines and communication corridors. Whether it was a Tsarist Russia or Soviet Union or now the Central Asian republics, there has always been a strategic ambition to open the routes to the warm water ports of the Indian Ocean.

Afghanistan which abuts Central Asia and is also considered part of greater central Asia has a geo-strategically pivotal position of being a land bridge connecting Central Asia to fast growing market economies of South

Asia. With the control of Afghanistan comes the control of the land routes between the Indian subcontinent and resource-rich Central Asia, as well as of a potential corridor to Iran and the Middle East. Thus stability and peace in Afghanistan and Central Asia offers tremendous potential for intraregional trade and economic prosperity.

Therefore, one of the most important objective for India and other powers in the region is to bring peace and stability in Afghanistan and improve connectivity between Central Asia and South Asia. The concept of Greater Central Asia which came into being around 2005-2006 was espoused by the U.S. The central theme of the concept was to build pipelines and corridors in Central Asia that avoid Russia. But India also was quite careful in associating itself with any negative aspects of this strategy which perhaps could go against the interests of Russia even though one of the main premises of the concept was to link Central Asia with South Asia through multi-modal corridors. At times, this concept was also sought to be linked with a kind of grand bargain with Pakistan on Kashmir issue which would lead to reconciliation between India. And thereafter Pakistan could be willing to give overland access to Central Asia. However, such formulations could not find any resonance in India given the complicated history of Indo-Pakistan relations.

The project of developing a power grid from the underutilized energy resources in Central Asia (hydro-power potential of Tajikistan and Kyrgyzstan and power stations based on Uzbekistan gas) with connections to Afghanistan initially and in later phases to Pakistan and India is part of the concept of integrating central with South Asia.

Development of transportation links and energy pipelines like Turkmenistan-Afghanistan-Pakistan-India (TAPI), Baku-Tbilisi- Ceyhan (BTC) and Baku-Tbilis- Erzhum (BTE) are all aimed at diversification of energy flows and economic linkages. In addition, there are a number of pipelines and corridors which are crossing the Central Asian land in all the directions but South; this void is sought to be filled by TAPI pipeline and many other infrastructure projects. But there are many practical difficulties and obstacles in the realization of greater Central Asia concept or strategy, the major one being worsening security environment in Afghanistan. Hence the prime need is to lay emphasis on not only intra regional cooperation but also inter regional cooperation. This would be an important part of the process of integration of Central and South Asia.

For instance with oil revenues in its coffers, Turkmenistan has reached out to neighbour Afghanistan. In July 2008 Turkmenistan agreed to explore and develop Afghanistan's oil and gas deposits in regions bordering on Turkmenistan, along with construction of a rail line, expansion of power supply lines and transport and communications network[1]. Uzbekistan and Afghanistan had signed memorandum of cooperation in the field of energy in November 2006 (progress on which is being reviewed annually)[2]. Power stations of Uzbekistan are energizing the power line built by India from Uzbek-Afghan border to Kabul. Tajikistan has also signed agreement with Afghanistan and Pakistan for export of hydro based power. Potential of expanding the electric grid to India for export of electricity is immense but is constrained by unstable situation and massive capital required for investments in this sector. Similarly, Kazakhstan has been supporting developmental projects in Kyrgyzstan and Tajikistan, the least developed nations among the CARs.

Poor economic strength of Kyrgyzstan and Tajikistan requires the alliance of several foreign investors to guarantee the feasibility of these costly power projects[3]. Spin off effects of these developments projects would contribute significantly to their economies.

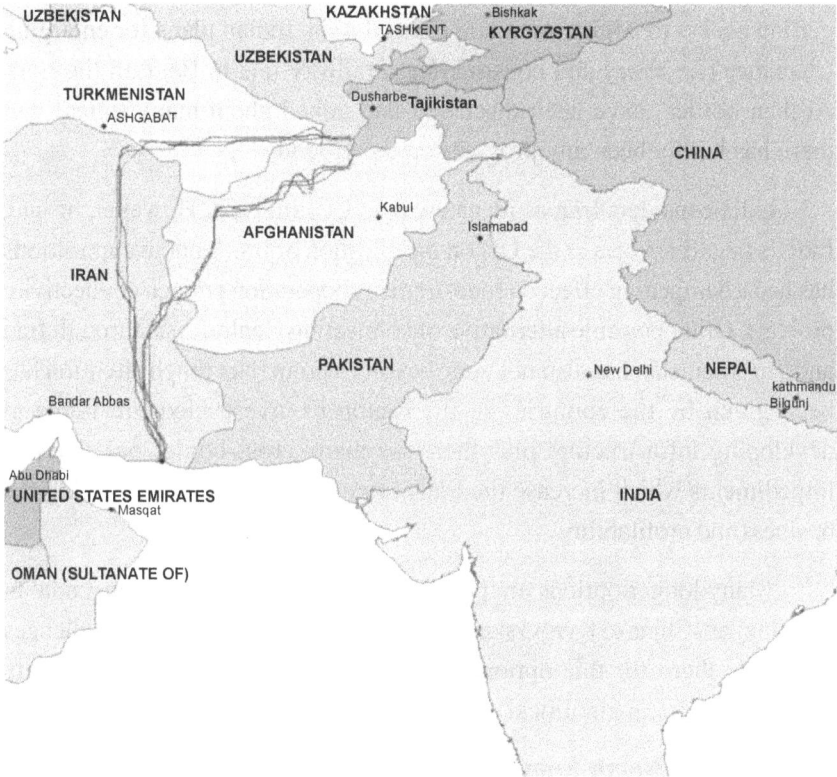

As the map shows there are many options and challenges as far as connectivity to Central Asia is concerned. The shortest route to CAR is through Afghanistan and Pakistan. However, due to obtuse policies of Pakistan and unstable situation in Afghanistan it may not be easy to realize this option in the near future. The alternative option is through Iran and Afghanistan; and India besides financing the Chabahar port in Iran, has also built a 218 kilometer Zaranj-Delaram road in Afghanistan's Nimroze province which   connects Chabahar port via Milak. This has opened the Indian market to Afghanistan to an extent.   This road connection to Afghanistan's Garland Highway has the potential to transport all goods to Afghanistan, Central Asia and beyond and increase economic cooperation amongst the region. The expansion of the Chabahar port and connecting it to the Zaranj-

Delaram Highway in Afghanistan has been central to India's strategy of getting access to Afghanistan and Central Asia. Indian plans for enlarging Chabahar five times and constructing a railway line to Bam on the Iran-Afghan border have been discussed and talked about many times, but there has hardly been any progress on the ground.

India considers Iran as its gateway to Central Asia. However, of late, India's negative votes at the UN on the question of Iran's nuclear ambitions has had a dampening effect on Indo-Iranian cooperation on such connectivity projects. Other possible alternative of connecting Central Asia through Iran and Turkmenistan has also not gone beyond a point. Not much attention has been given by the countries in the region to invest adequate funds in developing infrastructure plus there are many cross-border bureaucratic impediments which increase the transit time of commodities affecting the business and profitability.

Many longer options are possible for instance, through Leh-Ladakh, via Xingjian, China to Kyrgyzstan, Tajikistan and Kazakhstan. But challenges are really there for this option at least for short term as far as security environment and geopolitical challenges are concerned.

International North-South Transport Corridor

Another important option is the development of International North-South Transport Corridor (INSTC). Russia, India and Iran are the founding members and later on many countries enroute have joined the 6245 kilometers long multi-modal corridor project. This project is an ambitious effort to link Europe through Russia via Central Asian republics to South Asia and beyond to South East Asia. There are three corridors proposed; one is through the Caspian route, another route follows the west of the Caspian alignment and the third one which is through the Central Asian republics. (*refer Map 1 opposite*) There has been some improvement in the cargo traffic on these routes. For instance, 5 million tons of cargo is said to have been transported between India, Russia and Commonwealth of Independent States in 2009.

INSTC is considered to be 40 per cent faster and 30 percent cheaper.   But there are many contextual problems like different railway track gauges, double handling and many bureaucratic issues that cause delays. Full potential and the benefits which are supposed to accrue have not been realized so far. All these multi model corridors do have many economic, political and strategic implications. Some of the countries especially Kazakhstan was able to put money in North-South Transport Corridor. Turkmenistan is not part of this corridor so far but if they improve their infra structure in the region then proper linkages to Iran can be established. Even within Tehran-Chahbahar port's connectivity to the Iran's rail network is not optimal though this corridor uses the Bandar Abbas port. Bandar Abbas in Iran is of strategic importance as it is situated on the Strait of Hormuz leading to the Persian Gulf. According to Iranian officials   they desire to keep Bandar Abbas as the port for Russian and European trade. However, improvement of linkages and infrastructure between Bandar Abbas and Chabahar would provide much needed flexibility and redundancy.

Other Multi-modal Networks

The map shows (*refer Map 2 opposite*) the trans-Asian railway network that is being developed and coordinated under the aegis of the UN. There are different railway track gauges which create problems like double handling and therefore delay in trans-shipments and handling. There are many organizations and groupings which have been promoting infrastructure projects in CAR. Some of the nations in Central Asia consider these infrastructures converging in Uzbekistan which will need development of a lot of infrastructure and corresponding investments. Another important linkage is conceptualized by the USAID to link China to this central part of Central Asia through Kyrgyzstan and Tajikistan through multiple routes. Like this, there are number of projects in the Central Asian region to enhance high economic cooperation but more investments are for linking China to Central Asia and beyond to Europe rather than the North South kind of access where India and other South Asian countries could benefit.

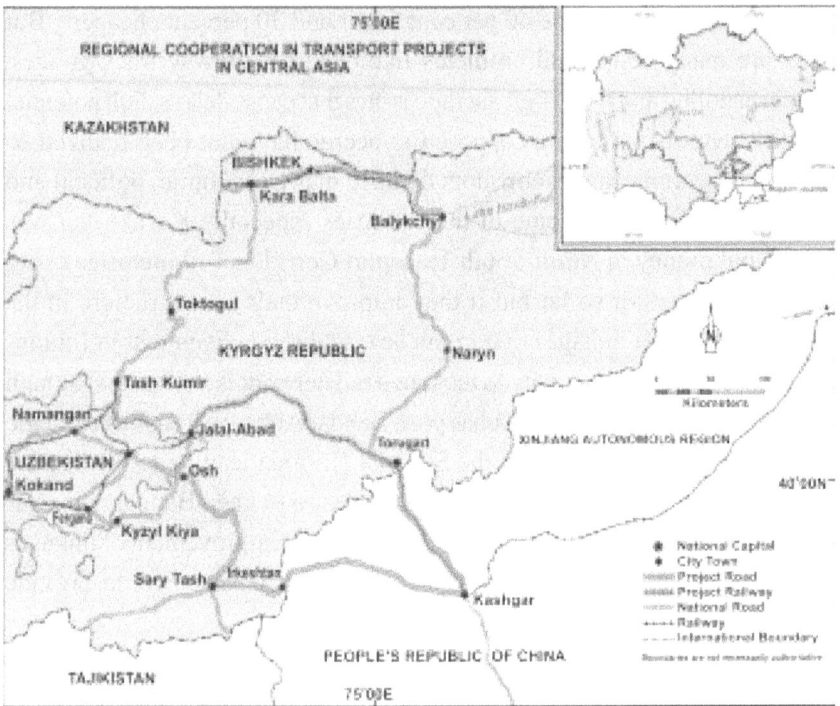

Linkages from China to Central Asian Republics

As this map shows, there are linkages from China to Tajikistan, Kyrgyzstan, and Kazakhstan and beyond. Some of the studies for such projects have been sponsored by USAID. These routes when fully developed have the potential to facilitate trade and cargo transport to and from CARs which would enhance region's competitiveness and profitability internationally. Many of the international institutions and banks are sponsoring east to west multi-modal corridors rather than North-South corridors and networks. In many ways some of the efforts of the US and the concept of the Central Asia strategy provide more inroads to China rather than to India or other powers. China has also supported the Karakoram high way which goes through Pakistan to Xinjiang and goes beyond Kyrgyzstan to Kazakhstan. There was a proposal, which is not feasible for many contextual reasons, for constructing linkages from Leh (Ladakh) via Tibet to connect with the Karakoram highway passing through Xinjian so that India could be connected to Kazakhstan or possibly to Kyrgyzstan. However, in the current geo-political climate that proposal seems to be far-fetched.

Northern Distribution Network- Basis for a New Silk Route

Supply Routes Key:

1. Pakistan Route- Pakistan, Afghanistan

2. NDN North- Latvia, Russia, Kazakhstan, Uzbekistan, Afghanistan

3. NDN South- Georgia, Azerbaijan, Kazakhstan, Uzbekistan, Afghanistan

4. KKT- Kazakhstan, Kyrgyzstan, Tajikistan, Afghanistan

An additional opportunity to improve our infrastructure of the Central Asian countries is putting in place of a Northern Distribution Network (NDN) by the US as an alternative route for supply of troops in Afghanistan. The NDN route to Afghanistan caters for 30 per cent of the supplies to the US and ISAF troops in Afghanistan. The three routes which are numbered 2, 3 and 4 in the given map can be used to develop the infrastructure in the transiting CARs. At a later stage the linkages through Iran and Afghanistan could be strengthened. The Garland Highway in Afghanistan has already been linked to Chabahar through Indian efforts. Therefore, NDN could perhaps become foundation for a new silk route. India has created economic opportunities in the region with increased cooperation with the US, Russia and Central Asian republics. NDN with additional linkages could become a modern silk route which would add to prosperity and security in the region. Further, the troops in Afghanistan are being supplied oil and gas among from indigenous sources in Central Asia i.e. from Turkmenistan and Kazakhstan utilizing the infrastructure available in these nations. This would further benefit the CARs and assist them in diverting more funds for developing their infrastructure.

Improving Regional Connectivity

While we discuss corridors one need to mention that there are multi modal corridors such as rail corridors, road corridors and even electricity grids. There is electricity supply from Uzbekistan and Turkmenistan that are powering the lights of Kabul. A rail line from Termez, Uzbekistan to Mazare Sharif in Heart province of Afghanistan has been completed. This is a manifestation of the intraregional cooperation which would add value to the whole infrastructure that is expected to come up in next decade.   And the electricity grid in the form of KASA 1000 project gives hopes that it will be extended to India in phases, though the problem stays with the first stage where number of issues are involved. The Afghanistan Pakistan Transit Trade which allows flow of goods is one direction that is from Afghanistan to India is, in essence, a retrograde condition.   India can not send its goods overland across Pakistan even though much gain could accrue to Pakistan due to transit revenues. It has been estimated by many economists that if

India was linked to Europe through CARs the transiting countries would be beneficiaries of not only transit revenues but their economies would also boom. On the other hand, Pakistan who as a member of SAARC has accepted South Asia Free Trade Agreement (SAFTA) in principle has failed to give it a practical shape, thus SAFTA remains a limbo because of the attitude of Pakistan.

Coming to the oil corridors there was some skepticism on the issue of the availability of gas in Turkmenistan which the ambassador of Turkmenistan has confirmed there is enough gas in Turkmenistan to meet the requirements of all these pipelines in all the directions. Whether, it is for China gas pipeline or commitments to Russia and prospects of providing gas to Europe through Nabucco gas pipeline or for that matter TAPI there are enough gas reserves in Turkmenistan. Recently, TAPI project has been in the limelight which is of immense importance to India. In October 2008 there was a discovery of proven gas reserves in Yoloten Osman which is 1000km east of Daulatabad. This has changed the entire strategic picture of the availability of gas; with this Central Asia becomes almost third or fourth in the availability of gas reserves in the world. Some of the pipelines which go towards Western direction are the well known BTC and there are many vintage oil and gas pipelines of Soviet Union era that go to Russia. China has come into Central Asia by laying an oil pipeline from almost Caspian Sea through Kazakhstan to China and a gas pipeline from Turkmenistan through Uzbekistan and Kazakhstan to China. In the process China is sucking out vast quantities of oil and gas to fuel its run away economic growth. There is also a possibility that if China can put money and connect the South Pars gas field in Iran it can avoid problems of the Malacca Strait dilemma by getting most of its oil and gas overland. The vulnerability of its hydro carbon supplies passing through the sea lines of communication would be reduced greatly.

Evacuating CAR Hydro Carbons for India

There are many alternatives and ways out to access the hydro carbon reserves for India among which TAPI is one substantive option. TAPI could play a vital role to integrating Central Asia with South Asia. A four nation talks were held in New Delhi in Apr 2011 to finalise the Gas Sales and

Purchase Agreement (GSPA). It was agreed to finalise the agreement by end Jun 2011. It is the policy of Turkmenistan to provide gas on borders; on the other hand India wishes to receive the gas on its border.The intervening risk is expected to be taken by a consortium which undertakes the risks and which can guarantee that gas would be delivered as planned. Of course, there will be of course rewards and penalties in case of violation.

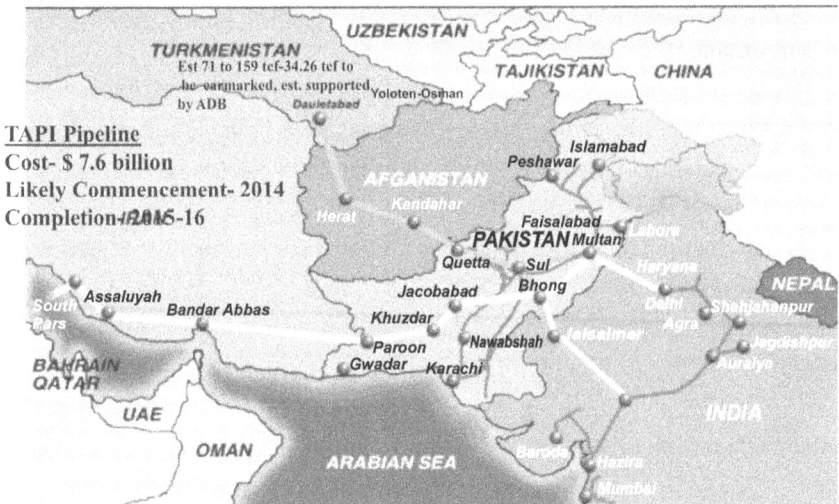

Turkmenistan-Afghanistan-Pakistan-India (TAPI) & Iran-Pakistan-India (IPI) pipelines

With the realization of TAPI pipeline Afghanistan is expected to get an amount that would provide one third of its development projects funding while creating additional domestic jobs. This will assist peaceful economic development of this country while helping to diversify Turkmenistan's gas export and meet energy needs of Pakistan and India. The Iran Pakistan and India line (IPI) is a limbo as far as India is concerned because of geopolitical issues.

Coming back to TAPI, the source for the gas is now unlikely to be Daulatabad; it is more likely that the gas would originate from Yoloten Osman gas field 1000 kilometers east of Daulatabad. However, there is going to be no change in the alignment of TAPI as Turkmenistan is in the process of constructing an East-west gas pipeline inside Turkmenistan which would link all the major gas fields. This would provide flexibility to the whole project in order to get gas from anywhere in Turkmenistan. Further, it is also visualized that TAPI, especially the Afghanistan section would be buried; there are also plans to place soldiers every hundred meters to take care of the security aspects.

Conclusion

To conclude, there needs to be legal and regulatory frame work to protect the interest of all these stake holders. One option is to create an International Pipeline Agency on the lines of International Atomic Energy Agency (IAEA) to ensure that exporters, importers and transit countries in cross-border pipelines abide by their various obligations. IPA could be tasked to detect non-compliance with the agreements signed by the parties, reporting of any disruption and conflict in cross-border pipelines, and enforcement of the various clauses of the agreement.

There is a need to spur the construction of allied infrastructure for improving the potential of the North South Corridor; evidently heavy investment besides political will of the stakeholders is required for this purpose. Further, both Kyrgyzstan and Tajikistan have immense hydropower potential but the same requires a lot of investment for exploiting this natural resource; finding a solution on water security issues with lower riparian countries is also very important. Over all Iran remains India's gate way to Central Asia due to Pakistan's policies; and many geopolitical challenges will remain in near future for India in improving its connectivity to Central Asian region. TAPI is increasingly becoming a viable project; however, security situation in Afghanistan has to improve considerably for the project to be realized.

Endnotes

[1] Turkmenistan News Brief, Issue 29 (2008), July 11-17, 2008 : Turkmenistan intends to finance construction of a branch line and expand power network towards Afghanistan by laying power lines. In particular it intends to increase power supply to Herat. Proposals have been prepared for construction of substations and 410 kms of 500Kilowatts power lines from Turkmenistan to Afghan border.

[2] "Uzbekistan, Afghanistan discuss energy cooperation" , Uzbekistan National News Agency, August 21, 2008 available at http://uza.uz/en/business/390/

[3] For details of China's mounting presence in Central Asia's electric power scene see Sebastein Peyrouse, "The Hydroelectric Sector in Central Asia and the Growing Role of China", China and Eurasia Forum Quarterly, Volume5, No. 2 (2007), pp.131-148.

INDIA-CENTRAL ASIA ECONOMIC ENGAGEMENT

Dr. Gulshan Sachdeva

Introduction

Indian economic reforms aimed at liberalizing highly controlled mixed market economy coincided with Central Asian economic transformation from a centrally planned economy to a market economy. Compared to Central Asian economic decline which lasted for many years, Indian economy slowed only for a year. Since 1992, India is making a successful transition from an excessively inward-oriented economy to a more globally integrated economy. As a result of new policies, it has become one of the fastest growing economies of the world. Despite some serious challenges, like energy security, poverty, infrastructure, regional disparities and internal security, there are strong indications that rapid growth will continue. Similarly, after a period of slow and negative growth, all central Asian economies started growing fast since 2000. This growth has resulted due to high commodity prices, reasonable infrastructure and human capital. The growth momentum provided confidence to leadership in the countries to push for much-needed economic reforms. As a result of this combination of factors, the central Asian regional growth performance has been among the fastest in the world since the late 1990s. Despite security and governance problems, economic growth has been good even in Afghanistan. These factors have created excellent opportunities for India and Central Asian region to create new economic linkages for mutual benefit.

Emerging New Dynamics

Apart from expansion, the Indian economy is also being diversified significantly in the last one decade. There has been rapid integration of the Indian economy within Asia, which has been reinforced by India's *Look East* policy that was initiated in the early 1990s. This is clearly evident from rapidly increasing India-China trade as well as India-Association of South Asian Nations (ASEAN) trade. Studies have shown that India's qualitative and quantitative engagement with the Asian economies is far deeper than commonly perceived.[1] India's economic linkages with west Asian countries have been traditionally quite strong, and more so now due to energy imports, 2.5 million Indian diaspora and good trade relations.

It is becoming clear that along with China and Japan, India would be playing an important role in an evolving Asian economic architecture. However, India will not be effective if its economic relations with Pakistan and Greater Central Asian (GCA) region remain marginal. There are many definitions of Wider or Greater Central Asia[2]. The GCA, in this paper, includes five former Soviet Central Asian republics plus Afghanistan. In this case, India needs to work for an economic policy framework, in which Pakistan; Afghanistan and Central Asian republics view the partnership benefiting them too. This policy framework will also improve India's energy security as it may finally get access to some of the energy resources in the Eurasian region. It can also fundamentally change India's sea-based continental trade. Simultaneously, it can generate tremendous opportunities of trade and transit for Pakistan, Afghanistan and Central Asia. Indians can find tremendous investment opportunities in the GCA, which in turn can transform their small and medium industries as well as agriculture. The growing realization of these opportunities has influenced policy makers not just in India, but also in Pakistan and Afghanistan. Many developments, viz., Afghanistan's membership to the South Asian Association for Regional Cooperation (SAARC), signing of South Asian Free Trade Area (SAFTA), Regional Economic Cooperation Conferences (RECC) on Afghanistan, emerging India-Kazakhstan partnership[3] and continuous interest in Turkmenistan-Afghanistan-Pakistan-India (TAPI) as well as in Iran-Pakistan-India (IPI) gas pipelines, have provided enough inputs to Indian policy makers to shape their newly emerging 'Look-West' policy.

Central Asian Energy Resources & India

In the last few years, energy diplomacy has also become one of the main agendas of country's foreign and security policy. India is seriously perusing nuclear energy option as well as import sources beyond the Middle-East. Indo-US nuclear agreement as well as consistent engagements with the countries of Eurasia, Africa and Latin America could be seen from this perspective.[4] In this scenario, new energy sources of GCA are going to play an important role in Indian energy strategy in the coming years. In the early 1990s, there was a lot of discussion about Central Asian region becoming another Middle East. These discussions and projected scenarios have become relatively sober. However, Central Asian republics definitely have 3 to 4 per cent of proven global oil and gas reserves. Similarly, production of oil and gas in the region has increased in the last few years.

As far as oil imports from GCA region to India are concerned, Kazakhstan could play an important role in diversifying Indian imports. Indian companies are trying hard to get a strong foothold in the region. Sakhalin 1 investment in Russia and recent purchase of Imperial energy by Indian public sector company, Oil and Natural Gas Corporation (ONGC), are efforts in this direction. Competition in the region is very fierce as China is also pursuing the same strategy. At the same time, rapidly growing trade and economic relationship between India and China also compel them to talk of building partnerships in other areas. Earlier both declared their intentions of cooperation in oil and gas biddings. India also mooted the idea of Asian regional cooperation in energy, and initiated a dialogue between principal Asian suppliers (Saudi Arabia, UAE, Kuwait, Iran, Qatar, and Oman) with principal Asian buyers (India, China, Japan, and Korea). These efforts showed some results when China National Petroleum Corporation (CNPC) and India's ONGC mounted a successful $573 million joint bid to acquire Petro-Canada's 37 per cent stake in the al-Furat oil and gas fields in Syria. Earlier they worked as joint operators in Sudan. India and China may be cooperating in other areas, but when it comes to Central Asian energy, competition is fierce. This was clearly illustrated in late 2005 when China outbid India to acquire PetroKazakhstan, Kazakhstan's third-largest oil producer with CNPC raising its bid to $4.18 billion. After trying for many years, India may finally be getting into the energy scene in the region. During the recent visit of Kazakh president to India in January 2009, India's ONGC Mittal Energy Limited (OMEL) and KazMunaiGaz (KMG), National Oil Company of Kazakhstan signed a Heads of Agreement for exploration of oil & gas in Satpayev Block in the Caspian Sea. OMEL is a joint venture between ONGC Videsh Limted (OVL) and Mittal Investments Sarl. The Satpayev block covers an area of 1582 sq km and is at a water depth of 5-10 m. It is situated in a highly prospective region of North Caspian Sea and is in close proximity to major fields, like Karazhanbas, Kalamkas, Kashagan and Donga, where significant quantum of oil has been discovered. It has estimated reserves of 1.85 billion barrels. Indian company will have 25 per cent stake and remaining 75 per cent will be with KMG.[5]

As far as gas imports are concerned, both Turkmenistan and Uzbekistan are important. Both have large amounts of proven gas. In the last fifteen years, both are trying to increase export volumes and diversify export routes. After troubled times of the 1990s, Turkmenistan gas production reached 2.2 tcf/y in 2006, making it the second largest producer of gas after Russia in the former Soviet space. The country plans to double its gas production by 2010. According to the latest data, it has proven gas reserves of 100 Tcf. In the last 12 years, there has been lot of discussion on the $7.6 bn TAPI gas pipeline. There have been some uncertainties – gas reserves in Turkmenistan, security situation in Afghanistan, and strained relations between India and Pakistan. Still, all parties are considering the proposal very seriously. This 1,680 km pipeline will run from the Dauletabad gas field in Turkmenistan to Afghanistan, from there it will be constructed alongside the highway running from Herat to Kandahar, and then via Quetta and Multan in Pakistan. The final destination of the pipeline will be Fazilka in Indian Punjab. India was formally invited to join the project in 2006. Finally, in December 2010, all the four countries have signed agreement in this regard. In a major departure from its previously stated policy of the seller delivering the gas at its border, India has agreed to take custody of the gas at Turkmenistan-Afghanistan border and will rely on an international consortium for safe transfer of the fuel through Afghanistan and Pakistan.[6]

Uzbekistan increased its gas production to 2.3 Tcf/y in 2007 but has concentrated mainly on the domestic sector. Indian public sector company Gas Authority of India (GAIL) has signed an MOU with Uzbekistan's Uzbekneftegaz for oil and gas exploration and production. The GAIL is also setting up a few Liquefied Petroleum Gas (LPG) in western Uzbekistan mainly for consumption in Uzbekistan.[7]

India-Central Asia Trade

At the time of the Soviet Union, Indian economic contacts with the republics of the USSR including with the Central Asian republics were through Moscow. Soviet Union used to be India's major trading partner. Since 1953, when the first trade agreement took place, seven long-term agreements were signed between the two countries up to the collapse of the USSR. This bilateral trade was conducted through a specific system of trade and payment, called Rupee Trade System based on annual plans. Important point of the system was payments in non-convertible currencies. In 1990-91 more than 16 per cent of Indian exports went to USSR and about 6 per cent imports came from it. The nature and character of the then Indo-Soviet trade and economic relations largely determined relations with Central Asia. In the post-socialist period, like other CIS countries, economic relations with the Central Asian region also declined considerably. In the last few years there has been some upward trend. Currently, the official two-way annual trade between India and the GCA region is more than US$ 1 billion (with about US$ 700 million exports). Apart from Afghanistan and Kazakhstan, economic relations with other countries are minimal. This trade is also restricted mainly to traditional items. The main commodities being exported from India are pharmaceuticals, tea, readymade garments, leather goods, jute manufactures, cosmetics, cotton yarn, machinery, machine tools, rice, plastic products, machinery and instruments, electronic goods, chemicals, etc. Imports from the GCA are restricted to fruits and nuts, raw cotton and iron & steel. Uzbekistan and Kazakhstan also export zinc to India[8]. The Export Import Bank of India has already identified many potential export items for this region.[9]

India Greater Central Asia Trade 1996-97 to 2009-10

(US $ million)

	2000-01	2001-02	2002-03	2003-04	2004-05	2005-06	2006-07	2007-08	2008-09	2009-10
Afghanistan	52.45	41.89	79.23	185.98	212.44	201.09	216.48	359.18	520.47	588.74
Kazakhstan	64.12	53.09	59.61	84.07	96.81	117.16	171.48	188.77	290.70	291.44
Kyrgyzstan	22.02	11.52	15.13	38.74	50.19	29.57	37.84	32.43	23.95	27.48
Tajikistan	4.10	2.56	8.73	8.42	10.68	12.13	15.42	22.21	34.17	32.57
Turkmenistan	3.83	6.30	15.70	28.55	26.12	31.18	45.94	45.65	53.50	46.15
Uzbekistan	19.98	23.80	25.62	42.84	52.81	50.57	63.60	56.52	116.27	84.00
Total GCA	166.50	139.16	204.02	388.60	488.75	441.70	550.76	704.76	1039.06	1070.38
Total Indian Trade	95096	95240	114131	141992	195053	252256	312149	414786	488991	467124
% of Total Indian Trade	0.175	0.146	0.178	0.273	0.250	0.175	0.176	0.169	0.212	0.229

Source: Department of Commerce, Ministry of Commerce & Industry, Government of India

Although India's trade with the GCA region looks quite insignificant, its importance should not be seen only within this limited context. With appropriate framework and foresighted policies, this region has the potential to alter the nature and character of India's continental trade. So far majority of Indian trade is conducted through sea. Border trade with China was stopped after India-China war in 1962. A limited opening has been made with China through Nathula Pass. Looking beyond the GCA region, it is clear that India trades a great deal with other CIS countries, Iran, and of course with the European continent. In 2007-08, India's total trade with these countries amounted to about US$ 110 billion. In the last three years, India's trade with this region is growing very fast, particularly with Afghanistan, Pakistan and Iran. Simple calculations on the basis of past trends show that India's trade with Europe, CIS plus Iran, Afghanistan and Pakistan would be in the range of US$ 500 to 600 billion in 2014-15.[10] These are quite realistic assessments. Actual trade has in fact surpassed many of these earlier predictions.[11] One reason perhaps was that Indian economy in between 2006 and 2008 grew above 9 per cent per year, one of the highest growths in recent history. Based on this one could predict trade with this region in the range of about $600 bn. Even after taking into consideration all the cyclical factors, the earlier prediction of achieving 500 billion by 2015 is very much within the reach. If political economy in the region improves and even if about 20 per cent of this trade is conducted through road, we are talking about US$ 100 to 120 billion of Indian trade passing through this region by 2015.

Investment Potential

The countries of this region provide good investment opportunities for Indian business. This is clearly shown by London-based Indian steel tycoon Laxmi Mittal. He owns 5.5 million ton capacity steel plant in Kazakhstan employing more than 50,000 people and from there it supplies to the Chinese market. To facilitate trade and investment with this region, the Indian policy makers in the last decade have created some institutional framework. Indian government has set up bilateral Inter-Governmental Commissions for trade, economic, scientific and technical cooperation with all Central Asian countries, which have been meeting on regular basis. These relations are further institutionalized through joint working groups in various fields, viz., IT, S&T, hydrocarbons, military-technical cooperation, etc. The Indian government also extends small lines of credit for the countries in the region to enable Indian exporters to export to these markets without repayment risk. In this scheme around 15 to 20 per cent of the contract value is paid as advance by the importers, the balance contract value is disbursed by the Indian EXIM Bank to the exporters on shipment of goods. The recovery of credit extended to the overseas buyer is taken care of by the EXIM Bank, without recourse to Indian exporter. To promote and facilitate trade, Double Taxation Avoidance Agreements have also been signed. In the banking sector also, improvement has taken place. Punjab National Bank has a full-fledged branch in Kabul and many other Indian banks have inter-banking arrangements with countries in the region. Canara Bank has links with Commercial Bank for Foreign Economic Affairs of Tajikistan, State Bank of India with Turan-Alem Bank of Kazakhstan, Commercial Bank of Kyrgyzstan, National Bank of Tajiistan, the State Bank for Foreign Economic Affairs of Turkmenistan and National Bank for Foreign Economic Activity of the Republic of Uzbekistan. In 2003, Indian Ministry of Commerce launched a *Focus CIS* programme. In the first phase, five Central Asian countries plus Azerbaijan and Ukraine were focused. Later, other CIS countries have also been included in the programme. The programme aims to promote business-to-business linkages, support trade fairs and different promotional meetings and seminars.

India has also signed many agreements with these countries for technical economic cooperation under International Technical and Economic Cooperation (ITEC). So far thousands of candidates from Central Asia have come to India under the programme in various disciplines, such as, diplomacy, banking, finance, trade, management, small industry promotion, etc. The highest number of seats allotted from Central Asia is from Uzbekistan, which sends about 120 candidates every year. Thousands of Afghan citizens have been able to participate in various short- and long-term study and training programmes in the last few years. The Federation of Indian Chambers of Commerce and Industry (FICCI) has set up Joint Business Councils with Kazakhstan, Uzbekistan and Kyrgyz republic.

Recently the governor of west Kazakhstan region invited Indian industry to invest in areas, like extraction of sunflower oil, wheat production, wool, leather, construction of elite housing complexes and five star hotels.[12]

Many Indian business organizations and think-tanks have identified areas of cooperation, like energy, food processing, textiles, tourism, information technology, education, consultancy services, petrochemicals, and construction.[13] Another area of major interest to Indian businesses would be to participate in the continuing privatization process in the region. Under Uzbek privatization programme, Indian Spentex Industries acquired the business of Tashkent-To'yetpa Tekstil, a state-owned spinning company in Uzbekistan for $81 million in 2006. The transaction comprised acquisition of two manufacturing facilities at Tashkent and To'yetpa that has an installed capacity of 220,000 spindles and a weaving capacity of 236 air-jet looms. Later, the company also acquired the assets to set up a dyeing facility there. The Vardhaman group is also planning to acquire a textile firm in Uzbekistan.Uzbekistan has announced many incentives to attract $300 million from Indian textile companies over the next three years. Uzbekistan and Kazakhstan are heavily marketing a bounty of fiscal sops to Indian textile firms.[14] Some other Indian companies like Punj Lloyd has also participated in oil pipeline projects in Kazakhstan. With offices in Almaty, Atyrau and Tengiz, Punj Lloyd has completed (1) KAM pipeline project for Petrokazakhstan Kumkol resources at Kyzylorda (construction of 16" X 177 Kms crude oil pipeline from Kumkol to Dhuzaly; (2) Large bore and small bore pipeline at wellhead with metering station for Tengizchevroil / PFD at Tengiz (construction of 410 Kms well connecting Flow lines 2" to 24" and Metering Station); (3) SGP Offsites & Utilities for Tengizchevroil / PFD at Tengiz (construction of pipeline fabrication and errection); and (4) Oil & Gas pipeline project - Kashagan Experimental Program for AGIP KCO (engineering, procurement and construction of export oil & gas pipeline 24" 150 kms).[15]

If some of the Central Asian countries are able to reform their land policies, there is a tremendous possibility of investment in the agricultural sector. Identifying investment opportunities country-wise, for Kazakhstan it could include oil and gas, power generation and distribution, telecommunication equipments, medical equipment and supplies, agricultural machinery, food processing and packaging, construction and engineering services, and mining. In Uzbekistan, focus could be on sectors such as energy sector, IT sector, mining sector, food processing and packaging, textile machinery and equipment, and tourism infrastructure. For Tajikistan investment opportunities are identified in mining and related equipment, medical and pharmaceutical supplies, textile machinery, telecommunications, agribusiness and related sectors. In Turkmenistan, potential areas for investment would include oil and gas industry (exploration, development services and equipment), electrical energy (equipment and services), chemical & mining industry, transportation, communications (equipment and services), environmental technology and services, and healthcare and medical industry.

Linkages through Regional Arrangements

In the past, India had adopted a cautious approach to regionalism, and was engaged in only a few bilateral/ regional initiatives, mainly through Preferential Trade Agreements (PTAs) or through open regionalism. The collapse of Doha Development Round of WTO negotiations has pushed many countries, including India, to look for alternatives to multilateral negotiations to improve their trade positions. For the last few years India has put its proposed regional trade agreements on the fast track. In recent years, it has concluded Comprehensive Economic Cooperation Agreements (CECAs) with many countries. These CECAs cover FTA in goods (zero customs duty regime within a fixed time frame on items covering substantial trade, and a relatively small negative list of sensitive items with none or limited-duty concessions), services, and investment and identified areas of economic cooperation. Such agreements include South Asian Free Trade Area (SAFTA), India-Association of Southeast Asian Nations (ASEAN) agreement, framework agreement for India-Bay of Bengal Initiative for Multi-sectoral Technical & Economic Cooperation (BIMSTEC) FTA, India-Thailand FTA, India-Singapore CECA, etc. India already had FTAs with Sri Lanka and Nepal. India-EU FTA, as well as India-Japan CECA are likely to be concluded soon. A trade and investment deal is also being negotiated with Gulf Cooperation Council (GCC), Southern Common Market

(MERCOSUR), South Korea, Chile, etc. India-Israel, India-Brazil, South Africa (IBSA) and India-Russia joint study groups have also been set up.

Compared to these broader trends, India's links with the GCA region have been relatively weak despite the fact the most of the Central Asian republics are members of a wide range of regional initiatives. Detailed analysis of these regional initiatives[16] reveal that these organizations are active in areas of transport, trade, energy, environment, customs, tourism, water, agriculture, food security, information sharing, and other social and cultural exchanges. In some cases, security issues are also covered. Overall, as a result of these initiatives, the countries in the region have made some modest gains in regional economic cooperation. However, there has also been growing realization that trade in Eurasia is shifting more towards continental rather than regional.[17]

Knowing that it does not have direct access to the GCA region and its difficult relations with Pakistan, India's major initiative has been cooperation in building North-South trade corridor. Russia, Iran and India are founder members of the International North South Transport Corridor (INSTC). Later many other countries, like Belarus, Kazakhstan, Tajikistan, Oman, Armenia, Azerbaijan, Syria, Bulgaria, Ukraine, Turkey, and Kyrgyzstan, have joined the project. The route links Indian Ocean (Mumbai port) with Bandar Abbas in southern Iran through maritime transport. Then the goods will be shipped from Bandar Abbas to northern Iranian ports on Caspian Sea (Bandar Anzali and Bandar Amirabad) through roads and railway and then will be dispatched to Astrakhan and Lagan ports in Russia.[18]

The main transport projects being undertaken in this programme with Indian involvement in the GCA are the development of a new port complex at Chah Bahar on the coast of Iran, from where a road goes north to the border with Afghanistan. India has also completed the construction of a 235 km link from Zaranj on the Iran-Afghan border to Delaram from where all major cities in Afghanistan and further north Central Asian republics are connected.

As discussed earlier, for India, it is the continental trade which is much more important than trade only with the GCA region. For this reason, any plan of linking India with Europe through the GCA region will be much more valuable than just having some regional or sub-regional initiative. In this context, the plans of Trans-Asian highway are very valuable to India. All Central Asian countries along with India and Pakistan are members of Asian highway. Similarly countries of the region are involved in one another UNESCAP project called Trans-Asian Railway. Most countries in the region are linked through different corridors of the project.

Air connections between GCA countries and India are prime example of tremendous business opportunities available when Indian market is linked to Europe through Central Asia. For greater regional integration, air transportation is going to play an extremely important role in the coming years. Since land and rail corridors are going to take time (due to heavy investments and other political/ security problems), air services at reasonable rates with reliable services could work wonders for the GCA region. Since air traffic in and out from the region may not be enough to sustain daily reliable services at economical rates, it has to be linked with the main traffic routes. Already there are about 30 direct weekly flights from India to all the important destinations in greater Central Asia. These flights are operated, as low-cost carriers mostly by the Central Asian airlines to/ from Delhi and Amritsar to Europe via Central Asian cities, like Tashkent/ Ashgabat. Once airlines from Afghanistan are able to establish their European connections, these will also be following the same route. In this way, Delhi could become the centre of air corridors for the entire region. This is very much possible as major modernization programme of Indian airports is already underway.

Unless the GCA countries open up politically and economically and ultimately become member of the WTO, there is going to be very limited regional economic cooperation in the short to medium run. In the meanwhile, India has concentrated more on Afghanistan and Kazakhstan for energy and trade cooperation. From Indian point of view, extension of SAFTA to the Central Asia could be useful. Already Afghanistan is a member, and Iran and China have been given observer status in the organization. Tajikistan, Uzbekistan and Kazakhstan could be encouraged to be associated in the grouping.

For India, these are still pieces of a much larger picture, which is basically development of entirely new India-Europe linkages through Central Asia. In fact, SAARC multi –model transport linkages, CAREC action plans and INSTC are all bits and pieces of already existing Trans-Asian highway and Trans-Asian railway plan. If India-Pakistan relations improve, it could be linked through Pakistan and Afghanistan, which will be useful, particularly for north Indian states. Some parts of India will be linked up with the plan through Mumbai port and INSTC. INTEC is already becoming an important component of the Trans-Asian railway network. Further synergies through SAARC and CAREC will improve its effectiveness and scope.

Conclusion

Due to economic policies initiated in the 1990s India's excessively inward-oriented economy has become one of the fastest growing economies in the world and its links with Asian economies have strengthened further. Although Asian economies have shown great dynamism in recent decades, yet a full-fledged Asian economic architecture is still evolving. India has formalized its economic relations with South and Southeast Asian countries through the establishment of SAFTA, BIMSTEC, India-ASEAN agreement and bilateral agreement with Sri Lanka, Singapore, Thailand, Afghanistan, Bhutan, Nepal, etc. The same trend would be followed with Japan and later perhaps with China, which has become its biggest trading partner. These arrangements indicate that India would be playing an important role in an evolving Asian economic architecture in the coming years and decades. India's role in this evolving architecture will be strengthened further if its economic relations with its immediate neighbour, Pakistan, and extended neighbours in Central Asia also become more dynamic. In these circumstances, India will have to work for an economic strategy, in which it is able to effectively engage Pakistan, Afghanistan and Central Asian republics in such a way that all of them become partner and see it as a great economic opportunity.

High economic growth in both Central Asian region and India is pushing policy makers to work for integration strategies. Afghanistan's membership to the SAARC, SAFTA implementation, increasing linkages between India and Kazakhstan, and Afghanistan's potential emergence as an important player in facilitating regional economic cooperation is shaping India's newly emerging 'Look-West' policy. This will be further strengthened with the signing of India-GCC FTA and positive developments on TAPI and IPI. With $1.3 bn. commitment, India is already playing a very constructive role in the reconstruction efforts of Afghanistan.

India's current trade with Central Asian region is very small and likely to remain modest in the coming years. However, importance of this region for Indian trade should not be seen only in the context of very small regional trade. By 2015, India's trade with Europe, CIS plus Iran, Afghanistan and Pakistan would be in the range of US$ 500 to $ 600 billion annually. Even if 20 per cent of this trade were conducted through road, US$ 100-120 billion of Indian trade would be passing through the GCA region. Recent developments indicate that India is finally entering the region in the areas of oil and gas, textiles and nuclear trade; these are the key areas for Central Asia. If Mittal Steel is considered 'Indian', India has been a dominant player in iron and steel for many years.

Compared to modest trade in South and Central Asia, continental trade is going to be much more important for India. As a result, plans for linking India with Europe through the GCA region will be much more valuable rather than just thinking in some regional or sub-regional context. Different infrastructural plans, like the SAARC multi-model transport linkages, CAREC action plans, INSTC, are all in a way different pieces of this grand design. Ultimately Indian trade volumes will be reaching Europe through these different schemes. Further synergies through SAARC and CAREC will improve its effectiveness and scope. With improvement in India-Pakistan relations, an important portion of Indian trade (particularly from the landlocked northern states including Jammu & Kashmir) will be moving through Pakistan and Afghanistan. With the possibility of this trade passing through GCA, most of the infrastructural projects in the region will also become economically viable. Creation of this infrastructure will create further incentives for regional and sub-regional cooperation. Once this happens, SAFTA could also be extended to Central Asia as well as to Iran in due course of time.

Endnotes

[1] See *India's Economic Integration with Asia*, A speech by Mr Jairam Ramesh, the then Minister of State for Commerce and Power, Government of India at seminar series on Regional Economic Integration, Asian Development Bank, Manila, 24 November 2008; Mukul G Asher, *India's Rising Role in Asia*, Discussion Paper No. 121, (New Delhi: RIS, 2007).

[2] See William Byrd, Martin Raiser et al., Economic Cooperation in the Wider Central Asian Region, World bank Working Paper No. 75 (Washington DC: The World Bank, 2006); S. Frederick Starr, ' *A Greater Central Asia Partnership for Afghanistan and Its Neighbours*', (Washington DC: Central Asia-Caucasus Institute & Silk Road Studies Program, 2005).

[3] For increasing India-Kazakhstan linkages, see P Stobdan, 'India and Kazakhstan Should Share Complementary Objectives', *Strategic Analysis*, Vol 33, No. 1, 2009.

[4] For details see Gulshan Sachdeva "Geo-economics & Energy for India" in David Scott (Ed) *Handbook of India's International Relations* (London: Routledge, 2011)

[5] http://timesofindia.indiatimes.com/Business/India_Business/ONGC-Mittal_signs_deal_to_take_25_stake_in_Kazakh_oilfield/articleshow/4027031.cms

[6] http://www.businessworld.in/bw/2010_12_08_Govt_Approves_TAPI_Gas_Pipeline_ Project.html

[7] 'GAIL to SET up LPG Plants in Uzbekistan' http://www.thehindu businessline.com/2006/05/02/stories/2006050201860300.htm

[8] For details see Gulshan Sachdeva, Regional economic Linkages

[9] *CIS Region: A Study of India's Trade and Investment Potential,* Occasional Paper No. 116 (Mumbai: Export Import Bank of India, 2007); Central Asian Republics, Afghanistan & Pakistan: A Study of India's Trade & Investment Potential, Working Paper (Mumbai: Export Import Bank of India, 2005).

[10] For details see Gulshan Sachdeva, "Regional Economic Linkages" in Nirmala Joshi (ed), Reconnecting India & Central Asia: Emerging Security & Economic Dimentions, (Washington DC, Washington: Central Asia-Caucasus Institute & Silk Road Studies Program, 2010) pp.115-179.

[11] Gulshan Sachdeva, 'India' in S Frederick Starr (Ed), *The New Silk Roads: Transport & Trade in Greater Central Asia* (Washington: Central Asia-Caucasus Institute & Silk Road Studies Program, 2007) pp.335-82.

[12] http://www.ficci.com/international/countries/Kazakhstan/kazak.pdf

[13] Ramgopal Agarwala, *Towards Comprehensive Economic Co-operation between*

India and Central Asian Republics, Discussion Paper No. 108 (New Delhi: RIS, 2006) [Online web] http://www.ris.org.in//dp108_pap.pdf; *Central Asia and Indian Business: Emerging Trends and Opportunities*, Seminar Proceedings, (New Delhi: Confederation of Indian Industry, May 2003).

[14] 'Central Asian Countries Woo Indian Textile Cos', *Business Line*, 22 January 2007.

[15] For details, see Punj Lloyd company website http://www.punjlloyd.com/subpage.php?opt=&page_cat=2&id=15

[16] See Gulshan Sachdeva, op.cit. 2010.

[17] See Nickolas Norling & Niklas Swanstrom, ' The Virtues and Potential Gains of Continental Trade in Eurasia', *Asian Survey*, Vol XLV11, No. 3. 2007.

[18] For details about the INSTC see www.instc.org

PROSPECTS OF ENERGY SECURITY COOPERATION BETWEEN INDIA AND CENTRAL ASIA

Dr. Jyotsna Bakshi

It is generally said that energy security comes for India next only to food security. India is home to some 17 per cent of the world's population and the fifth largest consumer of fossil fuels. Although India's per capita energy consumption at present is only 20 per cent of the world average, but with accelerated economic growth, India's energy consumption is bound to grow. India's commercial energy requirements are expected to grow at the rate of 5.2 to 6.1 per cent in the coming two decades.[1] India needs continuous availability of energy to sustain its economic growth momentum. Broadly speaking, India imports seventy per cent of its energy needs, out of which seventy-two per cent comes from the Gulf. The need for diversifying the import base is widely recognized.

For the next two to three decades, oil and gas are likely to remain India's second largest energy source after coal. India Hydrocarbon vision 2025 seeks energy self-sufficiency through increased indigenous production and active oil and gas diplomacy abroad by way of participation in transnational pipelines and acquiring equity oil and gas, etc. India is well endowed with gas hydrates that need to be tapped by harnessing appropriate technology. The availability of oil is generally believed to be limited in India.

Central Asia and Caspian Sea Region as a Source of Energy Supplies to India

India is scouring around the globe in a bid to get access to energy resources. Central Asia and Caspian Sea region also figures in prominently in this quest. The region is geographically closer to the Indian subcontinent and is of immense geopolitical and geo-strategic significance. It forms a part of India's 'strategic' and 'extended neighbourhood'.

According to EIA data, total proven oil reserves of the Caspian Sea region range from 2,320 to 6,683 million tons. Total proven gas reserves are estimated at 6,496 billion cubic meters. This amounts to four per cent of the total oil reserves of the world and five per cent of the total gas reserves.[2] In recent years, India has turned greater attention to Central Asia and Caspian Sea region with a view to diversifying its energy partners. However, India is seen as a late entrant in its pursuit of Caspian Sea and Central Asian hydrocarbon resources. In spite of considerable effort over the last few years, India's success in acquiring stakes in the oil and gas sector in Central Asia has been extremely modest so far.

This paper addresses the prospects of India-Central Asia energy security cooperation in all its dimensions that include hydrocarbons, hydroelectricity and non-conventional sources of energy. It is clear from the following discourse that the likely availability of oil and gas from Central Asia and Caspian Sea region may only partially meet India's growing energy requirements. India's geopolitical stakes in the region remain enormous. Partnership with Central Asian countries in modernization of and value addition to the hydrocarbon sector and developing non-conventional sources of energy holds immense possibility in a bid to raise India's presence and geopolitical profile in the region.

Geopolitical Advantages in Accessing Central Asian Energy Resources Outweigh Problems and Difficulties

Note may be taken of certain problems and difficulties attached with bringing Central Asian hydrocarbon resources to India. For instance, it is argued that the cost of oil production in Central Asia is two to three times higher as compared to the Gulf. Pipeline projects taking Central Asian gas to South Asia through pipelines will be fairly expensive. There are security concerns regarding the safety of pipelines. Moreover, there is uncertainty over the legal status of the Caspian Sea, which is hindering the oil and gas development in the area. It is believed that technical infrastructure for rapid development of petroleum sector in Central Asia is not fully developed.[3]

However, Geopolitical and geo-strategic gains in enhancing India's presence and role in Central Asia through energy and transport corridors, by far, out weigh the difficulties. Moreover, with rising oil and gas prices, the hydrocarbon imports from Central Asia may become economically viable.[4]

Central Asian Energy Scene: Hydrocarbons

Kazakhstan: Kazakhstan has the second largest oil reserves as well as the second largest oil production among the former Soviet republics after Russia. The country also has large reserves of natural gas. Production of both oil and gas is steadily increasing. Kazakhstan has proven oil reserves estimated according to EIA data at 30 billion barrel. Its proven gas reserves are estimated at 85 trillion cubic feet.[5] With the continued development of its giant Tengiz, Karachaganak, and Kashagan fields, the country is expected to at least double its current production by 2019. According to EIA, full development of its major oilfields could make Kazakhstan one of the world's top five oil producers within the next decade.[6]

In addition, Kazakhstan has huge reserves of uranium and can be an important source of uranium supplies to India in the expansion of India's nuclear energy generation programme.

The absence of contiguous borders and lack of good surface transport corridors have been a major hurdle in the way of expansion of multifarious cooperation between India and the Central Asian states. There have been several initiatives to develop transport routes connecting India with the Central Asian States. On February 22, 1997, India, Iran and Turkmenistan signed Tripartite transport corridor agreement to which other Central Asian countries also adhered. In 2008, India completed the construction of 218-km long Zaranj –Delaram road in Western Afghanistan. It provides an alternative outlet to the land-locked Afghanistan and Central Asian states to the world seas through the Iranian port of Chabahar. India has helped in the development of Chabahar port. By December 2011, Kazakhstan and Turkmenistan will complete works on railway Beyneu (Kazakhstan) - Etrek-Gyzylgaya (Turkmenistan) and Gorgan (Iran). It will create North- South Transportation Corridor from Central Asia to the Persian Gulf. This route can become an artery connecting India with oil and gas rich Central Asian states of Kazakhstan and Turkmenistan as well as with other Central Asian states. Given a more optimistic scenario, this route can also be used for bringing Central Asian hydrocarbons to India, either through swap deal or through pipelines.

Both India and Kazakhstan accord very high priority to cooperation and partnership with each other. President of Kazakhstan H.E. Nursultan Nazarbaev was invited as the chief guest for Republic Day celebrations in January 2009. The two countries signed the Declaration on Strategic Partnership during the visit. Several important agreements were signed at this time, including one on cooperation in hydrocarbon sector. The two sides also signed an initial agreement whereby India was to get 25 per cent share in Satpayev oil field in the Caspian Sea. The final exploration and production (E&P) contract was expected to be signed by February-end 2011 [7] which was finally signed on 16 Apr 2011.

However, if it was hoped that the signing of Satpayev oil field E&P agreement might lead to more such deals, that may not be the case. Kazakhstan has already received major foreign investments in the primary hydrocarbon sector. Thus, about $45 billion or sixty per cent of the total of $ 80 billion foreign direct investment in Kazakhstan so far has been in the primary energy sector i.e. exploration and production (E&P). During recently held International Seminar "India-Kazkhstan: Prospects for a Strategic Partnership" at New Delhi on January 18, 2011,[8] Kazakh scholars made it clear that there is already over investment in the hydrocarbon sector. Kazakh experts expressed the view that more investment in the primary energy sector will only add to inflation. Moreover, the bigger blocks are already occupied by the Russian, US and the Chinese companies. Only small and low-risk projects remain for Indian business.[9] Thus, it appears that major investment opportunities for India in the hydrocarbon sector are not in the primary E&P sector, but in modernization of oil and gas industries and in value addition like creation of petro-chemical complexes, refineries and pipeline construction, etc.

However, it may be expected that if India's presence in Kazakh economy grows in general, it may lead to several spin-off benefits in the primary energy sector also.

It is reported that Kazakhstan has been exporting its oil to the Gulf by a swap arrangement with Iran. According to a 1999 agreement, about one million ton Kazakh oil is delivered to the northern port of Iran while an equivalent amount of Iranian oil is delivered to the Persian Gulf port, which Kazakhstan can export outside. The swap arrangement can be another way for India of accessing Central Asian oil.[10]

Oil from Kazakhstan is already flowing to the Turkish port of Ceyhan via Baku-Ceyhan pipeline. India can buy it and bring it to the country across the Red Sea route through tankers.

Turkmenistan: Turkmenistan's natural gas reserves are often cited as the fourth largest in the world. According to another source, Turkmenistan ranks between top 3rd to 10th in terms of natural gas reserves. Turkmenistan plans to increase the annual production of gas from around 70 billion bcm in 2008 to 250 bcm by 2030. It is projected that 230 bcm out of 250 bcm would be exported: 70 bcm to Russia, 30 bcm to China, 30 bcm for (Turkmenistan-Afghanistan-Pakistan-India)TAPI, 14-15 bcm to Iran and 20-30 bcm to Europe.[11]

Earlier during the Soviet period, all the pipelines moved northward towards metropolis Russia. However, following independence most of the CARs are trying to diversify transport and pipeline routes. They are all following multi-vector foreign policy. With the commissioning of Baku-Ceyhan oil pipeline in May 2005, oil from Kazakhstan and Azerbaijan is moving west bypassing Russia and Iran as was desired by the US-led West. In past few years, China has made big in-roads in the Central Asian energy and transport sectors. In October 2005, Beijing succeeded in $4.18 billion takeover of PetroKazakhstan. Although the Indian bid for PetroKazakhstan was higher than the Chinese bid, however, last minute intervention by the Chinese President Hu Jintao, pressure and cash incentives appeared to have worked in China's favour. In December 2005, oil pipeline started flowing from Kazakhstan to China for the first time in history through Atasu-Alashankou pipeline. In December 2009, Chinese President Hu Jintao and the leaders of Turkmenistan, Uzbekistan and Kazakhstan gathered in eastern Turkmenistan to inaugurate a 1,833-km gas pipeline, running through Uzbekistan and Kazakhstan into China's Xinjiang region. The pipeline has the capacity of 30 bcm annually, which can be further raised to 40 bcm. The pipeline reduces Turkmenistan's total dependence on Russia.

The weakest link at present is the southern leg of oil/gas pipeline/s. However, if Turkmenistan-Afghanistan-Pakistan-India (TAPI) gas pipeline is constructed and gas starts flowing from Turkmenistan –Afghanistan-Pakistan to India, it will fill in the crucial gap in this direction. The best case scenario will be that gas from Uzbekistan, Kazakhstan and Azerbaijan is also fed into TAPI.

Uzbekistan: Uzbekistan is broadly self-sufficient in oil, but it has significant gas reserves estimated at 65 trillion cubic feet. It produces 2,387 billion cubic feet annually and consumes 1,858 billion cubic feet and thus is a net exporter of gas.[12] Uzbekistan is the key Central Asian country, which has borders with all other Central Asian states. Uzbeks constitute more than half of the population of Central Asia. Uzbekistan is well endowed with various valuable natural resources, including gold and uranium.

Turkmenistan-Afghanistan-Pakistan-India Gas Pipeline (TAPI)

The issue of Iran-Pakistan-India (IPI) pipeline has been hanging fire for a long time. Further progress was stalled on the issues of security and prices. For the security reasons, India has proposed an alternative offshore route from Iran to the maritime boundary between India and Pakistan off Kutch, from where one branch can come to India and the other can go to Pakistan. However, of late progress has been made in the direction of proposed Turkmenistan-Afghanistan-Pakistan-India (TAPI) gas pipeline. On

December 11, 2010, the intergovernmental agreement was signed by President Gurbanguly Berdymuhamedov of Turkmenistan, President Asif Zardari of Pakistan, President Hamid Karzai of Afghanistan, and Murli Deora, minister for oil and gas of India. The oil and gas ministers of the four countries also signed a framework agreement for TAPI.

If TAPI gas pipeline materializes, it will bring Central Asian gas to India for the first time in history. India attaches great importance to it also because India has deep interest in the stabilization and economic development of Afghanistan and in having a friendly and moderate government there. It is hoped that transit fee revenues from the TAPI gas pipeline —estimated at $ 300 million annually, may contribute to Afghanistan's economic development kitty. This figure amounts to equivalent to one-third of the annual budget of Afghanistan for development projects. It may create jobs for local people.[13]   It may also provide a chance to develop Afghanistan's own gas reserves in the Herat region. With a view to ensure the safety of the pipeline on the Afghan territory, it is proposed that segments of the pipeline will be buried underground. Local communities in Afghanistan will be given incentives to participate in safeguarding the pipeline. The government of Afghanistan has offered to deploy 7000 troops for the safety of the pipeline. The 1735-km long pipeline is to be built at the estimated cost of $ 7.6 billion. The lead role in financing the project will be played by the Asian Development Bank, which will finance $1/3^{rd}$ of the cost. This may open the way for other sources of financing the project. The pipeline will follow the Herat-Kandahar route. The northern route through Kabul is considered more difficult because of high mountain ranges. The pipeline will enter India at Fazilka in the Punjab. The capacity of the pipeline will be 33 billion cubic meters per year (bcm/y), of which India and Pakistan would each receive 14 bcm/y while Afghanistan gets five bcm/y. Initially it was thought that the gas for the pipeline would come from Turkmenistan's Daulatebad field. Now newly discovered "super giant" South Yolotan-Osman field, is being reported as the source of filling TAPI.[14]

It is likely that once the pipeline becomes operational, gas from Uzbekistan, Kazakhstan, Azerbaijan and even Russia can be linked up with it and it can meet increasing energy demand of South Asia.

If successfully executed TAPI gas pipeline project will greatly help in improving India-Pakistan and Pakistan-Afghanistan relations. It will have a salubrious effect on intra-South Asia cooperation as well as cooperation between the two neighbouring regions of South Asia and Central Asia. The shortest route from the India to Central Asia goes through Pakistan and Afghanistan. Given an optimistic scenario, the TAPI pipeline may also pave the way for opening of these routes for free movement of goods and peoples.

However, the security situation in Afghanistan-Pakistan region remains fluid. In the worst case scenario of further deterioration in the security situation in Afghanistan and Pakistan in near future, India would like to work on the option of bringing Turkmen gas to Iran and its Persian Gulf ports and from there move it via sub-sea pipeline via Qatar and Oman to India.

Kyrgyzstan and Tajikistan: Rich Hydroelectricity Potential

The mountainous republics of Kyrgyzstan and Tajikistan are the upstream states where about 80 per cent of the water flowing through Central Asia originates. Both Kyrgyzstan and Tajikistan possess huge potential for generating hydro electricity. The hydropower potential of Kyrgyzstan is estimated at 142 billion KWt/h.[15] The hydropower potential of Tajikistan is variously put at 300 to 527 billion KWt/h.[16] Tajikistan occupies 8th place in the world, 2nd place in the CIS and the 1st place in Central Asia in hydropower potential. The two countries currently utilize less than 10 per cent of their hydroelectricity potential.[17]

The running power of hydropower stations is cheap as no raw material is required. However, the construction cost is high. It takes 10-12 years to construct hydropower plants. Most of the hydropower plants operating in Kyrgyzstan and Tajikistan at present were built during the Soviet period. Both Kyrgyzstan and Tajikistan today lack internal resources to build the new HPPs (hydropower plants) on their own.

The Soviet Union spent billions of roubles in building an elaborate system of water reservoirs, hydropower stations and a network of canals to channel and utilize the water resources of Central Asia. Big reservoirs were built during the Soviet period on the territory of Kyrgyzstan and Tajikistan to supply water to Uzbekistan, Kazakhstan and Turkmenistan during the spring and summer to irrigate the thirsty crops of cotton and rice. These reservoirs were allowed to fill up in autumn and winter when the energy demand for heating is at peak in Kyrgyzstan and Tajikistan. Uzbekistan, Kazakhstan Turkmenistan used to supply oil, gas, coal and mazut (a heavy fuel oil made from refinery residues) to Tajikistan and Kyrgyzstan for heating in the winter months.[18] During the Soviet period, the sharing of water and energy resources was centrally controlled by Moscow authorities. Following the emergence of independent republics in Central Asia, frictions and disputes over the use of water and energy resources have become endemic.

Kyrgyzstan: The huge Toktogul reservoir built during the Soviet period on the lower reaches of Naryn River in Kyrgyzstan has the capacity to collect water on a very large scale, regulate its flow and guarantee water security to the entire region over the span of several years, including the years of water shortage. Almost 97 per cent of the total hydro-electricity generated in Kyrgyzstan is produced in the cascades of the lower Naryn River, including in the power station at the Toktogul reservoir.[19] The lower riparian states of Syr Darya, Uzbekistan and Kazakhstan are interested that the Toktogul reservoir mainly works in the irrigation mode. Kyrgyzstan wants water to be treated as a commodity and wants to be paid for it, to which the downstream states are vehemently opposed. When Uzbekistan introduced world price for its gas exports, which Kyrgyzstan could not afford to pay, the latter increased electricity production at Toktogul during winter to compensate for the lack of fuel. Increased electricity production at Toktogul caused winter flooding in Uzbekistan and Kazakhstan and disrupted flow of water to Syr Darya for irrigation in spring and summer causing damage to the crops in both cases. The construction of Kambarata -1 and Kambarata-2 water reservoirs and power stations at the higher reaches of Naryn river is seen as a solution to the problem as it would allow the water to fill up in the bigger Toktogul reservoir and generate electricity not only to satisfy the domestic requirements of Kyrgyzstan, but also surplus electricity for export to neighbouring countries. The construction of Kambarata-1 and 2 may take between 10 to 12 years and might cost about $1.2 billion, which is equal to the GDP of Kyrgyzstan. Therefore, the financing of the construction of the two projects might require foreign investment, the involvement of the private sector and the necessity to mobilize the neighbouring countries.

Russia has shown interest in investment in Kambarata-1 and 2 projects. It has so far spent $1 million in the feasibility study of Kambarata-1 and 2. However, Russia may invest the huge sum required only out of geopolitical and geo-strategic considerations. Recent developments show that the issue of Russian funding of the Kambarata project has become closely enmeshed with the domestic power struggle in Kyrgyzstan and the tussle over foreign policy orientation of the country. During President Bakiev's February 2009 visit to the Russian capital, Moscow offered a hefty aid package of $ 2.15 billion comprising $ 150 million in grant, $ 300 million loan at nominal interest rate and $ 1.7 billion investment pledge for the construction of Kambarata - 1 hydropower plant. In return, Moscow reportedly wanted the US airbase at Manas airport near capital Bishkek to be closed. On February 3, 2009, Bakiyev announced that the US airbase at Manas would be closed, but did not specify any time limit. However, the Kyrgyz President was essentially interested in getting financial advantage from both Moscow and Washington. Following some vacillation, in June 2009, Bishkek agreed to allow the US to stay at the base for a year in exchange for tripling of the rent. The USA agreed to pay $60 million against $17.4 million per year that it paid earlier.

In February 2010, it reported that Moscow was withholding $ 1.7 billion earmarked for the construction of Kambarata -1 hydropower project. It seemed that Moscow was annoyed at Kyrgyz government going back on the promise to close the Manas airbase.[20] Moreover, Moscow probably did not want to antagonize Uzbekistan, which is staunchly opposed to the construction of large new dams and power stations on the upper reaches of the inter-republican rivers for fear of water shortages. Thus, the construction of large hydropower dams in Kyrgyzstan does not appear to be possible in near term.

The Kyrgyz scholars talk of the need to form an energy consortium with the participation of Russia, China and Kazakhstan for the investment in the construction of the hydropower projects and electricity export to neighbouring countries. This would require a strong geopolitical and geo-strategic convergence of interests of all the sides. Moreover, with the political scenario within Kyrgyzstan and the whole region at large, still not clear, such a decision in near future does not appear to be likely.

Besides, the electricity sector of Kyrgyzstan requires reforms to prevent losses during distribution before anyone would come in with huge investments. In summer, Kyrgyzstan has surplus electricity, which amounts to 1 billion KW/h. The surplus electricity is exported to Russia via Kazakh grids. Kyrgyzstan is also exporting some electricity to China. During President Musharraf's visit to Kyrgyzstan in March 2005, there was much media hype regarding possible export of electricity from Kyrgyzstan to Pakistan. Pakistan has reportedly signed intergovernmental agreements with both Tajikistan and Kyrgyzstan to import electricity from them. Electricity is to be imported from Kyrgyzstan to Pakistan through Tajikistan and Afghanistan. The Pakistani analyst Asma Shakir Khwaja admitted, "Terrain and weather conditions are a clear impediment for this project", but added, "Yet both states appear determined to pursue it."[21] The scholars with whom I interacted in Bishkek, considered electricity export from Kyrgyzstan to Pakistan in near future as a "dream". The construction of high voltage transmission lines across difficult and hazardous terrain might require huge investments. Until the construction of Kambarata-1 and Kambarata-2, which would require huge investments, Kyrgyzstan would not even have enough surplus electricity for export to Pakistan. In the meanwhile, Pakistan in 2005 sought to create media hype for political reasons in order to raise its profile in Central Asia.

Tajikistan: Tajikistan is keen to utilize its hydropower potential to be able to export electricity and to produce aluminum on a large scale in order to improve the country's economy. However, Tajikistan currently produces a small fraction of its potential. Tajikistan faces shortages of electricity in autumn and winters owing to the reduced level of water in the rivers and reservoirs. In summer when snow melts and the water level rises from May to September, it has a surplus of 2 to 2.5 billion KW/h electricity. The surplus electricity is sold mainly to Russia and Kazakhstan through Uzbek power grids. Some electricity is also sold to Afghanistan. However, if Tajikistan wishes to export electricity in a big way, it would require huge investments in several mega hydropower projects, like Sangtuda -2 and Rogun hydropower stations. The work on these projects had begun during the Soviet period, but was abandoned following the collapse of the Soviet Union. Russia has shown interest in the construction of Sanctuda-2 and Rogun power plants. During Russian President Medvedev's visit to Dushanbe in July-end, the Sangtuda-1 hydropower project built on Vaksh River with Russian assistance was inaugurated. Russia owns 75 per cent stake in the project.

Recently, Russia took another initiative that appears to be aimed at acquiring a role for itself in Afghanistan-Pakistan direction, where the situation is rather fluid. Thus, in August 2009, the Presidents of Russia, Tajikistan, Afghanistan and Pakistan met in Tajik capital Dushanbe with a view to promoting quadripartite trade, building of road and rail infrastructure and exporting hydroelectricity from Tajikistan to Afghanistan and Pakistan. The four met again at Sochi on August 18, 2010. Section of the press viewed it as an attempt to pave the way for a new regional bloc.[22] It appears that all the major powers are jockeying for space and influence in this region. The USA is seeking permanent bases in Afghanistan. China is building roads, pipelines and hydropower plants in Pakistan-occupied Kashmir (PoK). It is reported to have sent 11000 troops to PoK in the name of assistance to flood-victims.[23] China may, thus, clandestinely change the geopolitics of the region in its favour. China is making concerted moves to get access to Afghanistan's mineral and metal resources, besides those of Central Asia. Pakistan's military-political establishment is keen to acquire "strategic depth" in Afghanistan and further north by excluding India from the region and by having a compliant pro-Pakistan government in Afghanistan.

In contrast, India consistently favours an inclusive and collaborative approach by the international community to stabilize Afghanistan and put it on the trajectory of economic development. India cannot remain oblivious to the processes taking place in its near and extended neighbourhood. Developments in Afghanistan have a direct bearing on India's security. In post-2001 period, India has emerged as a major donor to Afghanistan. It has already given $ 1.3 billion aid to Afghanistan for various projects from building roads, schools, hospitals, generating electricity, communication links to building the country's new Parliament House. India's development efforts are widely appreciated by the people and government of Afghanistan as well as by the international community in general. As a model of cooperation between South Asia and Central Asia, India has constructed crucial 220 kv double circuit electricity transmission lines from Pul-e-Khumri to Kabul involving the construction of over 600 transmission towers. The transmission lines pass over the Salang range crossing the height of 4000 meters. The project brings electricity to capital Kabul from Termez in Uzbekistan. Given a conducive environment, India can take up many such projects that may contribute to peace, stability and shared prosperity of the region.

Small Power Plants

In view of strong opposition of Uzbekistan to the construction of large power plants in countries like Kyrgyzstan and Tajikistan, perhaps the construction of small power plants is the answer to meeting Kyrgyzstan's and Tajikistan's crucial electricity requirements. Perhaps India should take up several such projects in these two countries with a view to enhancing its presence and profile in the region and further consolidate the immense goodwill that it still enjoys in its 'extended neighbourhood' in Central Asia.

Nuclear Energy

The share of nuclear power in India's energy mix is slated to grow in the coming decades. India has large thorium deposits that may be used in fast breeder reactors. The fast breeder reactors are still in the development stage. In the meanwhile, India needs to import uranium for its nuclear power plants. Kazakhstan has fourth largest proven reserves of uranium in the world.[24] Kazakhstan can be an important source for uranium supply for India. During the visit of Kazakhstan's President Nursultan Nazarbayev to India in January 2009, the two countries signed agreement for cooperation in civil nuclear field.

Uzbekistan is among the ten top countries with regard to uranium reserves. It can also emerge as an important partner in harnessing civil nuclear energy.[25]

Other Non-Conventional Sources of Energy

In order to create a niche for itself, India should not insist only on getting energy resources from Central Asia, but also offer what it can give them both in the field of conventional and non-conventional energy fields. This will create demand for Indian technology and products. Just now the Central Asian states are looking towards the West, Russia or East Asia as major partners. India should try to create a space for itself in Central Asian countries. India needs to be competitive by creating pockets of excellence in various fields. As a spin-off, it may also facilitate greater flow of energy from the region towards India.

All the Central Asian states are trying to promote renewable sources of energy, as the hydrocarbons shall not last forever. India can forge partnership with the Central Asian states in the promising field of research, development and production of renewable energy.

Wind Power: With vast wind-swept steppes, Kazakhstan is ideally suited for harnessing wind power as a source of energy. The same may apply to other Central Asian states to a lesser extent.

Bio-fuel Plants: Landmass of Kazakhstan —and to some extent of other Central Asian states also—can be used for cultivating bio-fuel plants. The issue requires further study as regards availability of water, the climatic conditions as well as suitability of soil, etc.

Solar Power: The southern Central Asian states like Tajikistan, Turkmenistan and Uzbekistan have plenty of sunshine for the large part of the year. India can cooperate with them in harnessing solar energy. For instance, on average Uzbekistan has 270 days per year with sufficient sunlight to operate solar devices. Solar heating systems are particularly suited for communities that are remote and difficult to access. During the Soviet period, Uzbekistan had a relatively well-developed solar power research, development and production base. Uzbekistan is still the largest centre of science in Central Asia.[26] India and Uzbekistan have a programme for cooperation in solar energy, which may be further activated to mutual advantage.

Biomass Energy: The Central Asian states are major cotton producing countries, so is India. India can fruitfully cooperate with the Central Asian states in harnessing new technologies for converting cotton waste for generating energy.

Joint Study of Mountain Glaciers: Mountain glaciers are sources of perennial rivers in both India and Central Asia. Of late concern is felt in both the regions about the shrinking of glaciers. The sides can undertake joint study and research of mountain glaciers in their region.

Geopolitics of Energy in Central Asia

In the initial post-Soviet period, the West tended to regard Russia as its main rival in Central Asia. It tried to build pipelines and transport routes bypassing Russia. However, of late power equilibrium in Eurasia is shifting because of China's growing presence in the region. So far, China has abstained from playing any significant role in the military security field. However, if its investments and stakes in the energy sphere in Central Asia further expand, it may seek a greater role in the military field also. Beijing is making generous payments to buy economic and political clout in Central Asia. At the fourth conference of the Council of SCO Prime Ministers on October 26, 2005 in Moscow, the Chinese Premier Wen Jiabao announced a $ 900 million export credit to SCO countries. He also announced that Beijing had earmarked $900 million in long-term, low-interest loans and grants for member states' infrastructural development and the training of technicians, etc.[27]

In the wake of the recent global financial crisis, that hit the economy of the Central Asian countries hard, Beijing opened its purse strings and offered generous credits to the countries of the region. In June 2009, it offered Turkmenistan $4 billion to develop its largest gas field, South Yolotan, close to the Afghan border. In the same month, the Chinese President Hu Jintao announced a $ 10 billion loan to SCO countries to tide over the global financial crisis. In April 2009, it offered oil rich Kazakhstan $ 10 billion loan for oil. Earlier in February 2009, China gave a hefty $ 25 billion loan for oil to Russian oil companies.

It may be noted that testifying before Senate Foreign Relations Committee in July 2009, the US special envoy for energy, underlined that the US needed to develop strategies to compete with China for energy in Central Asia. It seems a three-cornered great game is going on between Russia, the US and China for influence and control over the energy resources of Central Asia. China's increasing role in controlling energy sources of Central Asia has caused concern in Russia also. A commentary in fergana.ru website on April 10, 2008 was entitled "Russia, European Union, and United States are losing Central Asia to China." In an article in *Nezavisimaya Gazeta* (November 28, 2007), Victoria Panfilova remarked, "China is being smart in its strategy of penetration. Viewing the Central Asia as a protectorate, Beijing binds these countries to itself with credits." On its part, under President Obama, the US administration has taken measures to "reset buttons" in relations with Russia, but trust deficit between Russia and the West continues.

In the context of larger geopolitical game for control over Eurasian resources, it is in India's interest to enhance its presence and role in the region by expanding cooperation with the countries of the region in energy and other fields. These efforts may help in meeting part of India's energy requirements and at the same time promote her larger geopolitical and geo-strategic interests. India had the initial advantage of enjoying maximum goodwill in Central Asia. It still enjoys considerable goodwill. However, there is a need to take practical measures to translate it into mutually-beneficial cooperation.

Endnotes

[1]   Surya Sethi, "India's energy Challenges and Choices," in the book Eds. Ligia Noronha and Anant Sudarshan: *India's Energy Security*, Routledge Tailor and Francis Group, London and New York, 2009, pp. 19-21.

[2]   EIA, 2007 figures cited in Talmiz Ahmed, "Geopolitics of West Asian and Central Asian Oil and Gas: Implications for India 's Energy Security," in the book Eds. Ligia Noronha and Anant Sudarshan, no. 1, p. 67.

[3]   Ibid. pp. 76-77.

[4] Opinions differ on the issue of comparative cost of gas to be procured from Turkmenistan-Afghanistan-Pakistan-India pipeline. According to some recent reports, the cost of gas brought via TAPI is estimated at $ 10 per mmBTU, Qatar is asking for the same price for LNG (http://www.newscentralasia.net, December 13, 2010.

[5] http://www.eia.doe.gov/emeu/cabs/Kazakhstan/Profile.html. January 1, 2010 figures

[6] http://www.eia.doe.gov/emeu/cabs/Kazakhstan/Background.html. November 2010.

[7] ONGC Videsh Ltd (OVL), the overseas arm of the state-run firm, is to invest about $ 400 million in the prospective Satpayev oilfield. Peak output of 287,000 barrels per day (14.3 million tonnes a year) is envisaged from the 256 million tonnes of reserves in the field. Kazakh national oil firm KazMunaiGas will be the operator of the field, holding remaining 75 per cent stake. It has been reported that OVL will pay $26 million as signing amount to the Kazakhstan government. Besides, it will also pay $80 million as one-time assignment fee, Press Trust of India, December 6, 2010.

[8] The seminar was jointly organized by India Central Asia Foundation (ICAF), New Delhi, Kazakh Institute for Strategic Studies (KISSI), Almaty, Global India Foundation (GIF) and Maulana Abul Kalam Azad Institute of Asian Studies (MAKAIAS).

[9] Unpublished papers by Vyacheslav Dodonov and and Leila Muzaparova of KISSI. The Director of the Institute Dr. Bulat Sultanov invited Indian participation in Kazakhstan's "Strategy of Industrial-Innovational Development for 2003-2015," including in science, technology and higher education and value addition to existing sectors of economy. India missed the bus in mid-1990s by being late in investing in the primary sector in hydrocarbon E&P. It should not miss the bus again., he added.

[10] Ajay Patnaik, " *Geopolitics of Kazakhstan and Indo-Kazakh relations*," Research Papers on Regional Cooperation between Central and South Asia at http://www.kazembassy.in/RP_reg_corp.htm, retrieved on February 9, 2011.

[11] Binaya Srikanta Pradhan, "India-Turkmenistan: Engagement between Two Cultural Neighbours" in the book Ed. Jyotsna Bakshi, *Central Asia-India Dialogue: Building a Partnership on the Foundation of Rich Cultural and Historical Heritage*" Lal Bahdur Shstri Centre for Indian Culture, Tashkent and Mahatma Gandhi Indological centre, TSIOS, Tashkent, 2008, p. 90. At the time of the publication Binaya Srikanta Pradhan was Second Secretary, Political and Commercial and Head of Chancery in the Embassy of India at Ashgabat.

[12] EIA data as of July 14, 2010.

13   Robert M. Cutler, "Turkmenistan-Afghanistan-Pakistan-India Gas Pipeline gets Official Four-Way Go-Ahead," at http://cacianalyst.org, January 19, 2011.

14   Ibid.

15   T.T. Sarsembekov, A.N. Nurshev, A.E. Kozhakov and M.O. Ospanov, *Ispolzovanie i okhrana transgranichnykh rek v stranakh tsentralnoi Azii.* 2004. Izdatelstvo Atamura; Almaty. p. 89.

16   Ibid, p. 94.

17   S. Komilov, N. Rustamova, Energy Resources as Conditions for the Development of Economic Cooperation between the Central Asian Countries, Central Asia's Affairs, No. 3, July-September 2004, p. 35. Figures vary, some put the actual generation of hydroelectricity in Tajikistan just at 3-4% of the potential. See, for instance, "Commercial News – Tajikistan, June 2004, Jamshed Rahmonberdiev, BISNIS Representative in Tajikistan" at http://www.bisnis.doc.gov/bisnis/bisdoc/0406TJCommercialNews.htm.

18   ICG Report, Central Asia: Water and Conflict, May 30, 2002, p. 7.

19   *Proekt vodnoi strategii Kyrgyzskoi respubliki. 2003. Mezhdunarodny institut strategicheskikh isledovanii, fond imeni Ffridrikha Aeberta*; Bishkek, p. 13.

20   Jyotsna Bakshi, "Recent Developments in Kyrgyzstan: Domestic and Foreign Policy Concerns," Issue Brief at www.icwa.in, May 27, 2010.

21   Asma Shakir Khwaja, The Changing Dynamics of Pakistan's Relations with Central Asia, *Central Asia Caucasus Analyst*, February 23, 2005.

23   *Indian Express*, August 29, 2010.

24   Ajay Nath Jha, "Interview with Kazakhstan Ambassador to India Doulat Kuanyshev" at http://www.mediasarkar.com/index.php?option=com_ content& view=article&id=997:interview-with-kazakhstan-ambassador-to-india-doulat-kuanyshev&catid=114:web-blog-&Itemid=516

25   Dinara Ziganshina and Prof. Gleason, "Renewable Policy Research Project: Uzbekistan", *Energy and the Law*, March 17, 2008 at http://www.cawater-info.net/library/eng/ziganshina_renewable_policy_ research_project_e.pdf. According to the authors, there are at least 25 uranium reserves. Proven reserves of nearly 65,000 tons can be produced at a cost of $80 per kg. In addition there are a further 17,500 tons that can be produced at $80-130 kg and 47,000 tons that can be recovered at over $130 per kg.

26   Ibid.

27   Xinhua, October 27, 2005.

THE SHANGHAI COOPERATION ORGANISATION AND INDIA

Meena Singh Roy

In the recent years, the Shanghai Cooperation Organisation (SCO) has assumed a new geopolitical role in Central Asia. Established in 2001, the SCO has come a long way. It has gradually emerged as a significant regional mechanism in Eurasia. Its increasing influence and weight is being acknowledged in the international arena. The conventional notion that the Shanghai Cooperation Organisation is an anti-US organisation appears to be changing. Thus, US assistant secretary of state for south and central Asia, Robert O. Blake not only acknowledged during his recent visit to China that the SCO is a relevant regional organisation but also stated that the US would be interested in cooperating with it. As he noted "In Central Asia the Shanghai Cooperation Organisation seeks to bolster security, economic and cultural cooperation between China, Russia and Central Asia. We see the potential for greater U.S. –China dialogue on areas of mutual interest such as counter-narcotics and counter –terrorism in support of the SCO's effort".[1] This is a clear shift in American policy towards the SCO. Although, it has not made any decision on seeking any sort of status within the SCO either as an observer or as a dialogue partner but the US does seems to be inclined to cooperate with China in Central Asia by supporting the SCO efforts in the region. This change in the US view assumes importance in the run-up to the forthcoming annual summit meeting (June2011) of the SCO in Astana, Kazakhstan, where the focus is likely to be on regional security, membership expansion and economic cooperation.[2]

This increasing significance of the SCO gets reflected in some of the writings in West as well. In recent years some experts have also argued for stronger EU-SCO link. According to them by doing so the EU can help stabilise Central Asia, improve its energy security and strengthen its efforts to fight terrorism and drug trafficking.[3]

Importantly, inclusion of India, Iran, and Pakistan as observer states and of Sri Lanka and Belarus as dialogue partners suggests that the SCO is gradually expanding beyond Central Asian region into wider Southern Asian region. During the period 2005-07, the SCO finalised the Memorandum of Mutual Understanding (MOU) with the Association of Southeast Asian Nations (ASEAN), Commonwealth of Independent States (CIS), and Eurasian Economic Community (EurasEC). It has an observer status in the UN General Assembly, and maintains regular contacts with United Nations Economic and Social Commission for Asia and the Pacific (ESCAP) and United Nation Development Programme (UNDP). On January 21, 2008, the SCO signed the MOU with ESCAP.[4] However, it is not very clear how effective this mechanism will be in dealing with regional security issues and addressing the economic problems of Central Asian region, given its inherent constraints. There are two different views expressed by experts in CARs. While some are of the view that the SCO has not been an effective mechanism in dealing with security issues in Central Asia but it is good model to prevent competition and conflict between Russia and China. Others are of the opinion that this organisation brings two great powers together and sets a situation for close cooperation in the areas of security and culture. The SCO is "Window of opportunity" and choosing SCO for providing peace, security and stability in the region was an important strategic choice of regional countries. So far, it has turned out to be an effective regional grouping but nothing has been achieved in economic sphere because Russia and China are competing powers in the region. It is only their anti-US stand which has brought them together to cooperate under the SCO mechanism. Many in Central Asia are not very optimistic about the future of this organization. It is argued that the leading members of the SCO are not sure of what the organisation should be like. Moreover, there exists both competition and rivalry between China and Russia. Due to these limitations the SCO may not live up to the expectation.[5] However, despite its problems and limitations SCO's role and influence in the Eurasian region is likely to grow in future. The present study examines two important issues:

(1) What does it mean for India to be an observer state and how can it contribute in furthering the stability and economic development in the Central Asian region, which would be mutually beneficial?

(2) What would be the advantages and challenges for India if it joins the SCO as full member?

India and SCO

India joined SCO as an observer at its fifth summit meeting on July 5, 2005 in Astana. It is indeed the recognition of India's importance and the role, which it can play in the Central Asian region. Given India's past links with this region, its secular framework, growing economy and strong IT sector, India has much to contribute to the economic development of the Central Asian region. And it has consistently articulated its desire to play a meaningful and constructive role in the SCO. It was in 2009 at Yekaterinburg, Russia, that an Indian prime minister participated in a SCO summit for the first time. In the past few months, Indian officials have clearly stated that India is not only willing to play a greater role in Central Asia but is also interested in becoming a full member of the SCO. To add substance to India's growing focus on this strategically important region, Prime Minister Manmohan Singh paid a visit on 15-16 April 2011 to Kazakhstan. This will be followed by the visit of president of Uzbekistan, Islam Karimov, to Delhi in May. India is also planning some more high level visits to other Central Asian countries in the next few months. Enhancing trade and energy cooperation and fighting terrorism are driving factors for India in the SCO. India is capable of making a significant contribution in these two spheres. It regards economic cooperation as the best way of bringing stability to this region and also engaging China, which remains its major competitor. For India there are three major areas of cooperation under SCO - anti-terrorism, energy, and trade and transport corridors.

The Dynamics of Expanding the SCO - The Statute on the Procedure of Admitting New Members

On the Issue of admitting new members to the SCO, no final decision was taken till its ninth summit on June15 -16, 2009 in Yekaterinburg. The Special Expert Group was instructed to carry out its work on the draft document of regulations on the order of admitting new members. However, with a view to expand cooperation with new countries without giving them full membership within the SCO framework, Sri Lanka and Belarus were granted the status of dialogue partner of the organization. Despite India, Iran, Pakistan and Mongolia getting an observer status in SCO, the question of enlargement, mainly the full membership was discussed but criteria and regulations for admitting new members was approved only in its 10th summit meeting in June 2010 in Tashkent.

The statute on the procedure of admitting new members to the SCO was adopted at the SCO summit on June 11, 2010. As per the statute, any country wanting to join the SCO must be located in the Eurasian region, must have diplomatic relations with all the SCO member states and must have the status of observer at the SCO or Partner on dialogue. It must also maintain active trade; economic and humanitarian ties with the SCO members and it should not be under UN sanctions and should not be involved in an armed conflict with other state or states. If a country wishes to join the organisation it will have to send an official appeal asking for the SCO membership to the chairman of the council of the SCO head of state through the chairman of the council of foreign ministers of the organisation.[6] However, what is important to note here is that adoption of the statute does not indicate the organisation's automatic expansion. Any decision to accept a new member to the SCO will need the consensus of all member states. Therefore, the adoption of the statute only creates a legal basis for countries who are seeking full membership in the SCO.

During a media interaction at the end of the February 2011 Almaty international conference, SCO Secretary General made it clear that countries wanting to join the organisation should make positive contributions to it and not inject negativity. Earlier, during the course of this conference, it was pointed out that the SCO is an open organisation and its expansion is inevitable, although some technical issues need to be addressed first. In the current context, India, Pakistan and Mongolia are eligible for full membership, but Iran is not because of existing UN sanctions against it. While Mongolia has been a potential candidate for full membership, it prefers to continue as an observer and mainly seeks cooperation in the transportation and energy sectors. Both Afghanistan and Turkmenistan are part of the region and are welcome in the SCO, but they have not shown any interest in joining as either observers or full members.

The Chinese viewpoint on admitting new members, expressed during the SCO conference in Almaty, merits some attention. Chinese experts contended that the expansion of the SCO was inevitable, though, at the same time, they favoured a slow and cautious approach. Moreover, China would want the agreed-upon procedures to be observed. In this context, they raised some fundamental questions: Why should the SCO expand? What is the objective? And what does the SCO charter say about expansion? These, in their view, are some important questions that need to be discussed within the SCO framework before new members are admitted.

Russian experts, on the other hand, argued that augmenting financial resources is the main reason for expanding the SCO. At the moment, the organisation has a budget of some $4 million, which is not sufficient for financing various projects. China has promised $10 billion for projects but with the precondition that all the material used will have to be bought from China. The other reason for expanding the SCO, in the Russian view, is the need for reforming the organisation. The lack of consensus among SCO member states about the timing of inclusion of new members, final approval of the technical document on inclusion of new members and other related issues thus make the inclusion of new members at Astana unlikely. However, the technical document on the procedure for including new members is likely to get cleared at Astana.

India has been consistently articulating its desire to play much more meaning and constructive role in the SCO. In past few months, India has shown some interest in joining the SCO. Its current focus on building stronger partnership with this region indicates India's increasing interest and role which it is seeking to play in this region. India's inclusion as a full member of the SCO is backed by Russia and the Central Asian countries. In June 2010, Alexander M. Kadakin, stated: "Our position has all along been that we want India as a full-fledged member of the SCO."[7]

During a SCO conference in Almaty on February 22-23, 2011, Russian participants again reiterated their support for India's inclusion as a full member at the Astana summit. India is yet to formally apply for full membership. Before New Delhi formally does so, it must evaluate the advantages and challenges it may face as a full member.

Advantages

The first and the foremost advantage of joining the SCO as full member will provide India greater visibility in the affairs of the Eurasian region. In addition it will also provide a forum where it can constructively engage both China and Pakistan in regional context. Most importantly, cooperation in the three crucial areas –energy, transportation and terrorism can be facilitated through the SCO mechanism.

Energy

Some of the SCO member countries have energy resources (CARs, Russia and Iran) while others (China, Pakistan, Iran and Afghanistan) are transit countries for the supply of these resources. Therefore, energy cooperation remains an important issue for the SCO member countries. However, progress in the area of setting up energy club has not achieved much success. There is a difference of opinion on the issue of how to cooperate with each other within the SCO framework. While some members want creation of energy club, others emphasise on formulating an SCO energy strategy. Some of the members are also of the opinion that before formulating a regional energy strategy there is a need for the formulation of national energy strategy. However, as heads of States want to focus on energy issue there is a possibility that in the long run, SCO will be able to formulate a common energy strategy, which would be acceptable to all member states. It is in this sector that India needs to focus on its cooperation with all the SCO member states. The forward movement on the Turkmenistan-Afghanistan-Pakistan-India pipeline is a positive development. On December 11, 2010 India joined Turkmenistan, Afghanistan and Pakistan to sign a framework agreement to build TAPI pipeline. India and Pakistan will each get 33bcm of gas annually. The positive aspect of this pipeline is that it has the support of the Asian Development Bank (ADB) and the U.S. In fact, President Dimitry Medvedev has recently said that Russia will cooperate in the TAPI project. In October 2010 the Russian Deputy Prime Minister had also stated that Gazporam, the Russian company might participate in a consortium to build the TAPI pipeline. India has suggested that Gazporam join as one of the suppliers along with Azerbaijan, Kazakhstan and Uzbekistan. [8] The ADB has been making efforts to advance this project. The Penspen Company has prepared the project's feasibility report. Earlier the Head of Eni, Paolo Scaroni had signaled the desire to transport gas from Turkmenistan, Kazakhstan and Iran to Pakistan, India and China.[9] Future prospects for cooperation in energy sector under the mechanism of SCO can bring both consumers and producers together. The major consumers and producers of energy form part of the SCO.

Trade and Transport

One of the prerequisites to strengthen India's future relations with CARs is to impove the connectivity with this region. Lack of direct land route access to CARs has been the major impediment in expanding India's economic and trade ties with the Central Asian region. India wants Central Asia to be part of an extended trade network through north-south corridor. The SCO mechanism can be of great help to India and entire region if common strategy to build corridors can be worked out within SCO framework. In this context, President Islam Karimov called on the SCO countries to start joint project to build and reconstruct motorways and railroads and also to set up modern means of communication during the June 2010 SCO summit. [10]

Under the SCO framework, regional initiatives to connect the land - locked region of Central Asia will provide lot of opportunities both to the CARs and the countries neighbouring it. The construction of new corridors and revival of old routes through China to India would open the Central

Asian region to the world market, offering new prospects of economic cooperation and political stability. Integrating Central Asia with South and Southeast Asia through large- scale infrastructure development could ensure widespread economic growth for several years for this region. These routes in the past have worked as bridges amongst nations. The 'New Silk Route' under the SCO frame work can bring in economic prosperity and work as a confidence building measure amongst involved countries. India can benefit as a member country of the SCO if such large-scale transportation network are built within the framework of the SCO. India-Russia-China are already cooperating under this trilateral mechanism and India's entry into SCO will provide more opportunities to all three Asian powers to work together to enhance economic cooperation in the entire region of Central-South and West Asia.

Terrorism and Narcotics

Terrorism still remains the serious menace in the south and Central Asian region. It is expanding and becoming more international in nature. Today, international terrorist organisations are recruiting people from all over world to carry out terrorist activities. In addition, terrorism is also used as a tool/ method of interference in the internal affairs of another country. The main objective of the SCO is to counter these threats and challenges in the region. Given the size and nature of these challenges multilateral cooperation is the only way to address these threats. Integrated approach is required to deal with these challenges.

In this respect, SCO can provide an effective mechanism for all the regional countries to counter this menace through collective effort. While fighting terrorism India, CARs, China and Russia have much to offer to each other within the framework of SCO. China wants to address the problem of Eastern Turkistan terrorist groups, Russia wants to control the Chechen terrorist activities within Russia and India wants to control the activities of the extremist groups operating in Jammu and Kashmir region. The Central Asian States want to contain the extremist groups operating in the region.

Anti-terrorist centre in Tashkent can be an effective mechanism to address these concerns. Pakistan has also expressed its interest in 'optimal participation' in the SCO framework for greater economic integration, including customs cooperation, energy development, transport facilitation and investment promotion.[11] Islamabad is also keen to be associated with SCO's regional counter-terrorism structure (RCTS) and has suggested cooperation between the ECO and SCO in this regard. It has also endorsed the Russian and Chinese role 'in shaping a regional consensus on stabilising the Afghanistan situation'.[12] India at bilateral level has been addressing this issue with CARs and Russia. The threat emanating from Af-Pak region and increasing violence in Afghanistan is area of concern for all the SCO member states. In past three years the SCO seems to be providing greater attention to the Afghanistan issue. In future, after US-NATO exit the SCO may have to take more responsibility. In such a situation India as a full member will be able to address its concerns in Afghanistan. India's External Affairs Minister S.M. Krishna acknowledged the SCO's role in Afghanistan. He stated that "the SCO is uniquely fitted to provide positive contributions to the global discourse on Afghanistan. SCO can certainly add a critical regional perspective and play a constructive role in ensuring a peaceful and stable Afghanistan".[13] He also pointed out that India is ready to cooperate fully with the Regional Anti-Terrorism Structure (RATA) of SCO for exchanging information and working out a common strategy for combating terrorism.

Related to the issue of terrorism is the issue of Drug Trafficking and small arms proliferations. This is a major problem area faced by all the SCO member states. The Secretary General of the SCO stated during the recent Conference on the SCO in Almaty in February 2011 that the Anti-drug strategy of 2011-2017 of the SCO would be further intensified during upcoming Astana Summit. India has been working closely at bilateral level with Russia and CARs to address these issues. Now it has started cooperating with China as well. On January 15, 2006 the National Narcotics Control Commission and the Narcotics Control Bureau of the Ministry of Public Security of China   and the Narcotics Control Bureau of the Ministry of Home Affairs of India held the first bilateral meeting on drug   control cooperation in New Delhi.[14] Given India's experience to deal with these problems its active involvement under the SCO mechanism has much to contribute. As a full member India will be able to address these issues in much more effective ways under the regional framework. Irrespective of the might and capacity of the country, it is not possible for a single country to address the security challenges on its own therefore regional and international cooperation is required.

Challenges

If India joins the SCO, India will have to face the challenge of playing second fiddle to China and Russia, which have been the leaders since the SCO's inception. Moreover, given China's domination of the SCO, India's ability to assert itself will be minimal. India will also have to contend with China's use of the SCO for enhancing its own role not only in the Eurasian region but also in Southern Asia. In return for granting India full membership in the SCO, China may seek full membership in SAARC. What are the implications of China's entry into SAARC? Under these circumstances, India will have to analyse the implication of China's entry into SAARC and Pakistan's membership in SCO as full member state. It is important to note that the SCO Declaration of 2009 welcomed the end of an internal military conflict in Sri Lanka and expressed the hope for "establishing firm peace, strengthening security and stability in the country on the basis of ensuring its state sovereignty and territorial integrity, guaranteeing the right of all ethnic and religious groups." Sri Lanka's inclusion as a dialogue partner should be viewed against the background of China's increasing defence and strategic cooperation with Colombo with an aim of bringing it into its strategic fold.

Moreover, India will have to deal with the China-Pakistan nexus in the SCO, especially given the complementarity in Chinese and Pakistani interests in the Central Asian Republics China has always supported Pakistan's case in the SCO. An important question here that needs closer scrutiny is what does it mean for Pakistan to get this observer status in SCO and how it can use this forum to further its interests in the region if it is offered the full membership pushed by China? Islamabad's design to use this forum in its favour on the Kashmir issue needs consideration.

Pakistan is very keen and hoping to become a full-fledged member of the SCO. In this context Kazakh President Nursultan Nazarbayev also acknowledged that "the day when Pakistan becomes a full-fledged member is not far off." Within Pakistan, some analysts are of the opinion that Pakistan will have to play a pro-active role in the SCO framework in order to meet the new challenges and benefit from the new opportunities. They also believe that since the SCO has extensive experience in resolving boundary disputes, India and Pakistan as member-states can utilise this framework for settling bilateral border issues. Besides, SCO membership is also viewed as providing Pakistan an opportunity to expand its defence and security relations with Russia, as well as expanding the operational area of Pakistan's security and economic considerations. These perceptions on SCO and its utility for Pakistan should be seen in the light of Islamabad's anti-India rhetoric and its effort to balance India.

Both Pakistan and China are working on providing connectivity to Central Asia. Pakistan has offered to lay pipelines to enable China to procure gas and oil through Iran and the CARs. Both will soon undertake up gradation of the Karakoram highway to convert it into an all-weather corridor to facilitate bilateral trade. The importance of Gwadar and its use in times of any major conflict cannot be ruled out in future. It is also argued by strategists in Pakistan that the Gwadar Port may ultimately help the CARs to actively participate as ECO members and help open trade channels through Pakistan and can also go a long way in strengthening Pakistan's position in the region vis-à-vis India. To improve politico-economic ties with the Central Asian region, the creation of new organisation comprising Pakistan, Afghanistan, China, Iran and the five Central Asian states has been articulated in some Pakistani writings. It is believed that such an arrangement will effectively foreclose the possibility of "Indian design to isolate and encircle Pakistan in the region".

Today, India-Russia relations also need to be viewed in the light of India's increasing ties with the U.S and its increasing diversification of acquiring arms from West and Israel. At the same time, China's increasing economic cooperation with Russia and its investment in Russia's energy sector makes China an important strategic partner of Russia. Under these circumstances while Russia may try to balance China it would not like to annoy/confront China. While Central Asian countries are interested in India joining as full members but at the same time on some occasions they have expressed their concerns about Indo-Pak rivalry becoming part of the SCO. These are some of the complex issues which will have to be taken into considerations.

Conclusion

While there are many advantages for India in joining the SCO, it also poses many challenges. The success of India's engagement with the SCO will depend on how it is able to convert these challenges into opportunities. Moreover, India will have to pursue an active diplomacy with each member of the SCO to ensure smooth entry as full-member in the organisation. Given the uncertainties about the inclusion of new members and the lack of consensus among member states, India must proceed cautiously on the issue seeking full membership. It should wait till the final technical document on admitting new members is adopted. In the meantime, India must reenergize its efforts as an observer state to cement ties and engage with other members on issues relating to energy, connectivity and terrorism, drug trafficking and instability in Afghanistan. Given the current nature and functioning of the SCO, India needs to utilize its observer status in much more effective manner and boost its cooperation at bilateral level with the member states, particularly with Central Asian countries, Russia, China and Iran. All these countries have commonality of interests in Afghanistan. India should try and use the side room politics during the SCO meetings to shape the thinking of these friendly countries in favour of its interests.

Endnotes

1 Joshua Kucera, " Is the U.S. Warming to the Shanghai Cooperation Organisation", at http;//www.eurasianet.org/node/6311511 accessed on April 25,2011.

2 Meena Singh Roy, "Dynamics of Expanding the SCO", at http://www.idsa.in/idsacomments/DynamicsofExpandingtheSCO_msroy_0404

3 Oksana Antonenko, The EU should not ignore the Shanghai Co-operation Organisation, Policy Brief, London, Centre for European Reform, May 2007, at www.cer.org.UK

4 At present the SCO and UNESCAP are actively cooperating in the fields of economy,trade,transportation and communications, energy, environmental protection and sustainable development and use of information technology. "SCO and UNESCAP Secretariats conclude Memorandum of Understanding", at http://www.sectsco.org/html/01988.html.

5 Based on author's interactions with experts in Almaty and Bishkek during February 22nd to 3rd March 2011.

6 "SCO Heads of State Council meets in Tashkent", at http://www.sectsco.org/EN/show.asp?id=218 " Document on admitting new member to Shanghai bloc approved in Uzbek capital", Interfax news agency, Moscow in BBC Monitoring Global Newsline – Central Asia Political, June, 12, 2010, at http://www.monitor.bbc.co.uk

7 Sarwar Kashani "India has right to join SCO, not Pakistan: Russian envoy", at http://www.thaindia.com/newsportal/uncategorized/india-has-right-to-join-sco-not-pakistan-russian-envoy-interview_100377714.html

8 "Russia to back TAPI gas pipeline project in Central Asia", The Times of Central Asia, vol13no.4(653), January27,2011, pp.2; Atul Aneja, "India and Afghanistan:The way forward", The Hindu, January4,2011, pp.12;

9 "President: Turkmenistan remains interested in building gas pipeline to building gas pipeline to India through Afghanistan", at http://www.timesca.comindex.php? option=com_ content&task=view&id=208800& Itemid=11 (accessed on 6 March 2010)

10 "Uzbek leaders urges joint road projects among Shanghai bloc members",Interfax news agency, Moscow in BBC Monitoring Global Newsline –Central Asia Political, June, 12, 2010, at http://www.monitor.bbc.co.uk

11 Pakistan Foreign Minister Shah Mahmood Quereshi said this at the Moscow conference.

12 'Pakistan Committed to Afghanistan's Stabilization – Minister', BBC Monitoring Global Newsline – Former Soviet Union Political, March 28, 2009, at http://www.monitor.bbc.co.uk (Accessed March 30, 2009).

13 Remakes by EAM at the plenary session of Tashkent Summit of SCO, at http://www.mea.gov.in/speech/2010/06/11ss02.htm

14 Ministry of Foreign Affairs of the PRC, January 17, 2006.

INDIA-CENTRAL ASIA DEFENCE AND SECURITY COOPERATION: RETROSPECT AND PROSPECTS

Vinod Anand

Strategic environment around India is in a state of flux. This is particularly so in the Af-Pak region where the forces of radicalism, extremism and terrorism are gaining ascendancy. Worsening situation in Afghanistan and the re-emergence of Taliban has created security concerns for India and Central Asian Republics. In the late 90s when Taliban rose to the peak of power in Afghanistan it provided safe heavens to terror groups like Islamic Movement of Uzbekistan from Central Asia. Pakistan's ISI also used this opportunity to create training camps for so called jihad against India. Not only Pakistan was able to realize its concept of strategic depth in Afghanistan it sought to extend this concept to Central Asia by exporting fundamentalism and radical ideologies. In the aftermath of September 2001 attacks the US and its allies were able to defeat the Taliban with the help of Northern Alliance. India had extended help to Northern Alliance and had established some defence facilities in Tajikistan. From Indian perspective a strong defence and security relationship with Tajikistan, Uzbekistan and Turkmenistan is necessary as these countries are Afghanistan's neighbours. Similarly Kazakhstan and Kyrgyzstan are very important because not only they are contiguous to China but also because of secular Islamic majority nations. Further, fundamentalism and extremism emanating from Ferghana Valley shared by most of the Central Asian nations can affect all the secular nations in the neighbourhood.

With the United States expected to pull-out from Afghanistan in July 2011, India's linkages to the neighbors of Afghanistan i.e. Iran and Central

Asian nations become vital. As part of strengthening defence and security relationship the Indian Army Chief General V.K. Singh paid a four-day visit to Tajikistan in November 2010. According to an official statement, "Gen Singh's visit will further cement our defence relationship with a key friendly country in our extended neighborhood and provide an impetus to our defence cooperation road-map in Central Asia."

Central Asia is considered to be India's extended strategic neighbourhood as pronounced by Annual reports of India's Ministry of Defence. Discovery of hydro carbons and other natural resources has enhanced the strategic importance of Central Asian countries. In addition there are shared historical, civilisational and cultural links between India and Central Asians. While economic relationship is of immense significance and India and CARs have been endeavouring to strengthen it since the new states were created in 90s after the demise of the Soviet Union, the defence and security relationship has assumed added importance due to a number of contextual factors.

Central Asian Republics and India share the goals of anti-terrorism, security and stability in Central Asia and Afghanistan along with the curtailment of drug trafficking in the region. India has been cooperating on the issues of security both at bilateral and multilateral levels. It has Joint Working Group (JWG) on Combating International Terrorism with Uzbekistan; a JWG with Tajikistan on counter terrorism; and a JWG on international terrorism and other types of crimes with Kyrgyzstan. These JWGs have been having regular meetings to address threats arising from instability and fundamentalism in the region. At multilateral level India, as an observer, has been supporting the objectives of Shanghai Cooperation Organisation (SCO), which seek to ensure stability in the region, combat terrorism and extremist view points and is keen to play constructive and active role in SCO. India is also a member of Conference on Interaction and Confidence Building Measures in Asia (CICA) – a Kazakh sponsored initiative of eighteen Asian nations that includes CARs (less Turkmenistan). Many member states seem to view CICA as a useful instrument to pursue bilateral relations with individual states.

The defence services of CARs seek India's assistance in training their personnel in counter infiltration, counter terrorism, mountain warfare, coastal defence, deep sea diving, satellite imagery, Special Forces operations and signal intelligence. It is possible that India may become full member of the Shanghai Cooperation Organisation during its summit in June this year. SCO's Regional Anti-Terrorism Structure (RATS), established in Tashkent in 2004, provides a mechanism for intelligence sharing in narco-terrorism and proliferation of fissile material. Indian involvement in RATS is likely to lead to unprecedented interaction between the security forces of India and Central Asia.

So far there has been limited engagement in the sphere of defence cooperation between India and CAR. The key components of Indo-CAR defence relationship has been in the areas of intelligence sharing, training and assistance, servicing and upgrading of military hardware and import of transport aircraft from Uzbekistan. It needs to be remembered that in 2001 India had established a hospital in Tajikistan to treat anti-Taliban Northern Alliance fighters. India has also constructed an airfield at Ayni, northwest of its capital Dushanbe. Presently, India has a minor military presence in Tajikistan at the Ayni Airbase which stations nearly 150 Indian military personnel and an Air Force detachment of pilots and support staff for Mi-17 helicopters.

India has also extended assistance for the infrastructure requirements of the Military Training College in Dushanbe. During a visit to India, Tajik President Rakhmon observed: *'We are cooperating well in the field of defence training. We have agreed to institutionalize contact between our armed forces in specialised areas.'* Indian army has established a training team in Tajikistan for imparting English language training to military personnel. India is also in the process of setting up English-cum-IT labs and deployment of army training teams in Kazakhstan and Kyrgyzstan. Further, officers from all CARs (less Turkmenistan) have been attending military courses at India's premier military institutions.

India has purchased Uzbek-manufactured six IL-78 air-to-air refueller aircraft along with an agreement for repair of Indian transport aircraft at

Tashkent. Troops from Uzbekistan have also trained and exercised in counter-terrorism conducted at India's Counter-insurgency Warfare School.

Indian Navy has been in business with Kazakhstan and Kyrgyzstan for acquiring spares for thermal and electrical torpedoes. There is a degree of collaboration with Kazakhstan on research and development of underwater naval armaments. The torpedo testing facility at Issy Kul Lake (Kyrgyzstan) is of immense interest to DRDO for the indigenous torpedo programme.

The Kazakh Chief of Naval Staff, the Chief of Air Staff and the Chairman of the Chiefs of Staff Committee have visited India in 2008, 2009 and 2010 respectively to attend the Defence Expo and Aero India Expo. There have also been expressions of interest by both sides on setting up of joint ventures in the field of defence production. As of now the cooperation is mainly centered on purchasing of spare parts of torpedoes for Indian Navy. There are many Kazakh companies dealing with naval equipment and weapons who could supply spares of Russian origin equipment to India. For instance, JSC Kirov Mashzhavod has not only supplied spares for torpedoes but has also collaborated in research for joint development of a modern torpedo. The Defence Industrial Complex's another company JSC Ziktso produces all types of naval mines and RFI for supply of mines has been received from Indian Navy. Another Kazakh company JSC Gidropribor looks into R & D for naval armaments especially in the area of underwater remotely operated vehicles. There is a facility for overhaul of T-72 tanks and BMP-2s.

Military training for CAR armed forces mainly comprise training of officers under ITEC courses in various military institutions in India and training in UN related courses at Centre for UN Peacekeeping in New Delhi (CUNPK). English cum IT laboratory was established on gratis basis based on Kazakhstan's request at the Ministry of Defence, Astana in March 2007.

An Indo-kazakh joint Army Mountaineering Expedition to Mt Nun (Ladakh) was conducted in September, 2006. Six Kazakh Armed Forces personnel participated in the expedition. A joint Indo – Kazakh Army Mountaineering Team had successfully climbed Marble Wall peak in

Kazakhstan in September 2009. Joint mountaineering expedition between the two countries has been planned for Khan Tengri Peak in Kazakhstan in 2011. A joint vehicle expedition from Iran through Central Asia was planned in 2008. The proposal however did not fructify and the vehicle expedition is now being planned in 2011.

The officers from Kazakhstan, Kyrgyzstan, Uzbekistan and Tajikistan attend courses at NDC, DSSC, UN Training Centre, NDA, IMA, AEC College, HAWS and CIJW. Many cadets come from several countries to get trained in these Academies. CARs need to be encouraged to send their military officers to the NDA & IMA and other institutions. Such training would strengthen mil-to-mil relationship which is an essential part of defence diplomacy.

There are enough possibilities of cooperation in defence sphere since India's military hardware is of Soviet/Russian origin. Defence co-operation includes training of military personnel, joint exercises and purchase of military hardware. Kazakhstan also co-operated in India's space programme by allowing the launch of Indian satellite from its territory (Baikanour cosmodrome operated by Russia). Vacancies for Air force pilots to train in Indian Air force training establishments have also been allotted.

For the way ahead the following is recommended:-

(a) There is a need to sign a formal Defence Cooperation Agreement with Kazakhstan, Tajikistan, Kyrgyzstan and may be even Uzbekistan. Turkmenistan may be reluctant to do so, but at least a Defence Attaché needs to be posted there. Such steps would enable enhancement of contacts and commencement of military to military cooperation.

(b) Establishment of a joint working group with CARs on military to military cooperation similar to that of the Joint Working Group on Military –Technical Cooperation/JWG on counter terrorism is recommended. This would provide a structural basis for bilateral defence cooperation and enable identification of areas of mutual interest.

(e) There is a requirement of institutionalizing regular high level contacts to enhance defence cooperation. Regular bilateral defence and security dialogue could be institutionalised.

(f) There is a need to evolve an annual plan for military training as well as for military to military cooperation. Areas of Military to Military Cooperation need to be extended to the field of Counter Terrorism, Mountain Warfare, Special Forces Training and UN Peace Keeping Operations. Joint exercises could be initially commenced at Platoon level and as the experience is gained the levels could be raised company and higher levels in counter terrorism, Special Forces operations and mountain warfare.

(g) Joint production of weapons and equipment like it has been done with Russia in the case of Brahmos need to be undertaken.

(h) At the national level the possibility of establishing links between the National Security Secretariat of India and the National Security Council of CARs could be considered. Mutual visits by NSAs should be planned.

(i) Exchanges between the Intelligence agencies of the Central Asian countries especially on counter-terrorism and drug trafficking and other mutually acceptable subjects need to be enhanced. Regular meetings of the JWG on Counter –Terrorism needs to take place.

(j) Another area which the CARs can exploit is the rich experience of India's para-military forces by fostering cooperation between Border Guards – BSF/ITBP and the Central Asian border guarding forces.

Conclusion

Indo-CARs defence cooperation in both military technical field and in military to military area has vast potential. Existing cooperation needs to be enlarged to include more areas based on mutual benefits. At global and regional levels terrorism is becoming an ever expanding scourge which needs to be eliminated. Further, Indian and some of the Central Asian armed forces have contributed to peace keeping and have taken part in Special Forces operations and therefore can cooperate in this field to share each other's experience. Armed forces of CARs and India are rapidly modernising and there is enough potential to cooperate in the field of defence industrial production and establishment of joint ventures. Last but not the least is that there is more than adequate political will on both the sides to enhance defence cooperation in addition to cooperative endeavours in many other areas.

INDIA- CENTRAL ASIA ENGAGEMENT AND THE WAY FORWARD

Amb. Satish Chandra

Notwithstanding India's age old, cultural, commercial and political links with the Central Asian region its current relationship lacks content and depth as it is far below its actual potential. For instance, India's trade with all the Central Asian Republics (CARs) is less than $0.5 billion, as compared to China's trade of $26 billion; Russia's trade of about $20 billion; Iran and Turkey's trade of about $4 billion each and US trade of $2.7 billion. Poor connectivity is a major factor for India's minimal trade with CARs. The problem of land connectivity arises due to Pakistan's obduracy and absence of effective alternate routes. Besides, India's air connectivity with the entire CARs is also grossly inadequate with a total of only 18 flights per week.

The need for upgraded ties with the CAR's has both economic and politico-strategic impulses. It is not in India's interest to ignore a region with an area of 4 million sq kms, enormous hydrocarbon and mineral resources and a home to a very talented people numbering about 60 million. The compelling requirement of the CARs to upgrade their and develop their human resources provide India with enormous opportunities to intensify its links with each of these countries. The politico-strategic impulses arise from the fact that this region is in India's extended neighbourhood and whatever happens there is likely to affect it. Any increase of terrorism, fundamentalism and instability in the area cannot leave India, in the medium term atleast, unaffected.

There is a Great Game being played in Central Asian region and the major players are Russia, China and USA. Some regional countries also have ambitions of extending their influence in the region. The outcome of this new Great Game will also inevitably impact India. The Central Asian Republics have so far quite smartly balanced the struggle for influence in the area by the major players. For instance, in one of the CARs, a major power had an air base and the concerned CAR as a balancing exercise allowed another power to establish an air base in another part of the country. This sort of balancing is an ongoing process. But on the other hand, the CARs are quite vulnerable to the machinations of the major power players. This vulnerability could perhaps be somewhat reduced if the CARs had a strong institutionalised co-operative arrangement amongst themselves as do the ASEAN countries. Because of this co-operative arrangement, the ASEAN countries are able to set the tone for the manner of involvement for those who wish to be power players in the area. The non-conventional security threats emanating from religious extremism, terrorism, climate change, water etc. showed the necessity for co-operation amongst the CARs. Moreover, the issue of Afghanistan is significant, because any fall out from unstable Afghanistan would first affect the CARs. Therefore, the CARs need to work towards helping in re-establishment of stability in Afghanistan. In order to do so they need to recognize that the source of instability is Pakistan and they should adopt policies geared to addressing this.

The advantages of a greater Indian involvement in the region lies in terms of its past ties with these countries, its developmental model, its secular and democratic form of government, and its positive role in Afghanistan etc. In addition, unlike many other countries, India brings a non-threatening approach to its co-operative programmes in the area. Its major interest is to promote economic development and work along with the CARs for peace and stability. It is high time that India undertakes steps to enhance its ties with the CARs. India's 'Look West' policy geared to enhance economic ties with the Gulf and the Middle East in the 70's and 80's, its 'Look East' policy aimed at developing linkages with South East Asia dates to the 90's and the first decade of the 21st century. In this context, let it be said that India's 'Look North' policy is aimed at strengthening ties with CARs dates to the period 2010-2020.

What can and what should India do in specific terms to enhance its links with Central Asia? One of them is suggested by our Director that some of the VIF researchers should touch base with the CAR missions in Delhi and pen down concrete ideas for enhanced co-operation. Off-hand, the following are some of the things that could be done:

- India should do everything that is possible to promote peace and stability in Afghanistan as indeed it has been doing in the past. India not only should continue the economic co-operation programmes but also make concerted efforts to strengthen the Afghan army and build up its capabilities. As the US plans to scale down its forces over the next two-three years, there exists enormous possibilities in terms of training the Afghan forces. Moreover, India should urge Afghanistan to pressure Pakistan to revise APTTA so that Indian goods can transit to that country through Pakistan. This would help provide land connectivity to India, at least, to promote Afghan economic development. In this context, it would also be useful if the CARs could in their own interest urge Pakistan to provide land connectivity for India to Central Asia.

- The need for alternative routes necessitates that India along with the CARs push for early activisation of the North-South corridor, search for such an alternate route arises from the fact that Pakistan is unlikely to provide land connectivity to India.

- India should examine the possibility of sharply increasing air connectivity with the CARs.

- Although much has been spoken about TAPI and great hopes placed on it, India's problem with the project is the security of supply. In a conflict situation or in state of heightened tension, Pakistan is likely to stop supplies to India.

- Apart from its obvious interest in the mineral and hydrocarbon resources of the region, which it should seek to import, India should participate in the development of infrastructure in the region, particularly, the railroads in which India has considerable expertise and hydropower projects both mini as well as big if found feasible. India has undertaken such mini hydel projects in Afghanistan over the decades and this is an important area of co-operation with CARs.

- Enormous co-operation possibilities also exist in the areas which require minimal land or sea connectivity and movement of heavy equipment such as IT, pharmaceuticals, and management contracts. In man power, India offers great possibilities for co-operation. Human resource development is an Indian specialty and its high-tech programmes can be enhanced in areas of mutual interest.

- It may also be worthwhile to consider setting up world class institutes of technology and management as well as hospitals patterned on AIIMS in the CARs. In such areas connectivity plays a minimal role.

- India should also consider earmarking a sizable sum annually for investment in India-CAR projects.

- Finally, India should consider enhancement of high-level visits to the CARs. Such visits will energise Indian linkages with CARs.

CENTRAL ASIAN REPUBLICS COUNTRY BRIEFS

Sanjay Kumar

UZBEKISTAN

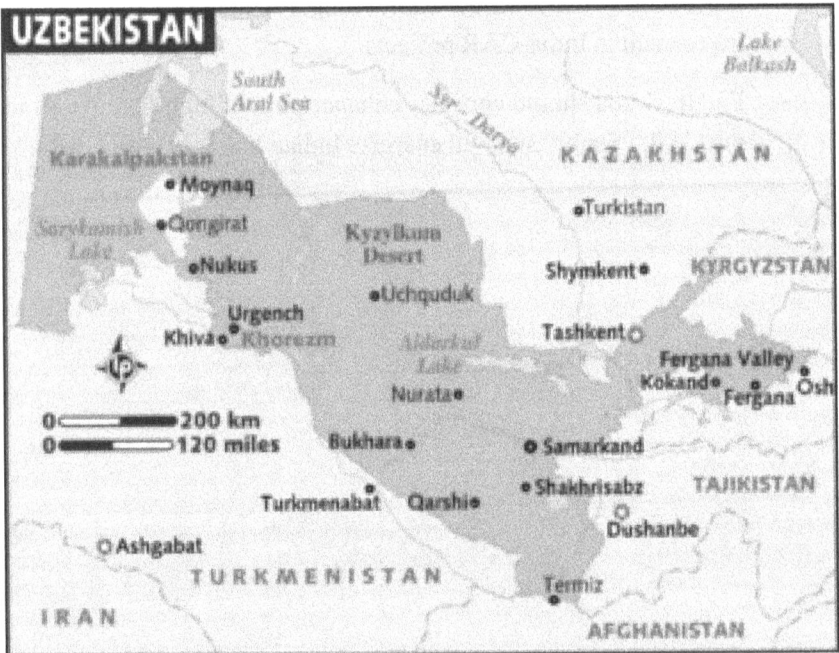

Source: lonelyplanet.com

General

Uzbekistan gained its independence in 1991 after more than a century of Russian rule - first as part of the Russian empire and then as a component of the Soviet Union. A landlocked country, Uzbekistan is positioned on the ancient Great Silk Road between Europe and Asia. It shares borders with Kazakhstan to the west and to the north, Kyrgyzstan and Tajikistan to the east, and Afghanistan and Turkmenistan to the south. Uzbekistan is the largest cotton producer in Central Asia; globally, it is the eighth largest natural gas producer and a major oil producing country. Uzbekistan's economy relies heavily on production of commodities such as cotton, gold, uranium, potassium, and natural gas. Post independence in 1991, Uzbekistan promised to evolve into a market economy. However, it continues to maintain rigid economic controls, which often repel foreign investors. The policy of gradual, strictly controlled transition has nevertheless produced beneficial results in the form of economic recovery since1995.

India - UzbekistanRelations

India and Uzbekistan have had shared historical and cultural ties even before the recognition of the later as an independent state in 1991. Prime Minister Jawaharlal Nehru accompanied by Smt. Indira Gandhi visited Uzbekistan in 1955 and 1961. Following Pakistan's defeat in 1965 war between India and Pakistan, the instrument of peace between New Delhi and Islamabad was signed in the Uzbek capital Tashkent on 10 January 1966. Prime Minister Lal Bahadur Shastri who signed the historical peace accord with Pakistan on India's behalf died tragically in Tashkent. His name has been commemorated - a street and school have been named after him and there are both a statue and a bust in his memory in Tashkent.

Post-1991, Indo-Uzbek relations have been characterized by frequent exchange of high level visits between the leaders of the two countries. During the last visit by an Indian Prime Minister to Uzbekistan in 2006, Sh. Manmohan Singh, India's current Prime Minister, signed eight inter-governmental agreements in oil & gas, mining, agriculture, textiles and education sectors. Thirteen agreements were signed between India and Uzbekistan during the third state visit to India by Uzbekistan's President

Islam Karimov in 2005. India and Uzbekistan have so far signed 61 bilateral documents in the form of Agreements/MOUs/Treaties/Protocols/Work Plans etc. Uzbekistan has also supported India's candidature for the non-permanent seat of the UN Security Council for 2011-2012.

According to the Department of Commerce, Government of India, Uzbekistan and India notched up a total trade turn over of USD 84.00 million in 2009-10, with goods worth USD 29.97 million imported from Uzbekistan and USD 54.03 million worth export to that country. As per trade statistics, major items of India's exports to Uzbekistan include drugs, pharmaceuticals, machinery & instruments, metal products, paper & wood products, meat & preparations. Raw cotton and non-ferrous metals constitute the largest item of Indian imports from Uzbekistan. Other principal items of import are petroleum, hide and skin, pulses, raw silk and services.

India's Trade with Uzbekistan, 2005-10

(Value in US $, million)

Trade / Year	2005-06	2006-07	2007-08	2008-09	2009-10
Import from Uzbekistan	26.13	33.91	16.20	70.74	29.97
Export to Uzbekistan	24.44	29.69	40.32	45.53	54.03
Total Trade Turn Over	**50.57**	**63.60**	**56.52**	**116.27**	**84.00**

Source: GOI, Department of Commerce

India's assistance for the development of Uzbekistan has been crucial through past several years. Computerization of three Uzbek Post Offices was undertaken and completed by Ministry of External Affairs/

Telecommunications Consultants India Limited in May 2002. Total grant allocated for the project was USD 75,000. During his visit to Uzbekistan in 2006, Prime Minister Sh. Manmohan Singh inaugurated an IT Centre in Tashkent, named after Pandit Jawahar Lal Nehru, for which a grant of USD 700,000 had been provided by New Delhi through the Centre for Development of Advanced Computing (C-DAC). Three credit lines of US$ 10 million each have been extended to Uzbekistan. The third credit line remained unutilized and was closed in July 2004. A "Dollar Credit Line Agreement" was signed between National Bank for Foreign Economic Activity of Uzbekistan (NBU) and EXIM bank of India on 21st August, 2008 in Tashkent. The agreement envisages providing a Credit up to an aggregate sum of US$ 10,000,000 (Dollars tem million) by the EXIM Bank of India to NBU to facilitate purchase from India of eligible goods by buyers in Uzbekistan.

Defence cooperation is an important aspect of India-Uzbekistan relations. The Indian Air Force flies six IL-78 MKI air-to-air refuelling aircraft, manufactured by Tashkent Aircraft Production Corporation (TAPC), Uzbekistan. Indian aircraft are being regularly serviced at the Chekalov aircraft plant in Tashkent. During the visit of President Islam A Karimov to New Delhi in 2005, India and Uzbekistan reached an agreement to fight terrorism on a long-term and sustained basis. The pact on cooperation in military and military technical cooperation, signed between Defence Minister Pranab Mukherjee and his Uzbek counterpart Kadir, provided for exchange of expertise, development, production, repair of equipment, training and joint exercises.

Uzbekistan Airways operates three flights to and from Delhi and five flights to and from Amritsar a week on a code-sharing basis with Indian Airlines.

TAJIKISTAN

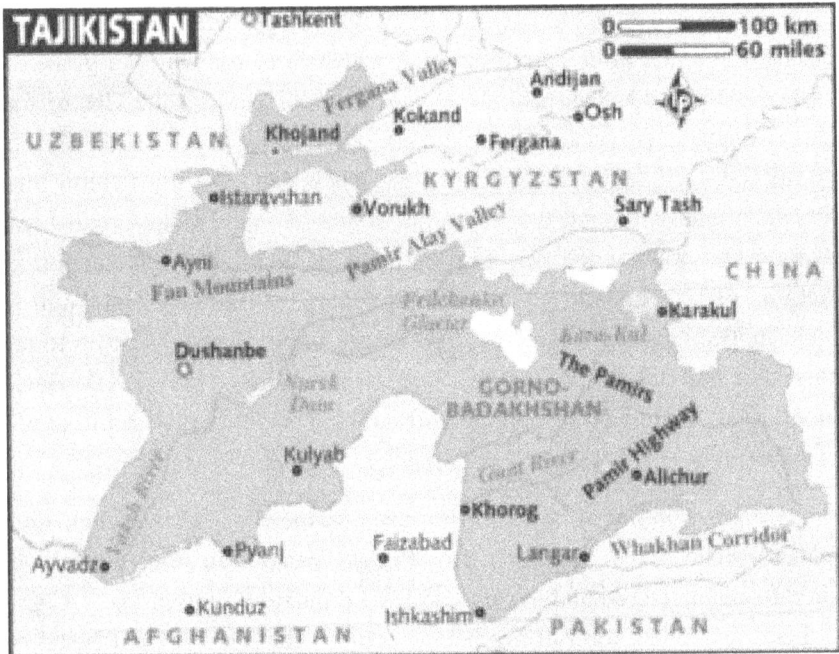

Source: lonelyplanet.com

General

Tajikistan is a mountainous landlocked country in Central Asia. Afghanistan borders it to the south, Uzbekistan to the west, Kyrgyzstan to the north, and People's Republic of China to the east. Tajikistan also lies adjacent to Pakistan's Chitral and the Gilgit-Baltistan region, separated by the narrow Wakhan Corridor. Most of Tajikistan's population belongs to the Persian-speaking Tajik ethnic group, who share language, culture and history with Afghanistan and Iran. Tajikistan is often referred to the category of countries having considerable deposits of precious metals and inexhaustible deposits of minerals used as construction and decoration materials such as marble, granite, volcanic tuff, limestone, and mineral springs. It is estimated that approximately 400 ore and other mineral deposits have been discovered, prospected and prepared for development in Tajikistan, of which 28 deposits are of gold with a general capacity amounting to about 429.3 tons. Tajikistan also takes the first place in the world for its hydropower resources (specific parameters) and according to the absolute parameters (300 billion kWt/h per year) – the eighth place. After independence from erstwhile Soviet Union in 1991, Tajikistan suffered from a devastating civil war which lasted from 1992 to 1997. Since the end of the war, newly established political stability and foreign aid have allowed the country's economy to grow. Trade in commodities such as cotton, aluminum and Uranium has contributed greatly to this steady improvement.

India - Tajikistan Relations

India opened its Embassy in Dushanbe in 1994 and Tajikistan opened its Consulate in Delhi in 2003, upgraded later to the status of a full fledged Embassy in 2006. Regular exchange of visits at the highest level has been taking place between the two countries ever since. President Pratibha Devisingh Patil paid a state visit to Tajikistan in September 2009 which enhanced bilateral relations. Prime Minister Vajpayee paid an official visit to Dushanbe in November 2003 and the Tajik President Rahmon visited India for the fourth time in August 2006. Further, there are regular interactions among various Ministries and Departments. Joint Working Groups and Inter Governmental Commissions on matters of mutual interest were constituted and they meet at regular intervals. India and Tajikistan share common perspectives on several international and regional issues.

Consequent to the announcements made during the visit of Tajikistan's President Rahmon to India in August 2006, Indian companies BHEL and NHPC have been engaged in the rehabilitation and modernization of the Varzob-1 Hydro Power Station (costing approx USD 17 million) in Tajikistan. Also, in response to an appeal made by President Rahmon for humanitarian assistance to overcome the crisis due to unprecedented harsh winter and shortages of power in Tajikistan during January-February 2008, India announced a grant of USD 2 million. (USD 1 million as cash assistance and USD 1 million in kind consisting of power cables generator and pump sets). In June 2009, USD 200,000 cash assistance was given by Govt. of India to overcome damages caused by heavy rains and floods in Tajikistan during

April-May 2009. After the flashfloods in Kulyab on 7 May 2010, the Government of India donated cash assistance of USD 200,000. After outbreak of Polio in Southwest Tajikistan, 2 million doses of oral polio vaccine were provided to Tajikistan by India. India's primary exports to Tajikistan include meat and meat products, pharmaceuticals, sugar, machinery and electrical items and while commodities imported by India from Tajikistan comprise mainly processed alumina.

India's Trade with Tajikistan, 2005-10

(Value in US $, million)

Trade / Year	2005-06	2006-07	2007-08	2008-09	2009-10
Import from Tajikistan	5.89	8.05	9.81	17.47	16.85
Export to Tajikistan	6.24	7.45	12.40	16.71	15.71
Total Trade Turn Over	12.13	15.40	22.21	33.18	31.56

Source: GOI, Department of Commerce

India is deeply interested in deepening defence cooperation with Tajikistan, the closest neighbour in Central Asia. Defence cooperation goes back to 2001 when Tajikistan Defence Minister Colonel General Sherali Khairullaev visited India, reciprocated by India's Defence Minister Shri George Fernandes' visit to Uzbekistan the next year. Defence cooperation however encompasses several areas including joint military exchanges. Indian and Tajik military personnel have conducted several joint exercises. Tajik military officers have been training regularly at India's National Defense Academy (NDA) at Khadakwasla since 1998. Besides offering military equipments including military jeeps and trucks and two Mi-8 helicopters, India also rebuilt and refurbished an air base at Ayni, outside the Tajik capital of Dushanbe.

Regular exchanges of cultural troupes between India and Tajikistan have been going on for past several years. Indian movies and songs are very popular in Tajikistan. The two countries signed a Cultural Exchange Programme (CEP) in 2006. Indian community in Tajikistan comprises of approximately 400 Indians, including nearly 300 students in the Dushanbe Medical College, and others in NGOs and other organizations.

East Air has started operating a weekly Dushanbe-Delhi flight since 15 February 2011.

KAZAKHSTAN

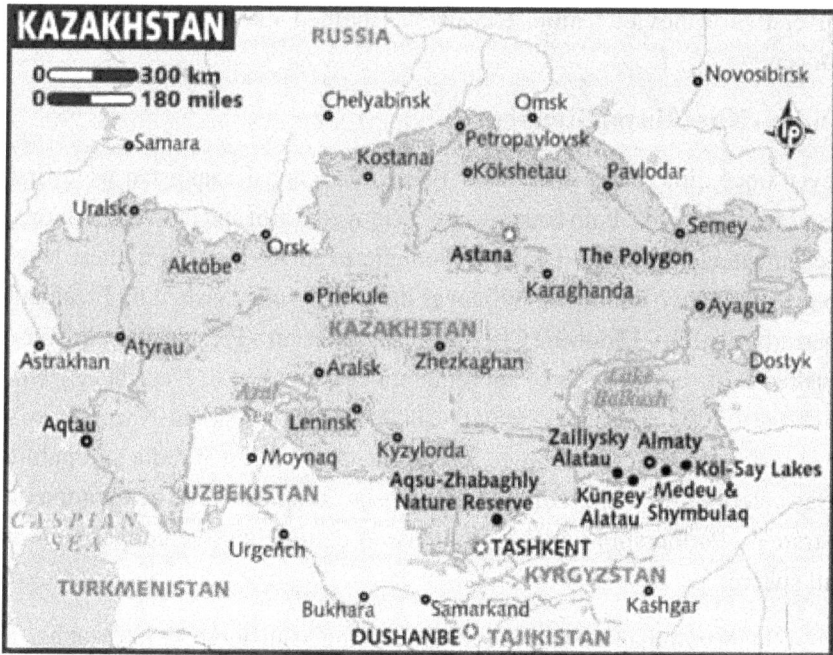

Source: lonelyplanet.com

General

The ninth largest country in the world area-wise, the Republic of Kazakhstan stretches over a vast expanse of northern and central Eurasia. Kazakhstan's territory is 2,727,300 sq km which is about 85 percent of India's territory but greater than the territory of Western Europe. While located mainly in Asia, a small portion of Kazakhstan lies in Europe. Kazakhstan borders with Russia, the People's Republic of China, and three other Central Asian countries - Kyrgyzstan, Turkmenistan, and Uzbekistan, and has a coastline on the Caspian Sea. The country has an abundant supply of accessible mineral and fossil fuel resources. Kazakhstan also has the second largest uranium, chromium, lead, and zinc reserves, the third largest manganese reserves, the fifth largest copper reserves, and ranks in the top ten for coal, iron, and gold. It is also an exporter of diamonds and potassium. A breakaway republic of erstwhile Soviet Union, Kazakhstan gained its independence on 25 December 1991.

India - Kazakhstan Relations

Ever since diplomatic relations between India and Kazakhstan were first established in 1992, both countries have enjoyed warm and friendly relations, accentuated further by regular diplomatic exchanges at the highest level between the two countries. India was the first country visited by President Nazarbayev in 1992 outside CIS region. Kazakhstan's President Nazarbayev visited India again on three subsequent occasions i.e. in December 1996, February 2002 and again January 2009. During President Nazarbayev's last visit to India in 2009, when he was the Chief Guest at India's Republic Day celebrations, both India and Kazakhstan adopted a joint declaration on Strategic Partnership which encompassed comprehensive cooperation in all spheres.

Sh. Narsimha Rao was India's first Prime Minister to visit Kazakhstan in 1993. This was followed by the visits of Vice President Sh. KR Narayanan in September 1996 and Prime Minister Sh. Atal Bihari Vajpayee in June 2002. Sh. Hamid Ansari, the current Vice President of India visited Kazakhstan from 6 to10 April 2008. During the visit of India's External Affairs Minister Shri S.M. Krishna to Kazakhstan from 11 to13 May 2010, a road-map delineating the major areas of cooperation with time frames was finalized and an agreement was also reached for cooperation in the fields of culture, arts, mass media and sports.

India and Kazakhstan actively cooperate under multilateral frameworks, including CICA, SCO and the UN organizations. Trade between India and Kazakhstan however do not match the existing potentials. Bilateral trade rose marginally from USD 290.71 million in 2009 to USD 291.45 million in 2010. Major commodities of export from India to Kazakhstan are tea, pharmaceuticals, medical equipments, machinery, tobacco, valves and consumer goods etc. Major items of import by India are asbestos, soft wheat, steel, aluminum, wool and raw hides. Prospects for cooperation in spheres of oil and gas, civil nuclear energy, uranium, agriculture, public health, information technology, education, culture and defence are promising. A fresh impetus to bilateral trade was added in January 2009, during President Nazarbayev's visit, with both countries agreeing to cooperate in the field of oil exploration and trade in uranium. A memorandum of understanding for cooperation in the field of space, extradition treaty and the protocol on the accession of Kazakhstan to WTO was also signed during this visit.

India's Trade with Kazakhstan, 2005-10

Trade / Year	2005-06	2006-07	2007-08	2008-09	2009-10
Import from Kazakhstan	90.86	83.18	111.99	131.68	136.54
Export to Kazakhstan	26.30	88.30	76.78	159.03	154.91
Total Trade Turn Over	117.16	171.48	188.77	290.71	291.45

Source: GOI, Department of Commerce

Indian Cultural Centre in Kazakhstan conducts classes in Yoga, Hindi and Kathak dances. India also trains specialists and scholars from Kazakhstan in various fields under ITEC program sponsored by Ministry of External Affairs and under the ICCR Scholarship programmes for international students. Since 1992 more than 700 specialists have undergone training under ITEC and more than 140 students have studied in India under ICCR programme.

India and Kazakhstan have an agreement on visa free entry for diplomatic and official passport holders. The first Bilateral Consular Consultations between India and Kazakhstan was held in Astana on 5-6 November 2009. There are about 2500 NRIs in the whole of Kazakhstan. This includes students studying medicine in Kazakhstan. Most of the NRIs are in the private sector and business (tea, pharmaceuticals etc). An India Association is in place, headquartered at Almaty, with branches in major cities of Kazakhstan.

KYRGYZSTAN

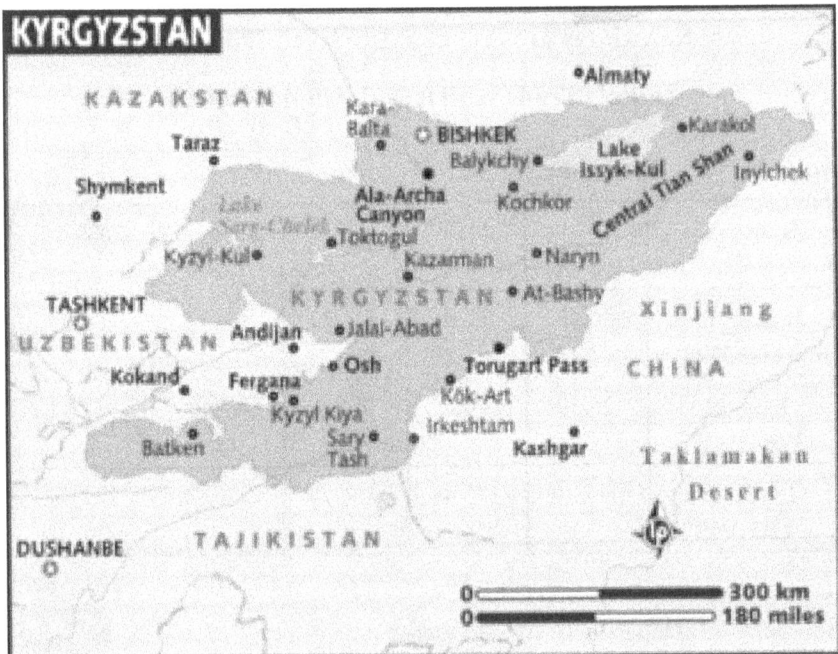

Source: lonelyplanet.com

General

Kyrgyzstan, a mountainous country – mountains constitute nearly 94 percent of its territory - located in the heart of Central Asia, sits at the heart of geo-political ambitions of several countries. It is home to Manas Air Base, a key transit point for US forces moving in and out of Afghanistan. A country of 5 million people, Kyrgyzstan's population comprises of 54 percent Kyrgyzs, 23 percent Russian and the remaining 23 percent other nationalities. About 700 Indian students study medicines in various medical institutions across the country. Kyrgyzstan shares borders with China to the south, Kazakhstan to the north, Uzbekistan to the west and Tajikistan to the south-west. The borders of the Republic of Kyrgyzstan generally follow natural boundaries - mountain ranges and rivers. Kyrgyzstan's total landmass is about the size of Switzerland, Belgium, the Netherlands, and Portugal combined. Kyrgyzstan has insignificant reserves of oil and gas and hence, it is generally dependent on imports to meet its energy requirements. The economy of Kyrgyzstan depends heavily on gold exports - mainly from output at the Kumtor gold mine. Other industrial exports include mercury, uranium, natural gas, and electricity.

India - Kyrgyztan Relations

Kyrgyzstan gained its independence from erstwhile Soviet Union on 31 August 1991. New Delhi was among the first to establish diplomatic relations with Kyrgyzstan in 1992; the resident Mission of India was set up in 1994. Relations between Kyrgyzstan and India have been traditionally warm and friendly, reinforced by several high-level visits. Important bilateral exchanges between the two countries include four visits to India by the former President Akaev: March 1992, April 1999, August 2002, and November 2003; other important visits from the Kyrgyz Republic to India included those of Mr. Apas Jumagulov, Prime Minister (May, 1997), Ms. Mira Jangavacheva, Vice-Prime Minister (March, 1997), Mr. I. A. Abdurazakov, State Secretary (April, 1997) etc. Lt. General I. Isakov, Kyrgyzstan's Defence Minister, visited India in November, 2005. From the Indian side, the late K.R. Narayanan and the late Krishna Kant, former Vice-Presidents, visited Kyrgyzstan in September 1996 and August 1999 respectively. Former PM, the late Narasimha Rao visited the Republic of Kyrgyzstan in September 1995. In 2003, two Indian cabinet Ministers, then EAM Shri Yashwant Sinha and then Raksha Mantri Shri George Fernandes, visited Bishkek in January and November respectively. Shri Murli S. Deora, Minister of Petroleum and Natural Gas led a delegation to Kyrgyzstan during SCO Summit on 15-16 August, 2007.

The Kyrgyz leaderships have been largely supportive of our stand on Kashmir and have welcomed the ongoing peace process. Kyrgyzstan also supports India's bid for permanent seat at UNSC and India's role in the Shanghai Cooperation Organization (SCO). Both countries share common concerns on threat of terrorism, extremism and drug–trafficking. Since the establishment of diplomatic relations in 1992, the two countries have signed several framework agreements, including on Culture, Trade and Economic Cooperation, Civil Aviation, Investment Promotion and Protection, Avoidance of Double Taxation, Consular Convention etc.

Trade turnover between Kyrgyzstan and India totaled USD 27.48 million in 2009-10, of which India's export to Kyrgyzstan contributed USD 26.84 million. Apparel and clothing (both knitted and crocheted as well as not-knitted and crocheted), leather goods, drugs, pharmaceuticals and fine chemicals, tea, transport equipments, machinery and instruments, electronic goods, residual engineering items are some of the important items in our export basket to Kyrgyzstan. Of these, apparel and clothing (knitted and crocheted as well as not-knitted and crocheted) constitute almost 45% of our total exports to Kyrgyzstan. Kyrgyz exports to India consist of Metalifers ores & metal scrap, professional instruments except electronics, leather, manufactures of metals, pulses, raw hides and skins etc.

India's Trade with Kyrgyzstan, 2005-10

(Value in USD, million)

Trade / Year	2005-06	2006-07	2007-08	2008-09	2009-10
Import from Kyrgyzstan	1.47	0.76	0.91	1.03	0.64
Export to Kyrgyzstan	28.09	37.08	31.52	22.92	26.84
Total Trade Turn Over	29.56	37.84	32.43	23.95	27.48

Source: GOI, Department of Commerce

Over the past two decades, India has contributed significantly to the development of Kyrgyzstan, offering both funds and technical assistance in setting up Information Technology development centers and potato processing plant. In 1995, India had extended USD 5 million in credit to Kyrgyzstan, most of which was later converted into grants. During former President Akaev's visit to India in November 2003, the Indian Prime Minister had announced a grant of US $ 2 million for setting up a mini hydro plant in Kyrgyzstan. Technical assistance under the Indian Technical and Economic Cooperation (ITEC) Program, particularly in terms of human resources development, is the cornerstone of India's economic involvement in Kyrgyzstan. Kyrgyzstan at present has been allotted 60 slots on an annual basis for civilian training under ITEC.

The Kyrgyz side has proposed to sign an agreement for cooperation in area of culture for the period from 2009-2011. The draft Agreement is presently under consideration by India. The Centre for Indian Studies set up in Osh State University in 1997 however has been useful in providing an exposure to Indian culture and civilization to academicians and intelligentsia in Kyrgyzstan.

There is no direct passenger flight between Delhi and Bishkek. The routes are Delhi-Tashkent-Bishkek and Delhi- Almaty by air and Almaty-Bishkek (By road).

TURKMENISTAN

Source: lonelyplanet.com

General

Turkmenistan, an independent neutral country in Central Asia, is located on the Eastern shore of the Caspian Sea. It borders Iran to the south, Afghanistan to the south and east, and Kazakhstan and Uzbekistan to the north. With Kara-Kum desert occupying eighty percent of the country's territory, Turkmenistan has an area of 488,100 sq km. Turkmenistan's population is estimated at 5,000,000, of which majority ethnic Turkmens are (85%); other sizeable minorities include Uzbeks (7%) and Russians (5%). Smaller minorities include Kazakhs, Azeris, Armenians, Ukrainians, Balochis, Koreans, and Tatars. An estimated eighty seven percent of the population practices Sunni Islam and eleven percent, Russian Orthodoxy. The literacy rate is ninety seven percent. Life expectancy is 68.3 years. Turkmenistan is rich in natural gas (estimated reserves of 20 trillion cubic meters) and oil (estimated reserves of 12 billion barrels). Other resources include coal, precious non-ferrous and rare metals, sulfur, gypsum, iodine, bromine, potassium and common salts, marble onyx, mineral waters. Turkmenistan was proclaimed as an Independent State in a nation-wide referendum on 27 October 1991 and the name adopted as Turkmenistan.

Turkmenistan produces cotton, wheat, rice, limited variety of vegetables and fruits but remains short of needs for its population. In view of continuous increase in domestic production of dairy products, butter, cheese and expansion of agro-food industry, there has been a remarkable reduction in Turkmenistan's imports of foodstuff. However, the country still depends on substantial import of various food items, viz., wheat-flour, rice, sugar, milk and milk products, fruits & vegetables, potatoes, etc. The economy of Turkmenistan grew by 9.2% in the year 2010.

India - Turkmenistan Relations

Turkmenistan and India enjoy close, friendly and historical ties. Turkman Gate was built in Delhi in 1650s. Being the richest country in natural gas in Central Asia, Turkmenistan is important for India's energy security. Four countries, viz., Turkmenistan, Afghanistan, Pakistan and India (TAPI countries) are working together on a gas pipeline project. On 11 December 2010, basic documents between the four countries were signed in Ashgabat in the presence of Presidents of Turkmenistan, Afghanistan and Pakistan and from India, Minister of Petroleum & Natural Gas, Shri Murli Deora. India enjoys a total trade turn over of USD 46.15 million with Turkmenistan, of which exports to Turkmenistan includes USD 36.15 million and imports from Turkmenistan includes USD 10 million. Exports from India to Turkmenistan comprise mainly electronic and electrical items, machinery, woven apparel and pharmaceuticals, frozen meat and tyres, while import from Turkmenistan comprise mainly raw cotton and inorganic chemicals.

India's Trade with Turkmenistan, 2005-10

(Value in US $, million)

Trade / Year	2005-06	2006-07	2007-08	2008-09	2009-10
Import from Turkmenistan	12.35	11.95	8.55	12.10	10.00
Export to Turkmenistan	18.33	33.99	36.09	41.40	36.15
Total Trade Turn Over	30.68	45.94	44.54	53.50	46.15

Source: GOI, Department of Commerce

Major visits from India to Turkmenistan includes: PM Shri P.V. Narasimha Rao, 19-21 September 1995; EAM Shri Jaswant Singh, May 1999; MOS (P&NG) Shri Dinsha Patel, 13-15 February 2006; MOS (EA) Shri E.Ahamed, 1-4 October 2006 & 14 February 2007; Minister of Water Resources Shri Saifuddin Soz, 23- 25 December 2006; Vice President Shri Hamid Ansari, 4-6 April 2008 ; EAM Shri S.M. Krishna, 18-19 September 2009; MOS (PK) Smt. Preneet Kaur, 8-9 February2010, MOS (P&NG) Shri Jitin Prasada, 19-20 September 2010; Minister (P&NG) Shri Murli Deora, 10-12 Dec.2010.

Among the high level visits to India from Turkmenistan include: President Saparmyrat Niyazov, 18-20 April 1992 & 25-26 February 1997; Deputy Foreign Minister Boris Shikhmuradov, 02-04 December 1992; Dy. Prime Minister & Foreign Minister, 18-20 April 1995, 07-08 April 1997 and April 2000; Dy. Prime Minister & Foreign Minister Rashid Meredov, 20-22 January 2008; President Gurbanguly Berdimuhamedov, 24-26 May 2010.

At present there are about 1,250 Indians nationals in Turkmenistan. Prominent among them are engineers (working in oil and gas industry), technocrats (working for Mitsubishi and a French construction company), businesspersons (in trading, pharmaceutical company), etc. Majority of Indian nationals in Turkmenistan are construction workers for a French construction company, Bouygues.

Turkmenistan Airlines has 8 flights a week to India – 2 flights to Delhi and 6 flights to Amritsar.

AFGHANISTAN

Source: lonelyplanet.com

Afghanistan, which is a landlocked and mountainous country, sits at the crossroads connecting the Middle East with Central Asia and the Indian subcontinent. It is bordered by Pakistan in the south and east, Iran in the west, Turkmenistan, Uzbekistan and Tajikistan in the north, and China in the far northeast.

India and Afghanistan historically have shared close cultural and political ties, and the complexity of their diplomatic history reflects this fact. India supported successive governments in Kabul until the rise of the Taliban in the 1990s, and was among the first non-Communist states to recognize the government installed by the Soviet Union after its 1989 invasion. But like most countries, India never recognized the Taliban's assumption of power in 1996 (only Saudi Arabia, Pakistan, and the United Arab Emirates recognized the Taliban regime). During the period in which Taliban ruled Afghanistan, India lent moral support to Northern Alliance, a rebel group that fought bitterly against Taliban. A hijacked Indian civilian plane was flown to Kandhar in southern Afghanistan in ....During the course of negotiations held for the release of hijacked passengers, the Taliban wanted their government be recognized by New Delhi in lieu for their support, a request India did not heed to. Following the 9/11 attacks and the U.S.-led war in Afghanistan that resulted, ties between India and Afghanistan grew strong once again. India has restored full diplomatic relations, and has provided hundreds of millions of dollars in aid for Afghanistan's reconstruction and development. Since 2001, India has offered $1.2 billion for Afghanistan's reconstruction, making it the largest regional donor to the country. India is also reconstructing a road in the remote southwestern Afghan province of Nimroz. The project is being carried out by state-owned Border Roads Organization.

Bilateral trade between India and Afghanistan has been on the rise, reaching $358 million for the fiscal year April 2007 to March 2008. India hopes its investment in the Iranian port at Chabahar will allow it to gain trading access to Afghanistan, bypassing Pakistan. Pakistan currently allows Afghanistan transit rights for its exports to India, but does not allow goods to move from India to Afghanistan.

CONTRIBUTORS

Lt General R K Sawhney, PVSM, AVSM

Lt General Ravi Sawhney is a former Deputy Chief of Army Staff and in-charge for UN forces deployment. He also held the crucial post of Director General Military Intelligence (DGMI) and also headed the Unified Command set up in Assam to tackle insurgency for over two years. After retirement, General Sawhney has been keeping an eye on Afghanistan and Burma and has been writing and speaking extensively on the defence matters. Presently, he is a distinguished fellow at the Vivekananda International Foundation.

Amb Kanwal Sibal

Mr Sibal is a former Foreign Secretary to the Government of India (2002-2003). He holds a Masters degree in English and a Bachelor's degree in Law. He has also spent a year at Oxford. Besides, Mr Sibal has served in numerous countries including Tanzania, Portugal and Nepal. He has also served as ambassador to Turkey, Egypt, France and Russia, apart from the Deputy Chief of Mission in the US.

Brig Vinod Anand (Retd)

Brig Anand is a senior fellow at the Vivekananda International Foundation (VIF), New Delhi. He holds a post-graduate degree in Defence and Strategic Studies and an alumnus of Defence Services and Staff College and College of Defence Management. Earlier he was a Senior Fellow at the Institute for Defence Studies and Analyses, New Delhi. Brig Anand has also been a Senior Fellow at the United Service Institution, New Delhi. He has authored monographs entitled *'Multi Vector Policies of CAR and India', 'Strategic Environment in Central Asia and India' 'Joint Vision for Indian Armed Forces',* and also co-authored a book entitled *'Defence Planning in India:*

Problems and Prospects'. Brig Anand is also a visiting faculty at Indian Institute of Mass Communication, Jawaharlal Nehru University Campus, New Delhi.

Dr Alexander Lukin

Dr Lukin is the Director, Center for East Asian and Shanghai Cooperation Organization Studies, Moscow State Institute of International Relations University of the Ministry of Foreign Affairs of Russia. He graduated from Moscow State Institute of International Relations in 1984, followed by a doctorate from Oxford in 1997 and another doctorate from Russian Diplomatic Academy in 2007. Dr Lukin has served in the Soviet Foreign Ministry and Soviet Embassy to the PRC. Apart from having held senior research positions at various institutions in Europe and the US, Dr Lukin has also written extensively on Russo-Sino relations and on East Asia. He is also a member of the Russian National Committee of The Council for Security Co-operation in the Asia Pacific (CSCAP).

Amb TCA Rangachari

Mr Rangachari served as India's Ambassador to Algeria, France and Germany. He is one of the notable experts on China in India. Since his retirement from the service, he has been extensively writing and lecturing on many topical issues relating to India's foreign policy, strategic and security matters.

Mr Tarakov Lev Yuryevich

Mr Yuryevich is the Editor-in-Chief and Director of *Newspaper Liter.* He graduated from Kiev Naval Political Academy in 1988. Since then he served as officer with a rank of Lieutenant Commander and political worker in Northern Navy. From 1992 onwards, Mr Yuryevich occupied many positions such as top specialist, main specialist, deputy director, director of the main department of expert and analytical work and timely information of the Ministry of Press and Mass Media of the Republic of Kazakhstan. He was appointed as divisional manager, deputy, principal deputy of the Center of Analysis and Strategic Research under the President of the Republic of Kazakhstan in 1994 and became the Director the Center in May 1997. Mr

Yuryevich was appointed as Vice-Minister of Information and Social Consensus of the Republic of Kazakhstan in December 1997. In May 1998, he was appointed as the Director of the Press Service of the President of the Republic of Kazakhstan. He became the deputy General Manger of Liter Media in 2009. Mr Yuryevich was also awarded an honorary award *Kurmet*.

Nivedita Das Kundu, Ph.d

Prof Nivedita Das is a Foreign Policy Analyst, presently working with the Indian Council for Social Science Research, New Delhi. Earlier she worked as a Research Fellow at the Indian Council of World Affairs, New Delhi and as an Associate Fellow with the Institute for Defence Studies and Analyses (IDSA). She was also a post doctoral fellow at Woodrow Wilson International Center for Scholars in Washington DC USA. She has received her Doctorate from School of International Studies, Jawaharlal Nehru University, New Delhi. Her research interest includes: geopolitical issues, foreign policy and strategic dimensions of security with the focus on Russia and the former Soviet States and multilateral organisations like SCO, BRIC, CSTO, NATO and EU. She has contributed widely on these research areas nationally and internationally. She has authored a book "Russia and it's Near Abroad: Strategic Dynamics and Implications" and edited two books, "Russia-India-China: Evolution of Geopolitical Strategic Trends" and "India-Russia Strategic Partnership: Challenges and Prospects", her forthcoming edited Book "India-Azerbaijan: The Silk Route Connection", is presently under the publication process.

Dr Davood Moradian

Dr Moradian is the Director General of the Foreign Ministry's Centre for Strategic Studies and Senior Policy Advisor to the Foreign Minister of Afghanistan. After earning his undergraduate degree at the University of London, he secured his doctorate in international relations from the University of St. Andrews, Scotland. He has also taught International Relations at his alma mater. Prior to joining the Ministry of Foreign Affairs, Dr Moradian was the chief of Presidential Programmes at President Karzai's Office.

Dr Laziz Tursunov

Dr Tursunov represents the Institute of Strategic Research and Studies (ISRS), Tashkent, Uzbekistan.

Brig Gurmeet Kanwal (Retd)

Brig Gurmeet Kanwal is the Director, Centre for Land Warfare Studies (CLAWS), New Delhi. Brig Kanwal has held several command and staff appointments including that of an instructor at the School of Artillery, Devlali, Director, MO-5 in the Military Operations Directorate at Army HQ and Deputy Assistant Chief of Integrated Defence Staff (Doctrine, Organisation and Training branch). He has also served as a Military Observer in UNTAG, Namibia; commanded an Artillery Regiment in active Counter-Insurgency operations in the Kashmir Valley and an Infantry Brigade on the Line of Control during Operation Parakram.

Brig Arun Sahgal PhD (Retd)

Brigadier Arun Sahgal, PhD (Retd) is Consultant with Institute for Peace and Conflict Studies, and Visiting Fellow, Vivekananda International Foundation. He was founder Director of the Office of Net Assessment, Indian Integrated Defence Staff, created to undertake long-term strategic assessments. Other academic pursuits include Head, Center for Strategic Studies and Simulation, United Service Institution of India, Senior Fellow, Institute for Defence Studies and Analyses. Research areas include scenario planning workshops for Indian and International participants, geo-political and strategic dimensions of Asian security with focus on China, India's neighbourhood and Indo-US strategic relations. Recent works include study of Nepali Maoists, and Madhesi Movement in Nepal, co-authored books include '*Relinking India and Central Asia: Security and Economic Dynamics*' by John Hopkins University, Washington, book on Sino – Indian CBM's, by IPCS. Other works include Net Assessment studies on Pakistan, Myanmar, Sri Lanka, and India – China Military Balance 2020. He was a member of National Task Force on Net Assessment and Simulation, under NSC and continues to support them through consultancy assignments.

Prof Nirmala Joshi

Prof Joshi is the Director of India-Central Asia Foundation, an independent think-tank, New Delhi. She received her PhD from the School International Studies, Jawaharlal Nehru University, New Delhi. She was a Professor and Chairperson of the Centre for Russian and Central Asian Studies, School of International Studies, Jawaharlal Nehru University. Prof Joshi was also Director of University Grants Commission (UGC) Programme on Russia and Central Asia at JNU. She was also member of the Indo-Russian Commission for Co-operation in Social Sciences. Prof Joshi was a Visiting Fellow at the Institute of Oriental Studies, Moscow and Ford Foundation Visiting Scholar at the Columbia University. She was also invited by the US Government to tour Centres of Soviet Studies in the US under the International Visitor Programme. She was a Fellow at the Salzburg Seminar in 1989.

Dr Arun Mohanty

Dr Mohanty is an Associate Professor at the Centre for Russian and Central Asian Studies, School of International Studies, Jawaharlal Nehru University, New Delhi. He has obtained his PhD from the Academy of Science USSR. Dr Mohanty has also taught at Moscow State University, Moscow. Apart from being a member of Russian Academy of Social Sciences, he is also the Editor-in-Chief of Eurasian Report. His expertise includes Russian Foreign and Security Policy, Russian Economy and Indo-Russian bilateral relations. During his two decades of stay in Russia and after, he has authored a number of books and articles on the above matters both in Russian as well as in English.

Dr Sanjay Kumar Pandey

Dr Pandey is an Associate Professor at the Centre for Russian and Central Asian Studies, School of International Studies, Jawaharlal Nehru University, New Delhi. Dr Pandey secured his doctorate in Soviet Studies at Jawaharlal Nehru University in 1995. He has been a Charles Wallace Trust Visiting Fellow, Centre of South Asian Studies, University of Cambridge in 2009. Dr Pandey has also been an Observer for the Presidential Election in Uzbekistan, December 2008. Dr Pandey, apart from Russia and Central Asia, writes on identity and federalism as well.

Dr Gulshan Sachdeva

Dr Sachdeva is an Associate Professor at the Centre for Russian and Central Asian Studies, School of International Studies, Jawaharlal Nehru University, New Delhi. He secured his PhD in Economic Science from the Hungarian Academy of Sciences, Budapest. As a Team Leader and Regional Cooperation Adviser, he has worked with the Asian Development Bank and with The Asia Foundation projects respectively at the Afghanistan Ministry of Foreign Affairs in Kabul. . He was Visiting Professor at the University of Antwerp, University of Trento (Italy) and Corvinus University of Budapest. He was also Visiting Fellow at the Institute of Oriental Studies Moscow, Institute of Oriental Studies, Almaty and Cambridge Central Asia Forum. Earlier, he was Director of the Europe Area Studies Programme at JNU. He is author of *Economy of the Northeast (2000),* various, monographs, project reports and 60 research papers in scholarly journals and edited books. He is a member of the governing board for the India-Central Asia Foundation.

Dr Jyotsna Bakshi

Dr Bakshi is a Visiting Senior Fellow at the Indian Council of World Affairs (ICWA). She has secured her PhD from Punjab University. She has also occupied the India Chair Professor at the University of World Economy and Diplomacy, Tashkent, Uzbekistan from 2006 to 2009. Dr Bakshi served as an Associate Professor at the Centre for Indian Studies at Osh State University, Kyrgyzstan from 2002 to 2005. She has also been a Research Fellow at the Institute for Defence Studies and Analyses, New Delhi. Dr Bakshi has also done two years' research fieldwork at the Institute of Oriental Studies, Moscow (Academy of Sciences, USSR). Moreover, she has a Kandidatskii Minimum Diploma in Russian language from the Department of Foreign Languages, Moscow Academy of Sciences, USSR.

Dr Meena Singh Roy

Dr Roy is a Research Fellow at the Institute for Defence Studies and Analyses, New Delhi. She holds a PhD from the University of Delhi. Dr

Roy has been Senior Research Scholar in the Department of African Studies, University of Delhi. She has also been associated with Institute of Commonwealth Studies and School of Oriental & African Studies (London). Dr Roy has done Vision 2020 and net assessment reports on Central Asia. She has also worked on India-Central Asia Relations, Issue of Terrorism, Energy issues, Regional Cooperation in Central Asia and India Iran Relations. She has been part of team publishing energy newsletters and Defence and Disarmament Review section of Strategic Digest at IDSA.

Amb Satish Chandra

Having joined the Indian Foreign Service in 1965, Satish Chandra went on to take up important diplomatic assignments in the Indian missions in Vienna, Karachi, Washington D.C., Algiers, and Dhaka. Later, he served as India's Permanent Representative to UN Offices in Geneva, Ambassador to the Philippines and High Commissioner to Pakistan. He was also Secretary to the National Security Council Secretariat. Ever since his retirement in 2005 as Deputy National Security Advisor, he has been actively engaged in writing on national security and strategic matters. Presently, he is a distinguished fellow at the Vivekananda International Foundation.

About the Editor

Brig Vinod Anand (Retd) is a postgraduate in Defence and Strategic studies and is an alumnus of Defence Services Staff College and College of Defence Management. He has authored monographs titled *'Multi Vector Policies of CAR and India'*, *'Strategic Environment in Central Asia and India'*, *'Joint Vision for Indian Armed Forces'*, and also co-authored a book titled *'Defence Planning in India: Problems and Prospects'*.

Presently he is a senior fellow at the Vivekananda International Foundation, New Delhi and visiting faculty at Indian Institute of Mass Communication, Jawaharlal Nehru University Campus, New Delhi. Besides writing on a wide variety of strategic issues he writes on Pakistan, Afghanistan and Central Asia, Information Warfare, Joint Operations and Perception Management. His papers and research articles have been published in Indian and Foreign Journals and Newspapers.

www.ingramcontent.com/pod-product-compliance
Lightning Source LLC
Chambersburg PA
CBHW070809300326
41914CB00078B/1912/J